William Samuel Wilson

The Ocean as a Health Resort

A practical Handbook of the Sea for the use of Tourists and Health-Seekers. Second Edition

William Samuel Wilson

The Ocean as a Health Resort
A practical Handbook of the Sea for the use of Tourists and Health-Seekers. Second Edition

ISBN/EAN: 9783337190361

Printed in Europe, USA, Canada, Australia, Japan

Cover: Foto ©Lupo / pixelio.de

More available books at **www.hansebooks.com**

THE
OCEAN AS A HEALTH RESORT

A Practical Handbook of the Sea

FOR THE USE OF

TOURISTS AND HEALTH-SEEKERS

BY

WILLIAM S. WILSON, L.R.C.P. LOND., M.R.C.S.E.

WITH A CHART
SHOWING THE OCEAN-ROUTES AND ILLUSTRATING THE PHYSICAL
GEOGRAPHY OF THE SEA

SECOND EDITION

LONDON
J. & A. CHURCHILL, NEW BURLINGTON STREET
1881

PREFACE TO THE FIRST EDITION.

FREQUENT conversations with the many fellow-passengers I have met in the course of more than one voyage to the Australian colonies have led me to believe that a small handbook, such as the present, might be of considerable use to the constantly increasing class of travellers who, without previous experience of the sea, determine to try its invigorating or curative effects. I found that many had started with exceedingly dim notions as to what lay before them in their sea-life; that some were inadequately provided with those necessaries of personal outfit which, though perhaps trifling in themselves, are, especially in the case of an invalid, so indispensable to comfort during a long voyage; and that others had formed no definite plans for their stay in the country for which they were bound.

In the following pages I have endeavoured, first, to give such practical information as to routes, shipping lines, outfit, and all other preliminary matters, as may enable even the most inexperienced traveller to make a judicious choice of a voyage and ship, and to provide himself with all that he will require for the passage out and home. Next, I have tried to present a faithful picture of life at sea, and of what is to be expected in the way of accommodation, food, and amusement during a long voyage; and I have also described the climate and weather usually experienced during a passage to and from Australia, and have given some hints as to the management of the health, especially in the tropics. A chapter has been devoted to the various objects of interest that are met with at sea, an intelligent appreciation of which will not only lessen the tedium of a long voyage, but will also, by keeping the mind employed, greatly assist the beneficial effects of sea-life. Lastly, some account has been given of Australia and South Africa, with special reference to climate and the localities most suitable as a residence for such invalids as, having made the voyage to either of those countries, intend to remain there for a longer or shorter time.

It has been my wish throughout this work to give not only reliable, but also thoroughly *practical*, information; and if this has led me at times to lay stress on seeming trifles, it must be remembered that comfort or discomfort at sea—particularly as regards invalids—is vastly dependent on little things, which to those on shore and in health might appear of the smallest consequence. Again, many of the details given may appear ridiculously unnecessary to those with any previous experience of the sea, but here again it must be borne in mind that this handbook has been written especially for those who have no such knowledge whatever.

Although the voyage to Australia by the Atlantic route has, on account of its many advantages for invalids, been selected as the typical health-voyage, particulars have been given of various other sea routes which, though not so suitable for the great majority of those travelling for health—especially if suffering from any affection of the chest—would yet be most enjoyable, and prove of the greatest benefit to those requiring change of scene rather than direct climatic treatment.

The great advance which has recently taken place in the construction of large, powerful, and commodious steamships for the Australian voyage will no doubt lead eventually to such improved accommodation for passengers as will not only cause vessels of this class almost entirely to supersede sailing ships for passenger traffic, but will also remove many of the objections that now exist to steamers in the case of invalids. Some of these objections, however—such as the too rapid transition from one kind of climate to another—must always remain; and for the present, some of the fine sailing ships which still run to Australia, and are specially arranged for the comfort and convenience of passengers travelling for health, will, I think, afford the most favourable opportunities for reaping the full benefits of a sea-voyage.

I cannot close this short preface without expressing my acknowledgments and thanks to my friend and fellow-traveller, E. Mawley, Esq., F.M.S., for his valuable assistance in compiling the chapter on marine meteorology, and for the complete table of observations taken by him during a homeward voyage from Australia round the Cape of Good Hope.

In conclusion, I venture to hope that these pages may

not only prove useful to those who are seeking in a voyage, a means of regaining health, but that they may also be found to contain some few hints which may be of service to the larger class of travellers who go to sea for business or for pleasure.

SANDOWN, ISLE OF WIGHT,
    July, 1880.

PREFACE TO THE SECOND EDITION.

THE favourable reception of this work since its first appearance in September last having already necessitated a second edition, an opportunity for revision and correction occurs sooner than had been anticipated.

All information with regard to shipping matters has been carefully brought down to the latest date, and in accordance with the suggestions of friends and reviewers several additions have been made to the work, which will, it is hoped, add materially to its usefulness. The specific action of the ocean climate upon the health has been fully considered, and statistics have been given showing its influence in the prevention and cure of pulmonary complaints.

Finding that many tourists and health-seekers now visit New Zealand in preference to Australia, I have added a chapter giving a brief account of the former country, and describing the nature of its climate.

The chapter on marine meteorology has been very carefully revised by Mr. Mawley, whose present position on the Council of the Meteorological Society gives him every facility for obtaining the latest information with regard to the scientific observation of the weather at sea. Mr. Mawley has also furnished useful tables for ascertaining the relative humidity of the atmosphere, and for estimating the force of the wind.

The map which accompanies this volume has been considerably enlarged, and in other respects improved, and will, it is hoped, be found useful both for reference as to routes, and as a track-chart.

Notwithstanding the steady progress of steam during the past year, especially in the case of the Australian passenger lines, those tourists who prefer, on the score of health, a sailing vessel to a steamer will find that their interests have by no means been overlooked. Several of the leading firms now despatch in the autumn fine ships of about 2,000 tons register, specially intended for passengers visiting the Australian colonies in search of health. These vessels make the return voyage by way of the Cape of Good Hope, calling generally at Cape Town and St. Helena, and thus meeting one of the great difficulties hitherto experienced by invalids with regard to the homeward passage.

Sandown, Isle of Wight,
June, 1881.

CONTENTS.

CHAPTER I.

CURATIVE EFFECTS OF THE OCEAN CLIMATE.

                                                                                                      PAGE

Conditions of sea-life favourable to the restoration of health—Rest and change of scene—Facilities for being in the open air—Purity of the air at sea—Special properties of sea-air—Equability of temperature—Sedative influence of a humid atmosphere—Bracing effects of change of climate—Diseases in which a sea-voyage has been found of benefit—Consumption—Bronchitis—Asthma—The after-effects of inflammation of the lungs, pleurisy, etc.—Nervous complaints—Diseases of joints—Debility—Overwork 1

CHAPTER II.

THE VARIOUS HEALTH-VOYAGES.

Choice of voyages limited—The voyage to the West Indies—The Royal Mail Company—The voyage to Brazil and the River Plate—Pacific Steam Navigation Company—"Red Cross" line etc.—The climate of Brazil—The voyage to the Cape of Good Hope—Union Steamship Company—Messrs. Donald, Currie and Co.'s "Castle" line—The voyage to India by the Suez Canal—Peninsular and Oriental Company—British India Steam Navigation Company—The Peninsular and Oriental Company—The voyage to Australia: three routes—the Indian route—the Pacific route—the Atlantic route—The latter voyage most suitable for invalids—Pacific Mail Steam Ship Company 22

CHAPTER III.

TIME OF STARTING—CHOOSING A SHIP.

Best time of starting for the West Indies—Healthiest months in India—Reversal of the seasons in the southern hemisphere—The best time of year for Brazil and the Cape of Good Hope—Importance of leaving England in the early autumn—Choice of a ship—Respective advantages of sailing vessels and steamers—Tonnage of sailing vessels—Iron, wooden, and "composite" ships—Poop ships and flush-deck ships—Australian steam-lines—The "Orient" line—Messrs. Houlder Bros'. steamships—The "Colonial" line—Messrs. Wigram's steamships—Australian lines of sailing vessels: Messrs. Green's "Blackwall" line—Messrs. Wigram's sailing ships discontinued—Messrs. Devitt and Moore—Messrs. Anderson, Anderson and Co.—Messrs. G. Thompson's "Aberdeen" line—Messrs. Trinder, Anderson and Co.—Messrs. Houlder Brothers and Co.—Mr. J. H. Flint's "Colonial" line—Various other firms—New Zealand lines: The New Zealand Shipping Co.—Messrs. Shaw, Savill and Co.'s "Passenger" line—The Australian ports 44

CHAPTER IV.

PRELIMINARY ARRANGEMENTS.

Securing a passage and engaging a berth—Personal inspection desirable—Hints on choosing a berth—Furnishing the cabin in sailing vessels—Articles of cabin furniture provided by the owners—Furniture to be provided by the passenger himself: bedding, folding-chair, lamp, bookshelf, carpet, bath, swing-tray, etc., etc.—Trunks and boxes—Travelling chest of drawers—Outfit of wearing apparel—Outfitters—Stores: medicines and sundries—Joining the ship—The ports of departure . . . 64

CHAPTER V.

LIFE AT SEA.

The Australian voyage—Commencement of the voyage—Sea-sickness—Daily routine—General arrangement of the ship—Meals on board ship—Quality of the various articles of food in sailing vessels—Supply of water—Unavoidable defects of the dietary on long sea-voyages—The quantities of provisions consumed during an Australian voyage—List of officers, crew, etc., of a large

passenger ship—Mode of indicating the time: the "bells"—
Taking the noon "sights"—Agreement of passengers amongst
themselves — Reading — Open-air games — Quoits — Cricket—
"Bull-board"—Shooting sea-birds—Athletic sports—Dancing—
Theatricals, concerts, etc.—Newspapers—Chess tournaments—
Sailors' amusements—"Crossing the line"—"Burying the dead
horse"—Sailors' songs—Speaking passing ships—Sending home
letters—Excursions in the ship's boats 77

CHAPTER VI.

COURSE, CLIMATE, AND WEATHER.

Course of a sailing vessel bound for Australia—The "regions" of the
ocean—Climate and weather experienced in the various portions
of the Australian voyage—The English Channel—Bay of Biscay
—Northern region of prevailing westerly winds—The calms of
Cancer—Region of north-east trade-winds—The equatorial calms
or "doldrums"—Equatorial rains—Region of south-east trade-
winds—Calm-belt of Capricorn—The southern region of prevailing westerly winds—Course of sailing vessels between the
longitude of the Cape and Australia—The "roaring forties"—
Occasional gales—Rapid alteration of apparent time—Temperature—Reversal of the characteristics of the winds—Effects of
the cold weather on invalids—Land sighted on the outward
voyage—Canary Islands—Cape Verde Islands—Tristan d'Acunha 104

CHAPTER VII.

MANAGEMENT OF THE HEALTH AT SEA.

The treatment of sea-sickness—Regulation of the diet—Exercise—
Bathing—Ventilation of the cabin — Closet arrangements—
Management of the health in the tropics—Sleeping on deck
— Tropical colds — Ulcerated sore-throat — "Prickly heat" —
Languor tropicus—Necessity of fresh air for invalids . . 124

CHAPTER VIII.

OBJECTS OF INTEREST AT SEA.

Colour of the sea—Composition of sea water—Waves—The southern
constellations—Auroras—Shooting-stars and meteors — Lunar
coronas and haloes—Waterspouts—Sunsets at sea—Vertical sun
—Living creatures of the sea—Whales—The Greenland whale—
Finbacks—The sperm whale—Food of whales—The enemies of

the whale—Dolphins and porpoises—Sharks—Pilot-fish—Catching a shark—Saw-fish and sword-fish—The Bonito—Barracouta—Flying fish—Turtles—Lower forms of marine life—Capturing crustacea, jelly-fish, etc.—" Portuguese man-of-war "—Mode of obtaining microscopical objects—The phosphorescence of the sea—Sea-birds—Mother Cary's chicken—Soland goose—The albatross—Sea-birds south of the Cape; their number and variety—Cape-hen—Mutton-bird—Cape-pigeon—Boatswain-bird—Whale-bird 139

CHAPTER IX.

END OF THE VOYAGE—FUTURE PLANS.

Approaching the Australian coast—Cape Otway—Bass' Strait—Port Phillip Heads—The "Rip"—Port Phillip harbour—Sandridge—Warehousing cabin furniture—Melbourne hotels—Deciding on length of stay in the colonies 179

CHAPTER X.

THE HOMEWARD VOYAGE.

Various homeward routes—Steamship routes—Sailing routes—The voyage round Cape Horn—Homeward route round the Cape of Good Hope—Limited choice of ships for this route—Its advantages for invalids—Length of passage—Course, climate, and weather—South Indian Ocean—Mauritius hurricanes—Course round the African coast—Calling at Cape Town—Course after leaving the Cape—A day at St. Helena—Island of Ascension—The Azores—Passing ships—Sunsets in the Indian Ocean—Marine zoology—Sargasso Sea 186

CHAPTER XI.

AUSTRALIA: ITS CLIMATE, CITIES, AND HEALTH RESORTS.

Discovery—Population, area, etc.—The aborigines—Rivers—Mountains—Government—Industries and productions—Droughts and floods—Mineral wealth—Exports—Railways—The climate of Australia generally; modifying influences—Climate of Victoria—Climate of South Australia—Climate of New South Wales—Climate of Queensland—Climate of Tasmania—Influence of the Australian climate on disease—Melbourne—Climate of Melbourne—Hot winds—Ballarat—Sandhurst—

CONTENTS. XV

Geelong—Victoria unsuitable for invalids in summer—Selection of a suitable climate—Tasmania as a summer residence—Crossing Bass' Strait — Launceston — Hobart Town—Climate of Hobart Town—Fruit in Tasmania—From Hobart Town to Sydney—Beauty of Sydney harbour—Sydney — Climate of Sydney—Health resorts of the interior—Queensland—Brisbane —Darling Downs—Adelaide—Climate of Adelaide . . . 202

CHAPTER XII.

NEW ZEALAND.

Position—Area—Discovery — History — Divisions—Government — Geographical features —Harbours—Productions, industries, and exports—Railways—Cities and principal towns—The Maories—Scenery and points of interest—Lake Wakatipu—The Southern Alps—The Island of Kawau—The volcanic district—Hot lakes and geysers—The pink and white terraces of Rotomahana—Forests—Flowers and fruits—Animals and birds—Reptiles—Fishes—The climate of New Zealand—Hints to invalids . . 238

CHAPTER XIII.

SOUTH AFRICA.

Districts comprised in South Africa—Cape Colony—Population—Rivers—Mountains—Industries and productions—Exports—Ports—Cape Town—Suburbs of Cape Town— Railways—Cape wines—Port Elizabeth—East London—Natal—Durban—Pietermaritzburg—Orange Free State—Elevated plains of the interior—Bloemfontein—The Transvaal—Climate of Cape Town and its neighbourhood—The " Cape Doctor "—Health resorts of the interior—Graham's Town—Cradock—Colesburg—Bloemfontein —Conveyances—Cobb and Co.'s coaches—Passenger carts—Mail carts—Private conveyances—Ox waggons—Climate of the inland plains; its dryness — Thunderstorms — Droughts — Meteorological observations—Influence of the climate on disease 279

CHAPTER XIV.

THE METEOROLOGY OF THE OCEAN.

Instruments required for taking observations—Barometer—Thermometer—Thermometer screen—Hygrometer—Method of determining the humidity of the air—Observations of shade-temperature—Surface temperature of the sea—The meteorological journal—Estimation of the amount of cloud—Direction and force of the wind—Observations of rainfall not reliable—Special meteorological conditions at sea—Distribution of storms—Log and meteorological tables of a voyage to Australia—Log, meteorological tables, and weather report of homeward voyage by Cape of Good Hope 303

CONCLUSION.

THE HEALTH-VOYAGE OF THE FUTURE 330

APPENDIX A—Outfit required for a voyage to Australia . . 339

APPENDIX B—Names and addresses of some of the principal shipping firms 341

APPENDIX C—Beaufort scale of force of wind—Table of relative humidity 344

INDEX 347

ERRATA.

Page 9, line 6, for "83" read "79."

Page 38, line 21, omit the words "and other lines."

THE OCEAN AS A HEALTH RESORT.

CHAPTER I.

CURATIVE EFFECTS OF THE OCEAN CLIMATE.

Conditions of sea life favourable to the restoration of health—Rest and change of scene—Facilities for being in the open air—Purity of the air at sea—Special properties of sea air—Equability of temperature—Sedative influence of a humid atmosphere—Bracing effects of change of climate—Complaints in which a sea voyage has been found of benefit—Consumption — Bronchitis — Asthma—The after-effects of inflammation of the lungs, pleurisy, etc.—Nervous complaints—Diseases of joints—Debility—Overwork.

ALTHOUGH the following pages will, it is hoped, be found useful by passengers of all classes, who are starting upon a long voyage without any previous experience of the sea, yet, as the work is written with more particular reference to those who are travelling in search of health, and may possibly be read also by members of my own profession, the opening chapter will be devoted to the consideration of two semi-medical questions, viz., first, the particular conditions of sea climate and sea life that exert a beneficial effect upon the constitution; and, second, the various diseases in which a sea voyage has proved most useful.

Every effort has been made here, as in other parts of the work, to avoid medical phraseology, and to render the meaning clear to all; but those readers who are not interested in subjects necessarily of a somewhat technical character may pass on at once to the more practical portions of the book.

The curative effects of the true ocean climate in certain cases of illness are becoming, year by year, better understood and appreciated. Ten or fifteen years ago it was quite an unusual thing to meet, even in the finest Australian sailing vessels, with any one taking a voyage solely for health's sake: now the favourite passenger ships, especially in the autumn, are half filled with invalids of every kind and degree, who are looking forward hopefully to testing the restorative influences of the ocean climate.

But although the remedial effects of a long voyage, especially in well-selected cases of chest disease, and the invigorating action of the ocean climate upon nearly all who go to sea are now fully recognised, not only by medical men, but by the public generally, the *modus operandi*—the way in which these beneficial results are brought about—is still only imperfectly understood, even by those who have given their best attention to the subject.

It is probable, however, that the rapid improvement which so generally takes place in the health while at sea may be attributed to some or all of the following causes:—

1. The entire change of scene, and the enforced rest from customary occupations.

2. The facilities for being constantly in the open air during the greater part of the twenty-four hours.

3. The habitual respiration, when on deck, of air free from those organic and inorganic impurities, and floating particles of dust and carbon, that are met with in even the purest air on land.

4. The presence in the air of certain substances, such

as saline particles, which may exert a specific beneficial effect upon the lungs and air-passages; also probable differences in the electrical conditions of the atmosphere and in the amount of ozone in sea air.

5. The greater equability of temperature at sea.

6. The sedative influence exerted on the constitution by a comparatively humid atmosphere combined with a high barometric pressure.

7. The bracing and hardening effect of almost constant sea breezes, and of the changes of climate experienced in passing through the different "regions" of the ocean.*

We will now briefly examine in turn each of these conditions of sea life.

1. *Rest and change of scene.* Owing to the intimate relation that exists between mind and body, change and mental rest will always constitute very important features in the treatment of every form of disease; but it is in nervous complaints—in cases of break-down from overwork and brain worry—that their good effects are perhaps most strikingly shown. At sea these two conditions can be enjoyed to an extent almost impossible on land. All the surroundings are different—every sight and sound is novel and unfamiliar. Business worries, letters, telegrams, are things of the past, and have faded out of the daily life, just as the distant shore has faded from the horizon. But it is not mental rest only that is obtained at sea. Bodily rest, often sorely needed, is also found in the floating home. The hurryings backwards and for-

* In completing my list of the causes influencing health at sea, I have availed myself of some of those suggested (I believe for the first time) by Dr. Faber in a series of valuable papers published in the *Practitioner* during 1876-7. As those papers did not come under my notice until the first edition was almost ready for publication, I was not able then to take advantage of several suggestions which I have found very useful in preparing the present edition.

wards, the hasty meals of active shore life, are no longer possible. The soothing, blunting effect of sea life,—an effect supposed by many to be in a measure due to the constant motion of the vessel,—soon aserts its influence; and bodily as well as mental exertion often becomes positively distasteful, especially in the hotter parts of the voyage, even to those who were before most active. The danger indeed is now of falling into the opposite extreme of taking too little bodily exercise for the needs of digestion and assimilation; and too little mental food to maintain a healthy condition of mind. But enough has been said to show how great a change and rest sea life will prove, not only to the harassed man of business, who has been living at high pressure until brain and body have alike given way, but also to the invalid, who, in spite of increasing bodily weakness, has endeavoured to carry on his customary avocations, when his strength was no longer equal to the task.

2. *Facilities for being almost constantly in the open air*. It is almost needless to enlarge on this head. On shore numberless causes combine to imprison us within four walls. Business duties, the calls of society, bad weather, the absence of adequate inducement, and, in the case of invalids, disinclination to undergo the fatigue of taking exercise, or of even dressing to go out,—these are a few of a long list of causes which on shore conspire to keep us indoors, and which any one can fill up from his own inner consciousness. At sea everything is reversed. There is but little temptation to remain below in the close and too often unsavoury atmosphere of the narrow cabins, when a few steps will take us into the pure sweet air of the sea. On deck there is to be found whatever the ship affords in the way of society, life, and animation, and from the deck are to be viewed the ever-changing sea and the expanse of sky and such natural phenomena

of air and water as the locality will yield. Nor is it necessary, at least in the warmer parts of the voyage, to undergo the slightest fatigue while in the open air. Lounging about on spars and coils of rope, or reclining more luxuriously in well-cushioned folding-chairs, is no great exertion, while the more thorough invalid may, if he thinks well, have his mattress brought on deck, and lie at his ease from morning till night, inhaling the health-giving ocean air.

3. *The habitual respiration, when on deck, of air free from dust and other impurities met with on land.* Most of us have, at some time in our lives, watched a beam of sunlight struggling through a narrow chink into a darkened room. Millions of motes, of whose presence we were previously unaware, are seen dancing in the light, and the path of the sunbeam is rendered luminous throughout its whole course. Were it not for these floating particles, the ray of light would be perfectly invisible until it fell upon some solid object. These motes, which are of course present in vast numbers in every breath we draw, constitute, when they have settled down by gravitation, that *bête noir* of careful housewives,—dust. Now if we allow some of this dust, which is everywhere floating in the air, to fall upon a perfectly clean piece of glass, and then examine it under the microscope, we shall be able to form an idea as to the nature of the particles we are receiving into our lungs. First, especially in cities and large towns, grains or flakes of carbon, *i.e.*, " blacks." This impurity is a very important one in large cities and manufacturing districts, where the lungs of those who have worked for many years in a soot-laden atmosphere are often found after death to contain large masses of carbon. We next find fragments of various tissues,—wool, silk, cotton, flax; minute hairs, particles of feathers, shreds of spiders' web; minute fragments of straw, and chips of brick, stone,

plaster, paint and varnish; tiny grains of sand; portions of the wings and legs of flies, spiders, and other insects: such are a few of the more ordinary constituents of dust. But there are things of greater importance sometimes present. In summer, and especially in the country, we find the pollen of various flowers, particularly of the grasses, carrying with them hay fever and hay asthma to those who are subject to such complaints. Then there are the spores and germs of various low forms of vegetable and animal life, some of which are looked upon with grave suspicion as the probable causes of disease. Many of the latter are extremely minute, and are only to be made out under the highest powers of the microscope; such as the omnipresent *bacteria, bacilli,* and *micrococci,* which have so much exercised the minds of scientists within the last few years.

But besides these suspended matters which find their way into our lungs, there are, especially in densely populated districts, many gaseous impurities calculated to be more or less prejudicial to health. Such are unconsumed coal gas and sulphurous acid gas, one of its impurities; ammonia, sulphuretted hydrogen, sewer gas, and the various noxious emanations from chemical works and manufactories of different kinds.

But far out at sea a very different state of things prevails. Here the air, if not absolutely pure, is probably the purest that can be found on the surface of the globe. Of dust there is none—if we set aside those very exceptional cases where the fine sand from the vast deserts of the interior is borne by the wind many miles away from land. The only "blacks" found at sea are those manufactured on board the ship itself, and this is one of the particulars in which a sailing vessel is so far superior to a steamer. The other floating and gaseous impurities of populous places are no longer present; and although I am not aware whether the more minute organisms are altogether absent from the air of remote ocean districts, yet the fact that outbreaks of infectious disease rarely, if ever, originate at sea would point to the conclusion that disease germs, if present at all, have been deprived of their vitality during their passage over wide ocean tracts. Within the ship, it is true, the air of the confined and sometimes crowded cabins is often far from pure; but this merely emphasizes the conclusion that in order to derive the full benefit from the pure sea air the invalid must spend every possible hour and minute on deck, and should only go below when compelled to do so by bad weather, hunger, or the needs of sleep.

4. *The presence in sea air of certain substances such as saline particles, etc., which act beneficially on the system.* Not only is the air purer at sea than it is on land, but it possesses certain peculiarities that are believed to exert a considerable influence on the health, especially in the case of invalids suffering from chest complaints. Saline particles in the form of finely divided spray are almost always present more or less in the sea air; but it is in rough weather, and more particularly during gales, that they most abound. Then the sea dust, blown in dense clouds from the crests of the waves, fills the air like a fog, and blots out the more distant objects. The constant inhalation of these particles, containing as they do the important constituents of sea water, may be expected to produce a very specific, and in most cases beneficial, effect upon the lungs and air-passages. But there are other peculiarities of the ocean climate, which, though perhaps less palpable, are possibly equally important. Ozone, or *peroxide of hydrogen*, as it is sometimes called, is one of these. Its nature, properties, and action on the human frame are still only imperfectly understood, but it is believed to exert considerable influence upon the

health—possibly, for the most part, through the respiratory system. It is almost always absent from the atmosphere of large cities; and is present in very variable quantities in the air of inland districts generally; but in sea air it is almost always found to a considerable amount. Carbonic acid (*carbonic anhydride*) is another constituent of the atmosphere which varies in its proportion at sea and on land—the quantity being somewhat less in ocean air. As regards the special electrical conditions of the sea, there is still much to learn, but there is little doubt that in the case of delicate persons of a susceptible nervous organization these conditions are of considerable importance.

5. *The greater equability of temperature at sea.* The equability is principally that of daily range. Those sudden changes of temperature so frequent and trying in our own climate—changes often amounting to 15° or 20° or even more in the course of the twenty-four hours—are, far out at sea, almost unknown. Here the extreme daily limits of temperature are usually comprised within some 4° or 5°. The changes too from day to day are comparatively small, although, in the case of a vessel sailing northwards or southwards, these changes are steadily progressive as the ship passes from cooler to warmer latitudes, or *vice versâ*.

6. *The sedative influence exerted on the constitution by a comparatively humid atmosphere combined with a high barometrical pressure.* If we consider the active evaporation that is constantly taking place from the surface of the vast stretches of ocean which surround our globe, we should be prepared to find that the humidity of the air at sea is greater than that of dry inland districts. As a matter of fact, however, the humidity would not seem to be considerably greater than that of our own insular climate. The mean relative humidity of the air

at noon, as observed during a voyage from Melbourne to London, *viâ* the Cape of Good Hope, was found to be 77 (100 representing complete saturation), while in a dry locality in the neighbourhood of London the mean for the year, as recorded by Mr. Mawley in his pamphlet, "The Weather of 1880," was as much as 85. But this represents the mean of three observations taken respectively at 9 a.m., 3 p.m., and 9 p.m. A fairer comparison would therefore be with the mean of the three o'clock observation, which, for the year, gave 71·5. It must not be forgotten, however, that the dampness of the air at sea is much less variable than it is on land—the difference between the humidity of the night and day, and also from day to day, being very slight. Its effect upon the constitution is also probably modified by the presence of saline matters, and by other causes.

The high barometrical pressure experienced at sea is due principally to position—the recording instrument, as well as the passengers in a ship, being elevated only a few feet above sea level. On comparing the mean pressure, as deduced from the observations taken during the voyage mentioned above, with the average at Greenwich for the last thirty years, the apparent difference is very small, amounting only to a few hundredths of an inch. It must be remembered, however, that on land very few localities are either at or near sea level; while many are several hundreds of feet above that point. But for the sake of uniformity in meteorological reports, all observations are reduced to sea level before they are published. The great majority, therefore, of the inhabitants of the British Islands are practically subjected to an atmospheric pressure often lower by several tenths than that recorded at Greenwich or elsewhere.

We find that during a long sea voyage a passenger is exposed to an atmosphere slightly (and more uniformly) moister than that of England, and a barometric pressure which is also generally higher than that on shore. These two conditions combined are believed to exert a sedative effect upon the human frame—an effect which in some cases constitutes an important remedial agent. That this sedative action exists is shown by the decrease of body temperature which takes place during a sea voyage, and which amounts on an average to nearly 1°.

7. We now come to the last of the remedial conditions peculiar to sea life, viz., the *bracing and hardening effects of sea breezes, and of the changes of climate experienced in passing through the different regions of the ocean.* Air in rapid motion—in other words, wind—exerts a twofold action on the human frame. It abstracts heat by increasing the evaporation of the skin, and it stimulates the nerves of the surface. At sea there is considerably more wind than in most localities on land, and the voyager is more constantly exposed to its influence. There is also about sea air, as every one knows, a bracing and stimulating quality not found in the air of inland districts. In the trade-wind regions the specific effects of the ocean air-currents are most powerfully felt. Differing as these winds do in several respects from anything that is experienced on shore, we can scarcely wonder that they should exert upon many people an exhilarating effect peculiar to themselves. To many nervous invalids, in fact, the "champagne atmosphere of the trades" is a tonic and stimulant of the most powerful kind.

The bracing and hardening effects of the changes of climate experienced during a voyage to the antipodes are considered by Dr. Faber to be amongst the most valuable of the curative influences of a long voyage. Although not myself inclined to accord a first place to this particular condition of sea life, yet there can be no doubt that these changes from climate to climate, if not made too abruptly, are of great value in enabling a debilitated constitution to throw off that susceptibility to climatic influences which is often one of the most troublesome accompaniments of ill health, especially when the chest is at fault. The changes of climate experienced between the northern and southern limits of a voyage to Australia, though considerable, are by no means equal to the difference between winter and summer temperatures in England. In the two voyages, the meteorological tables of which are appended to this work, the range of temperature experienced was in one case 36°, and in the other only 29°; whereas in England it often amounts in the course of the year to 70°. The lowest temperature during these two voyages was in one case 48°, and in the other 56°; while the average lowest temperature at Greenwich is about 15°. Where the voyage is made in a sailing vessel, the changes of climate between the English Channel and the tropics, and again between the tropics and the southern limits of the ship's course, are gradual and progressive,—the change of temperature from day to day seldom amounting to more than 4° or 5°. The transition from our own climate to the steamy atmosphere of the equatorial region, and then again to the bracing and boisterous weather of the South Atlantic, may possibly exert upon the constitution something of the effect of a prolonged Turkish bath. However this may be, it is certain that the beneficial effects of a sea voyage begin to show themselves most decidedly amongst the passengers when the colder regions between the Cape and Australia have been reached.

It will be seen then, by those who have had the patience to read the foregoing pages, that we possess in a long sea voyage a combination of peculiar health influences which, in the aggregate, form a remedial agent of the most powerful character. The fact that some of these conditions are at first sight somewhat contradictory does not detract from their usefulness. Every physician knows that a judicious combination or alternation of opposite remedies will often prove most successful in the treatment of disease; and there is nothing in a gradual transition from climate to climate that need interfere with the benefit to be derived from the equability of temperature at sea, as regards a limited daily range; nor is there anything in the bracing effects of strong sea breezes to injuriously counteract the sedative influences of a humid air, high barometric pressure, and perfect rest. That the blending of these various causes of good, notwithstanding the drawbacks inseparable from sea life, very often achieves the happiest results is beyond dispute; and there can be little doubt that in proportion as the subject is more studied, and the hygienic conditions of passenger ships are improved, so will the "thalasso-climatic" treatment, not only for invalids, but for the jaded and over-worked, gain ground in public estimation.

If it be asked whether it would not be possible to enjoy at a well-chosen seaside health resort, the advantages to be derived from an ocean voyage, a negative reply must be emphatically given. At our own favourite sanatoria, as well as those on the shores of the Mediterranean, the sea air is, at the best, a sadly adulterated article. When the wind blows from the land, it will contain all the impurities peculiar to the district, which may be marshy, malarious, or otherwise unhealthy. There will also be the various insanitary emanations of the city or the town itself. But even when the wind blows off the sea, the air is far from being as pure as could be wished. Seaweed and other vegetable and animal matters in various stages of decay, to say nothing of the sewage which is so often discharged into the sea at these places, all give off their distinctive odours to mingle with the breeze. I have often been amused by hearing newcomers to seaside places remarking with enthusiasm upon the " delightful smell of the sea ;" whereas in fact sea air and sea water, when perfectly pure, have no perceptible smell whatever. It is not only in the matter of pure sea air that health resorts are wanting. The conditions of temperature, moisture, atmospheric pressure, and telluric influences are all different; and no one who has practically considered the subject can doubt that the true ocean climate is only to be enjoyed *at sea*, and at a considerable distance from land. Although a few of the other conditions which have been mentioned might, under favourable circumstances, be enjoyed on shore, most of them are peculiar to an ocean climate far removed from all land influences. Indeed, any one who has been to sea will know that not only does such a climate differ entirely in its effects upon the health and constitution from the *mixed* sea air that is to be obtained on our coasts, but also that an appreciable difference will be felt by delicate persons when approaching even within twenty or thirty miles of land. The peculiar combination of curative influences such as have been enumerated above is, in fact, only to be met with in a well-chosen sea voyage.

Health resorts on land have, however, their own important advantages, and are in some cases to be preferred, especially where a patient is too weak, or his illness is too far advanced to enable him to bear the inconveniences and deprivations of ship life. But they occupy quite a different sphere amongst the curative agents at the command of the modern physician, and can never take the place of the true ocean treatment.

It would be obviously out of place, in a little work

intended for general use, to attempt to give anything like a detailed account of the diseases in which a sea voyage has been found of benefit; but a few brief and very general observations on the subject may be found of use to non-professional readers. It should, however, be clearly understood that no *invalid* is recommended to take a voyage, except under the advice and with the sanction of his physician or regular medical attendant; for there are special circumstances and peculiarities in the case of every patient which can only be duly weighed by his own medical adviser, after careful and individual examination.

The principal complaints for which invalids have hitherto been sent to sea are consumption, bronchitis, asthma, the after-effects of inflammation of the lungs and pleurisy, nervous complaints of various kinds, scrofulous diseases of joints, debility, the effects of overwork, etc.

Consumption is the illness of all others for which it is now customary to prescribe a sea voyage, although it is only comparatively of late years that this has been the case. There can be no doubt that in the *first* stages of consumption a judiciously selected sea voyage is often of incalculable value. The one great point is to take the disease sufficiently early—if possible, when the first threatenings only have manifested themselves. Every physician is familiar with cases where, while the patient is still young, and the constitution otherwise sound, symptoms arise which, though they might be regarded as trivial by the patient himself, will be at once recognised by the medical man as of grave import, especially if there should be a family predisposition to lung disease. These are, in fact, the "premonitory symptoms" of what may prove serious pulmonary mischief. It is in just such cases as these that a sea voyage acts most beneficially. It will often eradicate the tendency to consumption, and establish the constitution for life. Even in those cases where the first stage of the disease is more fully established, a few months at sea will frequently arrest the mischief, and sometimes effect a permanent cure.

It is when the disease has passed into its later stages that the advisability of sending a consumptive patient to sea becomes more doubtful. Even then great benefit will sometimes be obtained; but the question whether the possible good that *may* result will weigh against the certain loss of home comforts and the many inconveniences of ship life, is one that can only be decided by the physician in attendance on the case.

Unfortunately but few statistics bearing on this subject have been recorded, but such as are obtainable all point one way.

First, as to the preventive influence of the sea climate in regard to consumption. The registration returns of deaths amongst sailors of the mercantile marine show that the proportion of deaths from consumption as compared with those from other causes is *ten times less* than it is amongst the English land population. But if we take only the deaths that occur between the ages of fifteen and forty-five (the usual period during which sailors remain at sea) we shall find the result still more favourable—the proportion of deaths from consumption as against those from all other causes being *sixteen times less* at sea than on land.

Next as to the remedial effects of the ocean climate in the treatment of consumption. Dr. Theodore Williams has published statistics of eighteen cases in which the sea treatment received a thorough trial. Of these eighteen cases, sixteen improved, one remained stationary, and only one became worse. As some explanation of the extremely favourable results shown in this series of cases, it should be mentioned that the patients were carefully selected for treatment by physicians of great experience, and that several of them made more than one voyage.

With regard to thirty-eight cases of consumption which have come under my own observation, the results were as follows: twenty-eight improved, four remained stationary, three became worse, and one died. These cases were by no means selected. In some of them the disease was very far advanced—this was particularly the case with the three patients who became worse during the voyage. As regards the case that ended fatally, the patient had been for some time in the colonies, and was being sent home without any reasonable hope of his living to reach his destination. But even including these four cases which ought not to have been sent to sea at all, the results are most encouraging, and will compare favourably with any series of cases treated in the most favoured health resorts on shore.

Bronchitis is a complaint in which the climate of the ocean seems to be less certain in its action than in consumption. Patients who suffer either from chronic bronchitis, or from winter attacks of acute bronchitis, often derive much benefit from a voyage, not only by escaping the English winter (if they sail in the autumn), but also from the greater equability of the climate at sea, and the opportunities afforded them of being almost constantly in the open air. The colder portions of the voyage are, however, sometimes trying to bronchitic invalids, especially as there is often a good deal of atmospheric humidity accompanying the cold; but I have seldom or never seen severe attacks of bronchitis occur at sea, and the improvement in the general health usually brought about by the voyage is alone a great point gained. If the destination be Australia or South Africa, the dryness of the climate of either of these countries will render them admirably suited either as a temporary or a permanent residence for most patients suffering from bronchial affections.

Asthma—often associated with bronchitis—is a complaint presenting so many varieties and individual peculiarities, that it is impossible to speak of it with anything like certainty. Some patients never suffer from asthma while at sea, whereas others have their most severe attacks on board ship. The only reliable guide will be the patient's own previous experiences. If he has found, for instance, that he is most free from asthmatic attacks when staying at the seaside, he may generally safely look forward to deriving benefit from a voyage; but if an inland climate or the smoke-laden atmosphere of cities suits him best, he should on no account attempt to go to sea, as it is probable that the pure and somewhat humid air of the ocean would only aggravate his sufferings.

Inflammation of the lungs (pneumonia) and *pleurisy* are diseases which sometimes leave behind them after-effects of a very serious character: the lungs may be crippled in various ways, or weakened and rendered extremely susceptible to climatic influences, while the general health may be also more or less affected. In these cases—especially if the patient is young and the constitution naturally a sound one—it is impossible to speak too highly of a sea voyage as a means of insuring complete convalescence. The unfailing supply of fresh air, the enforced rest, the voracious appetite that usually sets in, have the happiest effect, and the patient often returns home with a re-established constitution.

Nervous complaints. These are so numerous and so varied in their manifestations, that it is only possible to speak of them generally. It may, however, be stated broadly that for all those anomalous affections of the nervous system that are not accompanied by any actual disease of the brain or spinal cord, but which are often dependent either upon mental causes or derangement of the digestive organs, we have in a sea voyage a most valuable and successful mode of treatment. In fact, there are no cases in which, as a rule, the effects of sea life are more strikingly beneficial than in these. The voyage, however, should be judiciously chosen. Where the physical health is not materially affected, but the mind is more at fault than the body—as in hypochondriasis—voyages of more varied interest, such as those to the Mediterranean, India, China, etc., or the shorter trip to the West Indies, may sometimes be selected in preference to the somewhat monotonous, though more invigorating, voyages to Australia or the Cape. The change of scene, the different mode of life, and the varied social conditions, thus experienced usually exercise the most cheering influence, not only upon the bodily health, but also upon the mental state; so that the nervous patient, after a month or two at sea, is often altogether a different being from what he was when he sailed.

With regard to the more serious diseases of the nervous system, such as paralysis and epilepsy, it is necessary to speak much more guardedly; and it is only after all the circumstances of such a case have been carefully weighed by the medical men in attendance, that it will be possible to form a decided opinion as to the advisability of a sea voyage.

Scrofulous affections of joints and glands and all kindred affections may, in certain stages, be most successfully treated by means of a sea voyage. It would of course be inadvisable to send a patient to sea while suffering from the more acute forms of joint disease, as the constant surgical attention and the many appliances and comforts required by the sufferer could scarcely be obtained on board ship. But when the more active symptoms have subsided, and, as is so often the case, the disease assumes a chronic form, the slow and tedious convalescence may, in suitable cases, be wonderfully hastened by a sea voyage of some duration. On land, fresh air and change of locality can, as a rule, only be obtained at the expense of being jolted in a carriage or some other mode of conveyance equally objectionable for invalids of this class; whereas at sea the patient can, during the greater portion of the voyage, recline on deck, in an invalid chair, under the most health-giving conditions of climate, and surrounded by much that will serve to interest and amuse him.

Debility, though not in itself a distinct disease, is nevertheless a very definite condition. It may be brought about from a variety of causes. The patient who is recovering from a severe illness or the effects of a surgical operation, and whose convalescence is slow and tedious,—the professional man, or man of business whose bodily health has broken down through over-work,—the lad who has "outgrown his strength,"—these are a few instances out of many that could be given of the way in which a constitution may become enfeebled, and where, although no actual disease may exist at the time, a thorough change of scene and climate becomes necessary to restore strength or prevent the development of more serious complaints. For cases such as these a sea voyage is thoroughly suitable: the entire rest, the invigorating sea climate, and the fresh experiences of life on board ship, are just what are required to build up a weakened and debilitated system.

The effects of over-work, etc. Closely allied with such cases as the preceding, and also with the nervous complaints that have been previously considered, are those cases of "break-down" which are, it is to be feared, greatly on the increase amongst us. The causes are various, but generally mental, such as over-study, domestic troubles and bereavements, business anxieties, and the innumerable worries of modern life. In such cases as these the brain has not as yet given way—it is only overwrought, and as soon as the thoughts can be turned out of the groove in which they have so long been confined, it will probably recover itself. Here again a larger choice of routes is open to us than in cases of purely physical illness, and it is impossible to overestimate the benefit that will often accrue to an overtaxed brain from the happy combination of rest, fresh air, and constantly changing scenes to be found in a judiciously selected sea voyage.

There are doubtless many other cases, besides those that have been mentioned, which the physician will from time to time see fit to send to sea; but the foregoing will probably include most of the disorders from which the great majority of invalids met with on board ship are found to be suffering. In by far the greater number of such cases the patient will improve during the voyage; and, in fact, *properly selected* cases will seldom fail to do so.

But the improvement in health will not be confined only to actual invalids. Those who are travelling for business or pleasure will almost always derive marked benefit from the voyage; and if they are strictly careful in carrying out the rules as to diet and exercise that are given in the following pages, they will generally experience an astonishing increase in strength and vigour by the end of the passage.

At the same time, those who take a voyage, whether as invalids or otherwise, must not fall into the mistake of looking upon the sea as a panacea for every ill, but must make up their minds to face many inconveniences and perhaps even a few dangers in their ocean life. They must remember, too, that the term "a good sailor" does not apply only to those who suffer little from sea-sickness, but that, in its wider sense, it means those who are able to adapt themselves easily and judiciously to a new mode of life—who are not unnecessarily alarmed by bad weather, or the many little accidents of the sea—who have sufficient resources within themselves not to be easily bored or depressed by the monotony inseparable from a long voyage, and who are able to "get on" harmoniously and pleasantly with their fellow-passengers. It is just those who are good sailors in this sense, who will derive most benefit from the sea, and who will be able in after-life to look back upon the voyages they have taken as being amongst the pleasantest experiences they have known.

CHAPTER II.

THE VARIOUS HEALTH VOYAGES.

Choice of voyages limited—The voyage to the West Indies—The voyage to Brazil and the River Plate—The climate of Brazil—The voyage to the Cape of Good Hope—The voyage to India by the Suez Canal—The voyage to Australia: three routes—The Indian route—The Pacific route—The Atlantic route—The latter voyage most suitable for invalids.

WE will now suppose that the reader, if an invalid, is under sailing orders from his physician; that he has been recommended to take a sea voyage for the benefit of his health, but that he has not yet received any definite instructions as to his route and destination. The world lies before him, and at first sight there would seem to be routes innumerable from which to choose. But practically the choice will be found to be much more limited than might be supposed. For the overworked man, indeed, or for the nervous invalid, to whom change of thought and scene are of more importance than climatic influences, there will be a tolerably wide field for selection; but in the case of those who are suffering from physical ailments, especially such ailments as affect the respiratory organs, the really suitable voyages are reduced to a very small number.

Excluding all sea passages of less than, say, fourteen days each way, as not affording sufficient time for the ocean climate to exercise an appreciable influence on the health and constitution, there remain the following voyages which may be considered more or less suitable:—

To   The West Indies.
„   Brazil and River Plate.
„   The Cape of Good Hope.
„   India, China, etc., by the Suez Canal.
„   Australia, etc., by the Suez Canal.
„   „   by the Pacific routes.
„   „   by the Cape of Good Hope.

Let us examine in turn the advantages and disadvantages of each of the above-named voyages.

THE VOYAGE TO THE WEST INDIES.—This voyage is specially suited for those who have but little time at their disposal, as the passage is comparatively a short one. It has also the advantage of being made in some of the finest and best-found steam-vessels afloat, with every surrounding of comfort and luxury that is possible at sea; while the ports touched at in the various islands present a constant succession of objects of interest to the traveller and naturalist. The charming description of these beautiful islands of the Atlantic given in Charles Kingsley's "At Last," will have rendered their wonders familiar to many readers.

The voyage to the West Indies should only be undertaken in winter, as in summer the climate is far from desirable for Europeans; but during the cooler months of the year—November, December, January, and February—most of the islands may be visited with confidence.

The steamers of the Royal Mail Steam-Packet Company leave Southampton for the West Indies on the 2nd and 17th of each month. The steamer that sails on the 2nd goes direct to St. Thomas; that which starts on the 17th calls first at the Island of Barbadoes. Both packets afterwards proceed to Jamaica, calling at various islands on their way. The voyage across the Atlantic, from

Southampton to either St. Thomas or Barbadoes, occupies, on an average, about fourteen days, and the trip may afterwards be indefinitely prolonged by proceeding in the Company's steamers to the various groups of islands, or to the adjacent ports of Mexico, Central America, or British Guiana. The Company have arranged various tours, occupying from six weeks to four months, and these afford opportunities for visiting an almost endless variety of places of interest.

The following is a list of the various islands and ports at which the steamers call:—

ISLAND OF ST. THOMAS.

ISLAND OF PORTO RICO.
- City of San Juan.
- Naguabo.
- Arroyo.
- Ponce.
- Mayaquez.
- Aguadilla.

ISLAND OF SAN DOMINGO.
- Porto Plata.
- Samaná.
- San Domingo.
- Jacmel.
- Port-au-Prince.

WINDWARD ISLANDS, etc.
- St. Kitts.
- Antigua.
- Guadaloupe.
- Dominica.
- Martinique.
- St. Lucia.
- Barbadoes.
- St. Vincent.
- Grenada.
- Trinidad.
- Tobago.

ISLAND OF JAMAICA—Kingston.
ISLAND OF CUBA—Havana.
ISLAND OF CURACOA.

THE VOYAGE TO THE WEST INDIES. 25

PORTS OF CENTRAL AMERICA, etc.
- Vera Cruz—*Mexico*.
- Belize—*Honduras*.
- Grey Town—*Nicaragua*.
- Port Simon—*Costa Rica*.
- Colon—*Isthmus of Panama*.
- Carthagena } *New Granada*.
- Savanilla }
- La Guayra—*Venezuela*.
- Demerara—*British Guiana*.

The following extracts from an article originally published in *Land and Water*,* and reprinted in a pamphlet form by the Royal Mail Company, will give, in few words, a capital idea of a West Indian Tour:—

"Let those of my readers whose only experience of the sea has been in a Channel or coasting steamboat imagine, if they can, a huge vessel of nearly 4,000 tons register, fitted with every comfort and convenience that modern science and skill can devise. Some of the passengers have already seen the ship, but those who have not at once commence a tour of inspection, and what do they see? A ladies' and smoking room on deck, a magnificent dining saloon amidships, and most commodious cabins, all provided with pneumatic bells, and furnished with best electro-plate fittings, which, together with glass and panelling of fancy wood, give a charming effect. It takes a long time to go over the ship and glance at the machinery, and no wonder, for there are upwards of thirty different steam engines used for various purposes, the steam for which is obtained from nine tubular boilers. No one need fear short commons as regards fresh water, on seeing a condensing apparatus sufficient to provide both passengers and crew with good drinking water, should the ordinary supplies by any accident be exhausted. The lifeboats and steam launches are hung on davits by a special method, so that two men, in a few

* Dec. 11th, 1880.

seconds, can lower them with ease and safety. Fire is well guarded against; for every compartment of the ship is separately fitted with an effective system of steam fire annihilators, on the Company's own plan.

"By this time lunch is ready, and shortly afterwards the bell rings for the friends of passengers to leave the steamer. . . . . Amid waving of handkerchiefs and lifting of hats, the magnificent vessel starts on her voyage, and every one settles down for two or three weeks to 'a life on the ocean wave.' There is considerable variety in a West Indian mail packet, and plenty of opportunity to practise French and Spanish; for there are generally a number of foreigners, among whom the Spanish Don predominates. There is also plenty of English society, consisting, for the most part, of Government officials and their families, naval and military officers, planters, and merchants. What with flirting, smoking, playing, reading, dancing, singing, and eating, the time soon passes. I have mentioned the gastronomic exercise last, but it certainly is not the least important occupation on board, for the meals, which are supplied on a most liberal scale, are coffee, biscuits, etc., in the morning, breakfast at nine, luncheon at 12.30, dinner, à la Russe, at five p.m., tea 7.30, and some indulge in supper afterwards.

"In about twelve days we reached St. Thomas, and never was the saying, 'Distance lends enchantment to the view,' more true than in this case; for although it looks pretty from the sea, a closer acquaintance proves it to be far from inviting. This is the head-quarters and one of the coaling stations of the Company in the West Indies, as well as the point from which the various intercolonial lines radiate.

"The scenery presented by the numerous islands, which are of every conceivable green, is magnificent, and Canon Kingsley compares them to 'an emerald with tints of sapphire and topaz hanging between blue sea and white surf below, and blue sky and white clouds above.' After sixteen hours' journey the steamer arrives at St. Kitts, and proceeds almost at once to Antigua, the most important of the Leeward Islands. Seven hours afterwards Guadaloupe, one of the French islands, is reached, and then Dominica, which possesses magnificent scenery and a boiling lake. Our next stopping place is St. Pierre, one of the principal cities of Martinique, possessing well-paved streets, a handsome opera house, and good hotels. After leaving Martinique, St. Lucia is the only island of call until we reach Bridgetown, the capital of Barbadoes, the residence of the Governor-General of the Windward Islands, and the see of a bishop. . . . . The broken patois of the negroes is most amusing, as well as the manner in which they call each other 'nigger,' as a term of reproach. Their Christian names are very elaborate, as also their white waistcoats and striped shirts on Sunday; but the black girls far outshine the men in finery, and appear once a week in gorgeous apparel.

"My next journey was to Trinidad, calling *en route* at St. Vincent and Grenada, the latter island being one of the most beautiful of the Caribbees, but so mountainous that I believe the only carriage belongs to the Governor, who can scarcely use it, whilst the streets are so steep that barrels of sugar roll down to the port of their own accord. No view can be more lovely than that afforded by the entrance to Port-of-Spain, the chief town of Trinidad, as it is approached from the sea through one of the three bocas or mouths. A great many French people reside in this island, as well as some Spaniards, and here I saw, for the first time, both Coolie and Chinese immigrants. The island is very picturesque, and produces a large quantity of cocoa, sugar, and cotton. The Pitch Lake is a curious phenomenon, usually visited by strangers, and behind the town is the Savannah and racecourse, around which is a charming drive. The Botanical Gardens and Government House are also in its vicinity, and the former contain the most wonderful trees and shrubs I have ever beheld. I left Trinidad for Demerara by the French Mail, and although there was not much to complain about, still the general arrangements and discipline were not equal to the Royal Mail. British Guiana has been much abused with regard to its climate, but I found the majority of the inhabitants in the enjoyment of perfect health, and I was so pleased with Georgetown, the people and the neighbourhood, that in spite of the kindness of the Barbadians towards me, I should certainly prefer living in Demerara. There is plenty of variety, and although the country is flat in some parts, it is very fertile, and produces splendid sugar. I managed to take a trip to Berbice, and also ascended the Essequibo river as far as the penal settlement, where the scenery is most beautiful and romantic, and consists of forests of cedar, ebony, and other valuable trees. The Kaiteur Fall, on the River Potaro, a tributary of the Essequibo, is nearly 750 feet high, and is alone almost worth the voyage from England now that it can be accomplished so quickly. Having learnt to eat pepperpot and brew milk-punch, which is better made in Demerara than elsewhere, I returned home after some further wanderings considerably wiser and more experienced than when I left old England."

With the exception of St. Thomas, which is seldom free from fever, and at which it is not advisable for Europeans to land, most of the islands may be visited in winter without risk, and the climate, although somewhat relaxing, is pleasant and enjoyable, and will form a most agreeable contrast to the rigours of an English winter; while the constant change of scene and the ever-varying interest render this voyage an admirable one for the over-worked professional man or the nervous invalid, as well as for the ordinary tourist in search of the novel and the picturesque.

For those, however, who are suffering from physical illness, especially if it have a pulmonary origin, the voyage to the West Indies is not so suitable. The time occupied in crossing the Alantic each way is not sufficiently long to allow of the sea climate exerting its full curative influence; and the climate of the islands themselves is not sufficiently good to constitute a really desirable health resort for consumptives. The fatigue also of landing and embarkation at the various ports would be trying for a confirmed invalid.

THE VOYAGE TO THE PORTS OF BRAZIL AND THE RIVER PLATE has, for invalids, considerable advantages over that to the West Indies. The time occupied in the passage to the various ports is approximately as follows:—

To Pernambuco	.	17 days.	To Santos	.	.	25 days.
,, Bahia	.	. 19 ,,	,, Monte Video	.	26	,,
,, Rio de Janeiro	.	22 ,,	,, Buenos Ayres	.	27	,,

The passenger, therefore, who chooses for his destination the most distant of these ports will have been at sea nearly four weeks; and although a considerable portion of the route lies near land, the greater part of the coasting is done in latitudes that are favourable to the invalid. Another point in favour of the voyage is that, while it has the advantage of being longer than that to the West Indies, it can be made under circumstances of equal comfort, as not only do the Royal Mail Company run steamers to Brazil and the River Plate, but there are also several other important lines of steam vessels sailing to those countries from various ports. Amongst these may be mentioned the following:—

The Pacific Steam Navigation Company, from Liverpool to the ports of Brazil every fortnight, calling at some or all of the following places *en route:* Bordeaux, Santander, Corunna, Carril, Vigo, Lisbon.

The Red Cross Line, from Liverpool to the northern ports of Brazil, every month, calling at Havre or Lisbon.

Messageries Maritimes de France, from Bordeaux to the ports of Brazil and River Plate, every fortnight, calling at Corunna, Lisbon, Dakar, etc.

The steamers of the Royal Mail Company leave Southampton for Brazil on the 7th, 9th, and 24th of each month.

The steamer that sails on the 7th calls at Carril and Vigo, and then proceeds direct to Monte Video and Buenos Ayres.

The packet which sails on the 9th calls at the following places: Cherbourg, Lisbon, St. Vincent (Cape Verd Islands), Pernambuco, Bahia, Rio de Janeiro, Santos.

The packet that sails on the 24th calls at Vigo, Lisbon, Pernambuco, Maceio, Bahia, Rio de Janeiro, Monte Video, and Buenos Ayres.

As regards the attractions presented by this voyage, I cannot do better than quote the following passage from Kidder and Fletcher's "Brazil and the Brazilians," which, although it refers to the homeward voyage, and mentions one or two places not now called at, will, *mutatis mutandis*, apply equally well to the outward passage: "I have sailed on many seas, but I know of no voyage which, all things considered, is comparable to that from Rio de Janeiro to England. We are out of sight of land but six days at the longest stretch, from Pernambuco to the Cape de Verds; while the average number of days at sea without stopping are two and a half. From Rio to Bahia there are but three days' steaming over summer waters, and the ten or twelve hours at the second city of the empire gives plenty of time for refreshing promenades or rides into the country. In less than two days we land at Pernambuco, where we spend from twelve to twenty hours, lay in a stock of fine oranges and pineapples— capital 'nauseatics'—and perhaps purchase a few screaming parrots or chattering monkeys to present to our European friends. We then steam for St. Vincent, Cape de Verds, where we remain a few hours; and next, steering northwards, in forty-eight hours we behold, 150 miles at sea, the tall Peak of Teneriffe, lifting itself more than 13,000 feet from the bosom of the ocean. Here we revel in peaches, pears, figs, and luscious clusters of grapes—in short, all the fruits of the temperate zone. We pass through the Canaries, and in thirty hours are at Funchal, where the fruit-dose is repeated. A walk upon the shore, 'if health bill clean,' is permitted, and after being bored a few hours by the pedlars and grape-vendors, we bid farewell to picturesque Madeira, and at the end of three days sail up the mouth of the Tagus, and anchor before Lisbon. When we leave Portugal, we steam along its coast and that of Spain, and in three days we land at Southampton. No such steamer voyage exists in the world; and those who are in quest of the strange, the new, and the beautiful, can nowhere so easily and so cheaply gratify their wishes in those respects as by the trip from Southampton to Rio, or *vice versâ*."

The climate of Brazil is on the whole a favourable one for Europeans, especially during the cooler months of the year. The northern portions of the state are of course tropical; but Rio de Janeiro, the capital, is situated only just within the tropics. Buenos Ayres and Monte Video, the cities of the River Plate, being situated many degrees further south, possess a much cooler climate.

The same authority I have quoted above gives the following account of the climate of Brazil:—

"No other tropic country is so generally elevated as Brazil. Though there are no very lofty mountains except on its extreme western border, yet the whole empire has an average elevation of more than 700 feet above sea level. This great elevation and those strong trade-winds combine to produce a climate much cooler and more healthful than the corresponding latitudes of Africa and southern Asia. The traveller, the naturalist, the merchant, and the missionary, do not have their first months of pleasure and usefulness thrown away, or their constitutions impaired, by acclimatising fevers. The mean temperature of Brazil, which extends from nearly the fifth degree of north latitude to the thirty-third degree of south latitude (almost an intertropical region), is from 81° to 88° F., according to different seasons of the year. At Rio de Janeiro, on the authority of Dr. Dundas, the mean temperature of thirty years was 73°. In December (which corresponds to June in the northern hemisphere) maximum 89·5°, minimum 70°, mean 79°. In July (the coldest month) maximum 79°, minimum 66°, mean 73·5°. I can add, from my own observations for several years, that I never saw 90° attained in the summer-time, and the lowest in the winter (June, July, and August) was 60°, and this was early in the morning. It must, however, be conceded that three months of weather ranging between 73° and 89° would be intolerable if it were not for the cool sea breeze on the coast, which generally sets in at eleven a.m., and the delicious land breeze, which so gently fans the earth until the morning sun has flashed over the mountains. In the interior the nights are always cool, and it may be added that 100 miles from the sea-coast the climate is entirely different. Rio is happily situated in its accessibility to the elevated regions. An hour's ride leaves you among the cascades and coolness of Zijuca. Six hours by steamer, railway, and coach lift you up to the mountain-city of Petropolis; or twelve hours will bring you amid the sublimities of the Sierra dos Orgöes and the silent and refreshing shade of Constancia, where at Heath's we may be far away from the dust, din, and diplomacy that are the constant concomitants of the commercial and political capital of Brazil." *

Lest the somewhat glowing description just quoted should convey a false impression as to the healthfulness of the climate, it is but right to add that of late years yellow fever has invaded the coast of Brazil, and that now nearly all the ports are subject to its visitations. Except, however, during an epidemic, the cases are not numerous, and I am assured that a casual visitor is not likely to run any risk from this cause.

Perhaps the best of the Brazilian ports for the invalid to stay at, if he contemplates remaining any length of time, will be Rio de Janeiro; for though the city itself is somewhat unhealthy, the high-lying localities mentioned above possess a fine and salubrious climate. It will, however, be still better to push on to the River Plate, and to take up quarters either at Monte Video or Buenos Ayres, both of these cities being almost entirely free from fever, and possessing a cooler climate than any of the Brazilian ports. Both Monte Video and Buenos Ayres are lively and interesting cities, and a stay of some duration may be very agreeably made at either of them.

THE VOYAGE TO THE CAPE OF GOOD HOPE.—This voyage, although scarcely so interesting to the general traveller as either of the preceding, is, for invalids,

---

* "Brazil and the Brazilians." Kidder and Fletcher.

perhaps the best of all the shorter voyages. A great part of the course lies through the central regions of the Atlantic, far removed from land influences; and the time occupied in the passage out and home is sufficient to allow the ocean climate to exert, to some extent, its specific effect on the constitution. In addition to this, the climate of South Africa is one of the best for pulmonary complaints that is to be found in the world.

There are two good lines of passenger steamers between England and the Cape—viz., those of the Union Steamship Company and those of the Castle Packets Company (Messrs. Donald, Currie, and Co.).

The steamers of the Orient line, which leave London at fortnightly intervals, also call (for the present) at Cape Town on their way to Australia, and take all classes of passengers.

The Union Company's mail steamers for the Cape of Good Hope leave Southampton every alternate Thursday, calling at Plymouth the following day. In addition to these, a steamer for Port Elizabeth and Natal is despatched every alternate Friday, calling at Cape Town to land passengers only.

The Castle Packets Company's steamers sail from London for Cape Town every alternate Tuesday, calling at Dartmouth on the following Friday.

All the Union Company's fortnightly steamers for Cape Town call at Madeira. Once in eight weeks one of the steamers calls at St. Helena. Ascension is only touched at on the homeward voyage.

Messrs. Donald Currie's steamers call at Madeira, and at intervals they also touch at St. Helena and Ascension.

The accommodation and fare on board both these lines of steamers are very good, and will compare favourably with other important ocean lines: all the latest improvements as regards ventilation, cabin fittings, etc., have been adopted by both companies.

The average length of passage from Southampton to Cape Town is now about twenty or twenty-one days; to Port Elizabeth, twenty-two or twenty-three days; and to Natal, about twenty-eight days. Some very rapid passages have however been made between England and the Cape. The *Pretoria* has made the outward voyage from port to port in eighteen days sixteen hours, including stoppages; and the *Durban* has made the homeward voyage in eighteen days nine hours. Both these vessels belong to the Union Company.

Although sailing vessels are sometimes advertised for the Cape, they are not adapted for passenger traffic; the accommodation and fare would scarcely be suitable except for those in robust health; and the want of society would also be a serious drawback.

The voyage to the Cape of Good Hope may be extended by taking the local steamers to Algoa Bay or Natal.

An account of the climate of South Africa and the localities most suitable for invalids will be found in another chapter.

THE VOYAGE TO INDIA, CHINA, ETC., BY THE MEDITERRANEAN AND THE SUEZ CANAL.—This voyage, from numberless descriptions, is familiar to every one as being the great high road to our Eastern possessions. It has the advantage of affording glimpses of many countries in the quick succession of a moving panorama; while the competition of many great lines of steamers render the passage rapid and luxurious. For these reasons the Indian voyage may sometimes be advantageously recommended in cases of nervous illness or mental strain, where amusement and change of scene are chiefly needed; but in other respects it can scarcely be regarded as a health voyage. The climate of the Mediterranean—whatever that of its coast-line may be—is not considered favourable for chest diseases; and the intense heat usually experienced in the Red Sea is trying to every constitution.

The Peninsular and Oriental Company's steamers sail from Southampton every Wednesday for Bombay, etc., *viâ* the Suez Canal. On alternate Wednesdays passengers have to change steamers at Suez, but at other times the whole voyage to Bombay is performed without transhipment.

In the "overland route," which is the quickest, passengers cross the Continent of Europe by railway to Venice or Brindisi; from thence they are conveyed by steamer to Alexandria, and instead of sailing through the Suez Canal they make the journey across the Isthmus by train, re-embarking at Suez for Bombay, etc., in one of the Company's steamers.

Besides the vessels of the Peninsular and Oriental Company, many other fine lines of steamers ply to India, China, and Japan through the Suez Canal, from various British and Continental ports. The accommodation and cuisine provided by most of these lines is excellent, and leaves little to be desired, but it is impossible, in the limits of the present chapter, to refer to each one separately. Special mention should, however, be made of the British India Steam Navigation Company, whose enormous fleet of seventy or eighty vessels plies to all parts of the world. The accommodation and fare on board these ships are said to be of the very best, and the great number of different places visited by the Company's packets will enable the passenger to vary his route in many ways.

The ports touched at by the Peninsular and Oriental steamers between Southampton and Bombay are Gibraltar, Malta, Port Said, Suez, and Aden.

The steamers for Calcutta, after leaving Aden, proceed

direct to Point de Galle (Ceylon), calling afterwards at Madras; those for China and Japan sail from Aden to Point de Galle, from thence to Penang, and passing through the Straits of Malacca, touch at Singapore, and afterwards sail northwards to Hong Kong, Shanghai, Yokohama, etc.

The time occupied in the voyage from Southampton to the various ports of the Mediterranean, India, etc., is approximately as follows:—

From Southampton to	Gibraltar	5 days.
,,	,, Malta	9 ,,
,,	,, Port Said	13 ,,
,,	,, Suez	14 ,,
,,	,, Aden	15 ,,
,,	,, Bombay	27 ,,
,,	,, Ceylon (Point de Galle)	29 ,,
,,	,, Madras	33 ,,
,,	,, Calcutta	37 ,,
,,	,, Penang	37 ,,
,,	,, Singapore	39 ,,
,,	,, Hong Kong	48 ,,
,,	,, Shanghai	54 ,,
,,	,, Yokohama (Japan)	57 ,,

As neither the passage itself to India and China by steamer, nor the climate of those countries, can be recommended for those whose first consideration is health, this voyage may be dismissed for the present, but it will be necessary to revert to it when speaking of the various Australian routes.

The days of the fine old East Indian sailing vessels, which used to convey passengers, troops, and freight to our Eastern possessions by way of the Cape of Good Hope, have passed away. The whole of the passenger traffic is now diverted to the Suez Canal, and even cargo is for the most part conveyed by that route; but a few sailing vessels still carry freight to China, etc., by the old route, and it might occasionally be possible for those so disposed to secure a passage on board one of those ships; but as they are neither fitted up nor victualled with a view to carrying passengers, the accommodation will necessarily be rough, and the absence of society and the tediousness of the voyage would deter most people, nowadays, from taking what was formerly one of the favourite and most luxurious of health voyages.

THE VOYAGE TO AUSTRALIA AND NEW ZEALAND.—This is the voyage which, in preference to all others, is now usually recommended to invalids—especially to those who are suffering from pulmonary complaints. Its length allows time for the ocean climate to exert its full effect upon the constitution; the destination is a healthy one; and the choice of steamers, "auxiliary screw" vessels, and sailing ships is almost unlimited.

There are now three great routes to Australia—viz., the Indian route, the Pacific route, and the Atlantic route.

(1.) *The Indian Route.*—The Peninsular and Oriental Company and other lines convey passengers for Australia by way of the Mediterranean, the Suez Canal and the Red Sea to Point de Galle, and from thence by another steamer to King George's Sound, Adelaide, Melbourne, and Sydney. The passage from Southampton to Melbourne by this route occupies about fifty-three days; it can, however, be shortened to the extent of two or three days by travelling "overland" to Venice or Brindisi, or it can be lengthened indefinitely by taking Indian or other ports on the way. Passengers may, if they prefer it, travel to Queensland by way of Singapore and Torres Straits. In this case they are conveyed on from Singapore by the steamers of the Eastern and Australian Mail Steam Company.

The high qualities of the Peninsular and Oriental Company's steamers are too well known to need comment, and the many comforts, the varied society and amusing incidents of this route will always recommend it as a pleasure trip. The disdavantages for invalids of the first part of the passage have been already pointed out; but after Aden has been passed, and the Red Sea left behind, the healthfulness of the voyage is much increased, although even now a great part of the course will lie through those equatorial regions which, of all parts of the ocean, are least desirable.

(2.) *The Pacific Route.*—This voyage may be made either by way of New York and San Francisco, or by the Isthmus of Panama.

In the former case the passenger may travel by any of the great Atlantic lines of steamers to New York, from whence a railway journey of over 3,300 miles across the whole breadth of the American continent takes him to San Francisco, where he joins one of the Pacific Mail steamers for Sydney, calling at Honolulu (Sandwich Islands) and Auckland (New Zealand) on the way.

The distances and the average time occupied on this route are as follows: but of course no one travelling for pleasure or health would think of making the journey in so short a time, and without resting at intermediate points.

	Miles.	Days.
* Liverpool to New York	3,000	10
New York to San Francisco	3,318	6
San Francisco to Honolulu	2,100	8
Honolulu to Auckland	3,879	15
Auckland to Sydney	1,300	4
Total	13,597	43

The first half of the railway journey from New York

* Handbook of Pacific Mail Steamship Company.

across the American continent can be varied to a considerable extent, according to individual taste, and can be made to embrace a great number of places of interest. The latter section of the journey is made by the Pacific Railway, and takes the traveller near some of the most magnificent scenery and most remarkable localities of the New World.

If, in order to avoid the long railway journey across America, the voyage is made by way of the Isthmus of Panama, the traveller can either proceed in the first instance to New York as before, and from thence take one of the Pacific Mail steamers to Aspinwall; or preferably, he can sail direct to the latter place from England by one of the Royal Mail steamers.

Colon (Aspinwall), on the northern or Atlantic side of the Isthmus, is connected with Panama, on the southern or Pacific side, by a railway line forty-seven miles in length. From Panama the Pacific Mail steamers convey passengers to San Francisco, where they are transferred to another of the Company's vessels for Sydney, *viâ* Honolulu and New Zealand.

Although both the Pacific routes are full of interest to the general traveller, neither of them can be regarded as suitable to the confirmed invalid. The long railway journey in the one case, occupying, as it does, many days and nights; the unhealthy climate of the Isthmus of Panama in the other case; the many changes and the relaxing latitudes common to both, render the Pacific routes inadmissible for the valetudinarian. At the same time it must be acknowledged that, for those who are sufficiently well to brave fatigue and heat, and whose first considerations are change and recreation rather than the curative effects of the ocean climate, there are few pleasanter ways of seeing the world than by combining the Pacific and the Indian routes—visiting Australia, for instance, by way of New York and San Francisco, and returning by way of India and the Suez Canal, or *vice versâ*. The Pacific Mail Steamship Company issue circular tickets for this tour round the world, and give every facility for breaking the journey at all points of interest which the tourist may desire to visit.

(3.) *The Atlantic Route.*—As the long sea voyage to Australia round the Cape of Good Hope is emphatically the invalid's route, it demands more careful consideration than either of the preceding. Although, perhaps, presenting less variety and interest than the others, its advantages for the invalid are at once apparent. The whole voyage is performed without transhipment or changes of any kind, so that the traveller can settle himself into his cabin, surrounded by such comforts as are possible to him, and feel that it will be his floating home until he is landed at his destination on the other side of the world. The duration of the voyage—from forty days to three months, according to the class of vessel in which it is made—is sufficiently long to allow the sea climate to exert its full constitutional effects; and, lastly, the portions of the ocean that are traversed by this route are, on the whole, the best that can be chosen. The voyage itself, and the regions of the ocean through which a vessel passes on its way to Australia by this route, are described in detail in other chapters; at present it will be only necessary to glance at the different classes of passenger ships available for selection by the intending voyager.

There are three descriptions of vessels in which the voyage to Australia or New Zealand may be made; viz., (1) Full-powered ocean steamers, (2) sailing vessels, (3) a combination of the two—viz., sailing vessels with an "auxiliary screw."

With the exception of the venerable *Great Britain*,

which plied for so many years between England and Australia without a rival, and which properly belonged to the class of auxiliary screws, Australian steam vessels are a comparatively recent institution.

About 1862, Messrs. Money Wigram added to their fine fleet of Australian sailing ships a few vessels such as the *Somersetshire*, the *Northumberland*, and the *Durham*, which, while they were built to sail with speed, were also furnished with screw propellers, worked by engines of moderate power, for use when the wind is light or contrary. These vessels, which have been for so many years favourably known on the Australian line, are for the present running to New Zealand at intervals as required.

Vessels of this class made the passage to Melbourne, under favourable circumstances, in from fifty to fifty-five days. Some of the newer ones have occasionally done it in forty-five days.

The first steam vessel built to perform the *whole* journey between England and Australia by steam, without the aid of sails, was despatched in 1874, and, despite all unfavourable prognostications, succeeded in making the voyage to Melbourne in about forty-nine days, including stoppage at the Cape to coal. Since that time many other full-powered steamships have been put on to the Australian line, the average time occupied on the passage being now only from forty to forty-five days.*

The lines of sailing vessels to Australia and New Zealand are now so numerous as to afford passengers an almost unlimited choice; and although some of the old well-known firms, such as Green's, still retain the foremost rank in public estimation, yet the competition is so great, that fairly good accommodation may be reckoned upon in the ships belonging to all respectable owners,

* The *Orient* has, I believe, made the passage in thirty-seven days.

if due care is taken in the selection, while the charges by some of these are considerably lower than in the case of the old-established lines.

The speed of sailing vessels has been greatly increased since the days when a voyage to Australia often occupied six months. It may now take from fifty-nine days (which is, I believe, the shortest passage on record) to 120 days, or, in *very* exceptional cases, even longer; while the average length of passage is about eighty days.

More detailed information as to the various lines of passenger ships to Australia, and the comparative merits of the different classes of vessels, will be found in the next chapter.

CHAPTER III.

TIME OF STARTING.—CHOOSING A SHIP.

Best time of starting for the West Indies—Healthiest months in India—Reversal of the seasons in the southern hemisphere—The best time of year for Brazil and the Cape of Good Hope—Importance of leaving England in the early autumn—Choice of a ship—Respective advantages of sailing vessels and steamers—Tonnage of sailing vessels—Iron, wooden, and "composite" ships—Poop-ships and flush-deck ships—Australian and New Zealand steam-lines—The "Orient" line—The "Colonial" line—The "Elder" line—Messrs. Wigram's steamships—Australian lines of sailing vessels—Messrs. Green's "Blackwall" line—Messrs. Wigram's sailing ships discontinued—Messrs. Devitt and Moore—Messrs. Anderson, Anderson, and Co.—Messrs. Trinder. Anderson. and Co.—Messrs. Houlder Brothers and Co.—Mr. J. H. Flint—Various other firms—New Zealand sailing lines—The New Zealand Shipping Co.—The "Passenger" line—The Australian ports.

HAVING selected his route, our traveller must next decide upon his time for starting. Of course in many cases he will have no option—he must go when he can; but where circumstances will allow a choice to be made, the time of year at which the voyage is commenced is a point to be carefully considered, not only with reference to the voyage itself, but also with regard to the climate of the country that is to be visited. Thus, hot countries should, as a rule, be visited only in winter; and even in those countries which possess a more moderate climate, some months are much more favourable than others. A brief consideration of the best time of year for making each of the voyages that have been mentioned may prove useful.

In the West Indies the seasons coincide with our own;

and it is only in winter that a European, and especially an invalid, would from choice visit these islands. One or two of the West Indian ports are scarcely altogether free from yellow fever and other infectious diseases even in winter, and of course in summer the risk of infection is everywhere greater; added to which, the intense heat during the hot months of the year would be trying even to the strongest constitutions. The best time, therefore, to start on this voyage is in the late autumn, so as to be in the West Indies during the months of December, January, or February. The necessity for starting so late in the year is a drawback to this voyage for those suffering from any chest delicacy.

In taking a voyage to India through the Suez Canal the time of starting is also very important. During the summer and early autumn the heat in the Red Sea is often most intense,—so much so as occasionally to prove fatal; while the pleasantest and healthiest months for Europeans in India are as a rule November, December, and January. The time of sailing should therefore be so arranged as not only to avoid as much as possible the period of extreme heat in the Red Sea, but also to arrive in India during the cool season. This is best done by leaving England some time during the month of October.

The seasons in countries situated in the southern hemisphere are of course the reverse of our own, and the time of departure must be arranged with due regard to this fact. The following simple table of the months which correspond with each other in the two hemispheres may be found of use:—

January corresponds with July
February ,, ,, August
March ,, ,, September
April ,, ,, October
May ,, ,, November
June ,, ,, December.

In Brazil the healthiest season of the year, on the whole, is the winter (corresponding to our summer)—the coolest month being July. An invalid visiting that country should therefore endeavour to start in the spring, about May. Unless it is intended to spend the following winter abroad, the Brazilian voyage is on this account an unsuitable one for patients suffering from pulmonary complaints, as they would be returning to England at the worst time of year—viz., in the autumn.

The climate of the Cape of Good Hope, if the locality be judiciously chosen, is at all times a good one for chest invalids; but the time of year when the country is to be seen at its best, and when the colony is altogether pleasantest for Europeans, is the spring—viz., about October and November. The best time, therefore, for leaving England will be in September, which is an admirable time for invalids who wish to escape the winter at home.

In the Australian colonies, as in South Africa, localities are to be found that are admirably adapted for invalids at all seasons of the year. Those, therefore, who choose the Australian voyage need be under no particular anxiety as to the time at which they will arrive at their destination. Speaking generally, the autumn—corresponding to our March, April, and May—is perhaps the most favourable time of year as regards climate. In many parts of Australia, however, the winter is delightful, while for seeing the vegetation in full perfection the spring is the most favourable time.

The climate of Australia and of South Africa, and the characteristics of the seasons in those countries, will be fully described in future chapters.

Having spoken of the best time for sailing, from the point of view of the country to be visited, it may be as well to say a few words as to the most favourable months for leaving our own shores in order to avoid the inclemencies of our climate and unnecessary discomforts at starting.

For invalids suffering from chest delicacy it will of course be very important to escape our English winter; and for this reason the autumn should in all cases be chosen, when practicable, as the time for commencing the voyage. It is true that cold weather will not altogether be avoided by those who start in the autumn on a voyage to Australia. For five or six weeks after passing to the south of the Cape of Good Hope a temperature will be experienced which, though seldom below 50°, will appear considerably lower on account of the humidity of the air and the strong winds that almost constantly blow in those regions of the ocean. But although the weather is cold and bracing, it is still the summer of those latitudes, as shown by the length of the days and the brightness of the sunshine. Those few weeks of cold weather are therefore very different in their effect on the constitution to the seven or eight months of fog, gloom, and rain which we so frequently experience in England.

The date of sailing should not be delayed too long. September, or, at the latest, October, should be the month chosen. Towards the end of September and the beginning of October the "equinoctial gales" are supposed to prevail round the British coasts, and some may prefer to avoid sailing during the time they are expected. But seafaring men take but little notice of these gales, which are very irregular in their occurrence.

The invalid should, if possible, avoid sailing during the winter months. The weather round our coasts is then often very severe, and the cold is all the more trying because the comforts of home have just been left behind. Sea fogs and violent gales frequently prevail during the winter season, and increase the discomforts, if not the dangers, of the first part of the voyage.

Besides these objections to commencing a voyage in winter, there is also the very important one of the rapid transition from the cold of England to the heat of the tropics, which cannot but be trying to those of delicate constitution at the commencement of a voyage.

From the foregoing remarks it will be seen that if the invalid is in a position to fix his own time of starting; if his destination should be the Cape of Good Hope or Australia; and particularly if he suffers from chest delicacy, the early autumn is the best time for him to commence his travels.

CHOICE OF A SHIP.—The next point will be the choice of a ship. If the voyage is to the West Indies, to Brazil, to India by the Suez Canal, or to the Cape of Good Hope, the choice will be confined to those steamers of one or more great lines which happen to be sailing at the time the traveller wishes to start. Nor would it be necessary in these cases to exercise any further selection, because the name of the company is usually a sufficient guarantee for the safety and comfort of each of its vessels. But when the contemplated voyage is to Australia or New Zealand by the Atlantic route, there will be a much wider choice. It will then be necessary to decide between sailing vessels, steamers, and vessels with an auxiliary screw; and if a sailing vessel be chosen, there will be the ships of various lines from which to select.

This brings us to the important question of the respective advantages to the invalid of sailing vessels and steamers. Putting aside the question of greater speed and economy of time, which, it is to be supposed, are not of the first importance to an invalid traveller, the principal advantages of a steamer over a sailing vessel are the (usually) superior cuisine and attendance, and the uniform rate of progress—the steam-power being specially of value as ensuring a rapid passage through those equatorial regions in which it is by no means desirable to linger. The currents of air produced by the movement of the vessel, and the greater facilities for ventilation by means of windsails, etc., will also be points in favour of steamers during the warmer parts of the voyage. Against these advantages, however, are to be set some very grave drawbacks. One of these is the constant vibration of the engines, which, continuing night and day, is very distressing to some invalids, especially to those who are suffering from nervous complaints. The disagreeable greasy smell from the engine-room, and the blacks which are sometimes sprinkled from the funnel, are also far from pleasant. The whole ship is also hotter on account of the furnaces and the radiated heat from the funnel, etc. I find that the maximum heat in the tropics is from $8°$ to $10°$ greater in the cabins of an iron steamship, than in those of a wooden sailing vessel. Again, the motion of a steamer is more uneasy than that of a sailing vessel, especially when the former is steaming against a head wind. But the most important disadvantage of all is the greater economy of space rendered necessary in steamers by the large amount of room taken up by the engines and coal-bunkers; by the extra expenses of steam, and the extra value of freight. The cabins are therefore smaller and more crowded. Thus, while in a good sailing vessel a cabin measuring ten feet by ten feet will contain only two berths, a cabin considerably smaller, viz., ten feet by seven or eight feet, will in a steamer be made to accommodate three passengers. In the more modern steamers, much is done to render the ventilation as satisfactory as possible, but the small cabin space, and the crowding together of its occupants, must always be, especially in the case of invalids, a serious drawback.

Vessels with an "auxiliary screw" would seem at first sight to combine all the advantages of sailing ships and steamers; and in some respects this is the case. They sail when the wind is favourable, and they have the advantage of being able to get up steam and hurry through those belts of calm in which a vessel with only sails to depend upon is sometimes detained for many days. The great objection of comparatively small and crowded cabins still, however, remains, and seems at present to be inseparable from steamers of all kinds.

Looking at the question from every point of view, there can be no hesitation in saying, that, for any one really travelling for health, a sailing vessel is more suitable than a steamer, especially if the invalid suffers from chest delicacy. Not only are the cabins more roomy and less crowded, but a certain air of quiet and an absence of bustle and hurry usually prevail on board a sailing vessel, which are seldom to be found in a steamer; and although those who are of an impatient disposition may chafe at the delay caused by calms and contrary winds, others only regard those hindrances as an agreeable change, and find them less monotonous than a uniform rate of progress.

But the most important points of all in favour of a sailing vessel for invalids suffering from chest delicacy are the greater length of time occupied in the voyage,—thus allowing the climate of the sea ample scope for its curative effects,—and the more gradual transition from cold to hot latitudes, and *vice versâ*. In a steamer, these transitions are so sudden and abrupt as often to be extremely trying to delicate constitutions; for although those changes of climate, by their hardening effect on the system, constitute an important factor in the benefit derived from sea voyages, yet if made too rapidly the shock is greater than can be borne by most invalids.

Bearing in mind, however, the extraordinarily rapid development of steam in connection with the Australian trade during the last five or six years, it is almost impossible to doubt that before long the whole of the passenger traffic will be absorbed by the great lines of steamers, and that the handsome and well-found Australian sailing packet will—unless a few are specially retained as invalid ships—become as much a thing of the past as the old East Indiaman. But although we may be inclined to regret this, we fortunately live in an age of progress, and the great improvements already made in the construction and arrangements of steamers warrant us in the hope that most of the objections which at present exist to this class of vessels in the case of invalids may before long be removed.

A few particulars as to the size and construction of the two classes of passenger vessels may be found of interest.

To begin with steamers. The great tendency of the present day is to increase not only the size but the power of ocean steam-ships. Each year sees vessels launched which are larger and more powerful than their predecessors. In saying this, no account is made of the *Great Eastern*, which was a prodigy, born before its time, and, like most prodigies, to some extent a failure. But the ships which are year by year added to the fleets of great existing lines are not experiments, but a cautious and successful advance upon former models.

It is little more than sixty years ago since the first steamer was constructed. It was merely a strong barge fitted with engines and paddle-wheels. The large ocean steamers of the present day are nearly all from 300 ft. to 520 ft. in length, and have a gross tonnage of from

2,000 to 8,500 tons. In size, construction, rig, and internal arrangement, steamers present an almost endless variety. In some the saloon and principal cabins are at the stern end of the ship; in others they are in front of the engine-room; and in others again they occupy the more central portion of the vessel. The saloon is in many cases placed longitudinally, with the sleeping cabins opening into it on either side; while in other ships it occupies a section of the whole breadth of the vessel. Some steamers are built with "poop-decks," and in this case the "poop," which is constructed above the main deck, contains the saloons and the best sleeping cabins. Other ships have "flush-decks," in which case nearly the whole of the accommodation is below. No two ships are altogether alike, and all have their distinctive features, and good and bad qualities.

The following description of the *Servia*, a new ship added to the fleet of the Cunard Company in March, 1881, will give an idea of the latest development of ship-building as applied to ocean passenger traffic.

"The dimensions of the *Servia* are—length, 530ft., breadth 52ft., depth 44ft. 9in., gross tonnage 8,500 tons. A better idea of the huge size of the vessel will be gained from the following facts. Her cargo capacity will be equal to 6,500 tons, with 1,800 tons of coal and 1,000 tons of water ballast, the vessel having a double bottom on the longitudinal bracket system. It is anticipated that the indicated horse-power will amount to 10,500. There are in all seven boilers, six of which are double and one single-ended, and all are made of steel, with corrugated furnaces, the total number of furnaces being thirty-nine. Practically the *Servia* is a five-decker, as she is built with four decks and a promenade. The promenade, which is reserved for the passengers, is very large and spacious. On the fore part of it are the steam steering gear and house, captain's room, and flying bridge. On the upper deck forward is the forecastle, with accommodation for the crew, and lavatories and bath rooms for steerage passengers, while aft are the light towers for signalling the Admiralty lights, with the look-out bridge on the top. Near to the midship house are the captain's and officers' sleeping cabins. Next to the engine skylight is the smoking-room, which can be entered from the deck or from the cabins below. It is unusually large for a smoking-room, being 30ft. long by 22ft. wide. Near the after-deck house is the ladies' drawing-room, to which access can be obtained either from the music-room or from the deck. Abaft of this, and in the upper end of the upper deck, is the music-room, which is 50ft. by 22ft. in dimensions, and which is to be fitted up in a handsome manner with polished wood panellings. Immediately abaft of the music-room is the grand staircase, which leads to the main saloon and the cabins below on the main and lower decks. For the convenience of the passengers there are no fewer than four different entrances from the upper deck of the ship to the cabins. At the foot of the stair leading to the saloon and also in the cabins the panellings are of polished Hungarian ash and maple wood. The saloon is very large, being 74ft. long by 49ft. wide, with sitting accommodation for 350 persons, while the clear height under the beams is 8ft. 6in. The sides are all in fancy woods, with beautifully polished inlaid panels. All the upholstery of the saloon is of morocco leather. Right forward of the after-deck are the pantries, baths, lavatories, and state rooms. The total number of state rooms is 168, and the vessel has accommodation for 450 first-class and 600 steerage passengers, besides a crew of 200 officers and men. For two-thirds of its entire length the lower deck is fitted up with first-class state rooms. The ship is divided into nine water-tight bulkheads, and she is built according to the Admiralty requirements for war purposes. There are in all twelve boats, and these are equipped as lifeboats, and have Hill and Clark's patent improved boat-lowering apparatus. The upper deck is of steel, covered with yellow pine, the main deck is of steel with a teak covering, and the lower deck is of steel with a covering of teak above the engine and boiler spaces. All the deck houses and deck fittings, which are liable to be carried away in a heavy sea, are made of iron and steel, and are riveted to the steel decks underneath. The *Servia* possesses a peculiarity which will add to her safety—namely, a double bottom, or iron skin. Thus, were she to ground on rocks, she would remain perfectly safe while the inner skin continued intact. There are three masts on the vessel, and the Cunard Company have adhered to their special rig, believing it to be more ship-shape than the practice of fitting up masts according to the length of the ship. On these masts there will be a good spread of canvas to assist in propelling the vessel."*

In some of the more recently built steamers, considerable improvements have been made as regards the ventilation and warming of the cabins: not a few are fitted up throughout with electric or pneumatic bells; and I believe it is in contemplation to introduce the electric light in some of the larger vessels.

We will now turn to sailing ships. Although vessels of this class have within the last fifty years undergone very great improvements, especially as regards size and speed, the advance has scarcely been so rapid as in the case of steamers. The rig has, at any rate to a landsman's eye, been but little altered—there are still the

* *Times*, March 3rd, 1881.

full-rigged ships, barques, brigs, brigantines, and schooners, of former days. Certain labour-saving appliances, such as double topsail yards, self-reefing topsails, donkey-engines, etc., have been introduced. These have been rendered necessary by the small crews—scarcely half those of former days—which, owing to competition and heavy expenses, even the largest ships are now compelled to carry. A wonderful increase of speed has been brought about by the application of scientific principles to the construction of modern sailing vessels. Little more than half a century ago a voyage to Australia often occupied more than six months; now it is frequently made in little more than two.

But it is perhaps in the matter of size that the greatest advance has been made. In old times the longest voyages used to be made in vessels of 40 or 50 tons burden. Even in the most flourishing days of the East India traders, there were but few ships of more than 1,000 tons, and their size was only excused on the ground that they might have to defend themselves or even to attack on occasion. They took out small armaments and a crew some sixty to a hundred strong. Now there are few passenger ships of *less* than 1,000 tons, and many are over 2,000 tons. Most of the sailing vessels carrying passengers to Australia and New Zealand have a registered tonnage of 1,000 to 2,000, and even the largest are now content with a crew of from thirty to forty men and boys, including officers and midshipmen, but exclusive of stewards.

Iron has been so rapidly superseding wood for ship-building purposes of late years, that the old-fashioned "frigate-built" ship, framed entirely of hard wood (generally teak or oak), is quickly disappearing. The new ships —which are generally of the longer narrower build to which the term "clipper" has been applied—are mostly either built altogether of iron, or are what are called "composite" ships—that is, they consist of a casing of wood upon an iron framework. There are still, however, some fine wooden ships remaining; and, where the choice can be made, wood is to be preferred to iron for several reasons, the most important of which is that wooden ships are cooler in hot and warmer in cold latitudes than iron ones. Composite vessels, whose sides are constructed entirely of wood, are free from any objection, and are often most comfortable and reliable in every respect.

The great majority of passenger sailing vessels are "poop" ships, and most of the first-class passengers are accommodated in the poop cabins. There are, however, a few very fine "flush-deck" ships, in which there is either no poop at all, or one only sufficiently large to contain the officers' cabins. In these vessels the whole of the passengers' cabins are on the lower deck. Flush-deck ships have one or two advantages over those with a poop. They generally afford a larger space for exercise, and the cabins are more protected in rough weather.* On the other hand, the ventilation in the cabins is not usually so good as it is in a poop ship, as the ports are not only smaller, but also being nearer the sea, they have to be closed more frequently. In fact, poop cabins are always liked on account of their airiness and cheerfulness.

Australian sailing vessels intended to carry passengers are, as we have seen, generally of from 1,000 to 2,000 tons register. As a rule, the larger the ship the steadier she will be in all ordinary weather; but some seafaring men hold that in really severe gales a ship of 1,000 tons will

* Flush-deck ships frequently have a smoking-room on deck. This is a very great advantage to invalids, as it affords them shelter during rough or rainy weather, and they are not compelled to go below and breathe the vitiated air of the saloon and cabin—always worse at such times on account of the skylights being closed.

behave better than one of 2,000. Speaking generally, and from personal experience, I am inclined to the opinion that the larger the ship the more comfortable she will be found in all respects under all ordinary circumstances.

The following description of the *Sobraon*, one of Messrs. Green's Australian packets, will give some idea of the dimensions and equipment of a first-class sailing vessel.

The ship in question is a "composite" ship—that is, she is built of solid teak, with iron beams and framework. She is of 2,130 tons register, 3,500 tons burden. Her length is 300 feet, her breadth 40 feet; extreme depth of hold 28 feet. The height of the mainmast, which in common with the other masts is of wrought iron, is 189 feet, 29 feet being below the main deck. The length of the main and fore yards is 90 feet; lower topsail yards 76 feet; upper topsail yards 56 feet; royal yards 44 feet. All the yards are of steel.

The following is a list of the sails, with the quantity of canvas contained in each:—

MAINMAST.

Mainsail	. 720 yds.	Topmast staysail	. 330 yds.
Two maintopsails	. 700 ,,	Topgallant ,,	. 260 ,,
Topgallantsail	. 280 ,,	Royal ,,	. 188 ,,
Royal	. 193 ,,		

FOREMAST.

Foresail	. 583 yds.	Royal	. 180 yds.
Two foretopsails	. 700 ,,	Topmast staysail	. 165 ,,
Topgallantsail	. 280 ,,	Three jibs	. 600 ,,

MIZENMAST.

Crossjack	. 300 yds.	Topmast staysail	. 327 yds.
Two mizentopsails	. 450 ,,	Topgallant ,,	. 210 ,,
Topgallantsail	. 190 ,,	Spanker	. 280 ,,
Royal	. 120 ,,		

Giving a total of 7,056 yards, or not far short of *two acres* of canvas.

Some idea may be formed of the expense of a suit of sails from the fact that a new mainsail costs nearly £100.

The *Sobraon* is built with a special view to carrying a large number of passengers. She has a flush deck, with only a very small poop, containing merely the officers' quarters. There is a deck-house, containing a smoking-room, two bath-rooms, and a handsome staircase leading to the saloons. The principal saloon is more than 100 feet in length, and is panelled in polished teak and maple. It will dine seventy or eighty people. There is also a prettily decorated ladies' saloon near the stern of the ship. On either side of the saloons are the sleeping cabins, and at one end of the principal saloon there is a piano. The second and third-class cabins are particularly roomy and well ventilated.

The reader will now, it is hoped, be in a position to make his selection of the class of ship which will best suit his state of health, his requirements, and the length of time at his disposal, and may turn his attention to the various lines of vessels which, in the case of a voyage to Australia or New Zealand will be at his disposal.

If it is decided to make the passage out by steam, the choice will be somewhat limited, as there are at present only a few lines of steamers running to the Australian colonies. They are as follows: but changes are so constantly occurring in all matters connected with shipping, especially at the present time, that the information given can only be taken as approximately correct up to the date of publication:—

1. The full-powered steamships of the "Orient" Steam Navigation Company (limited), associated at present with vessels belonging to the Pacific Steam Navigation Company, run every fortnight from London (South-west India Docks) to Adelaide, Melbourne, and Sydney. The steamers

of this line are splendid vessels, of about 4,000 to 5,400 tons register. They are provided with every accommodation for passengers, including steam heating apparatus, bath-rooms, smoking-room, ice-house, piano, library, etc., and make the passage out in about forty to forty-five days.* They embark passengers at either Gravesend or Plymouth, and call at St. Vincent (Cape Verd Islands) and at Cape Town on the outward voyage.

2. Messrs Houlder Brothers advertise a line of Australian Steamships comprising, according to their lists, some fine vessels of 3,000 to 4,500 tons register. These vessels have the advantage of containing only two berths in each cabin. It should be mentioned that the outward route of these ships is sometimes by the Suez Canal, and sometimes by the Cape of Good Hope, according to circumstances. The sailings take place at present at

---

* The following account of the *Orient*, one of the new steamships of the "Orient" Steam Navigation Company, is taken from the *Daily News* :—" The total length of the *Orient* is 460 ft., her width 46 ft. 6 in., and her depth 37 ft. 8 in. Her tonnage is 5,400. She is 4,000 horse-power nominally, but practically 4,500. She has accommodation for 136 saloon passengers, 138 second-class, and 300 steerage, with further capacity for 250 more. If needed for war purposes, she could take 3,000 troops and 400 horses. Every provision for safety in case of accident has been made. Cork life-belts are found in every bunk. The life and other boats are capable of taking off the whole of an average ship's party, and the ship is divided into seven water-tight compartments. Pipes are laid all over in case of fire, so that the vessel might be almost instantaneously flooded. The *Orient* is built expressly for the Australian and New Zealand trade, and, as already stated, is expected to do the voyage to Adelaide in thirty-five days. Her consumption of coal will not be far short of seventy tons per day. Her total weight, with full complement of passengers and freightage, will be about 10,000 tons—her four anchors alone weighing four tons each. The total cost will not be much less than £150,000. Her crew, including stewards, numbers nearly 150."

irregular intervals, but are well advertised beforehand in the public papers.*

3. Mr. John Henry Flint advertises, in connection with the "Colonial" line, steamers similar to the above for the Australian voyage. The sailings and full particulars are notified from time to time in the public prints.

4. Mention has already been made of the vessels belonging to the class formerly known as "auxiliary screws," owned by Messrs. Money Wigram and Sons. They comprise the *Somersetshire*, *Northumberland*, *Durham*, and *Kent*—vessels of from 2,000 to 3,000 tons register, all of which achieved a great reputation for comfort and convenience. The *Norfolk*, the last added to the list, is a vessel of a somewhat different class to the others. She has engines of greater power, and more nearly resembles the full-powered steamers, such as those of the "Orient" line. After a long and useful career in the Australian trade, these ships now run at intervals to the ports of New Zealand, in connection with one of the New Zealand passenger lines.

It will be seen, on looking over the above list, that a passenger wishing to proceed to Australia *by steam*, during any particular month, will, on an average, have two or three steamers from which to choose; and as each of these vessels will probably be of a different class, there will be no difficulty in arriving at a decision.

But when the voyage is to be made in a sailing vessel, the selection becomes a matter of some little difficulty, because there are so many great lines of passenger ships, many of which offer excellent accommodation.

Perhaps the best known of all the shipping firms is

* It should be borne in mind that the same vessels are sometimes advertised under different agencies, and would appear as if belonging to several different "lines."

that of Messrs. Green and Co., of Blackwall, whose magnificent fleet of East Indian and Australian vessels used in former days to rank next to the Royal Navy.

Since the discontinuance of the old passenger route to India by the Cape of Good Hope, the actual number of their sailing ships has been considerably diminished; but, on the other hand, they have built some very fine steamers for the Indian voyage through the Suez Canal. They still retain, however, a considerable number of Australian sailing packets—some being frigate-built ships of the older type, others iron and composite vessels,—many of which are amongst the largest and finest sailing ships to be found in the mercantile marine. Although perhaps not so well found, nor so fully manned, as in the palmy old East Indian days, Messrs. Green's ships still maintain their position in the very first rank of Australian passenger lines, and their vessels are in all respects thoroughly reliable. Some of them, such as the *Sobraon*, regularly make the return voyage by the Cape of Good Hope, and have obtained quite a reputation as invalid ships.

The firm of Messrs. Money Wigram and Sons was, many years ago, associated with that of Messrs. Green; and when the separation occurred, they took with them the original house flag, which, according to tradition, they won by lot. In addition to their auxiliary screw steamships, which have been already mentioned, Messrs. Wigram until recently owned a fine fleet of sailing vessels of much the same type as those of Messrs. Green and Co. For some years past, however, they have gradually reduced the number of their ships, until at the present time not more than one is retained on the Australian line, even if that has not also been already discontinued. Not a few who can look back to pleasant voyages in these comfortable vessels will feel some regret that the familiar flag will be no longer seen upon Australian waters.

Messrs. Devitt and Moore have for many years owned or chartered some of the largest and most popular passenger ships in the Australian trade. The firm has recently become associated with that of Messrs. Green and Co., both the lines being now under the same management. Messrs. Devitt and Moore's ships have achieved a great and deserved reputation, especially in the colonies, and the name of this firm may always be regarded as a guarantee for the excellence of their vessels.

In addition to these, there are many other firms of high standing which own lines of vessels for Australia and New Zealand. Amongst them the following may be mentioned:—

Messrs. Anderson, Anderson and Co.'s line of sailing ships for Adelaide, Melbourne, Sydney, Brisbane, etc. These ships, most of which are over 1,000 tons register, are despatched at frequent intervals from the Southwest India Dock. Two of these—the *Hesperus* and the *Harbinger*—now regularly make the return voyage by the Cape of Good Hope, and are therefore well suited for invalids going out and returning by sailing vessel.

Messrs. Geo. Thompson's "Aberdeen" line of clipper ships has long been favourably known amongst the Australian sailing lines. Messrs. Thompson own a large number of vessels, and they frequently despatch four or five ships in one month—some to Melbourne, and some to Sydney or other ports.

Messrs. Trinder, Anderson and Co.'s ships of the "Elder" line sail from the London Docks for Adelaide generally twice in every month. Their vessels are also occasionally despatched to the other Australian ports. Several of the ships belonging to this line make the return voyage by way of the Cape of Good Hope. The

Torrens, which is specially recommended by Messrs. Trinder and Co., as an invalid ship, leaves London each year in October, and calls at Cape Town and St. Helena on her way home.

Messrs. Houlder Brothers and Co.'s line of clipper ships are despatched from the South-west India Docks for Melbourne, Adelaide, etc., several times each month; also from Liverpool to Sydney, Melbourne, and Adelaide every month.

Mr. John Henry Flint's "Colonial Line" of steam and sailing ships comprises some fine vessels belonging to the latter class. The ships of this line are usually despatched to Sydney or Melbourne.

Other well-known lines are the "Thames and Mersey Line" of Messrs. Gavin, Birt and Co., the "Victoria Line" of Messrs. John Potter and Co., the "London Line" of Messrs. Taylor, Bethel and Roberts, and the "White Star Line" of Messrs. Ismay, Imrie and Co. Some of those firms despatch ships from Liverpool as well as from London. The ships of the "Scottish Line" of Messrs. M'Ilwraith, M'Eacharn and Co. run chiefly to the ports of Queensland, and are despatched from London or Glasgow.

Amongst the lines of passenger ships to New Zealand may be mentioned those of the "New Zealand Shipping Company" and the "Passenger Line" of Messrs. Shaw, Savill and Co. The fine vessels belonging to both these lines sail at frequent intervals to the various ports of New Zealand.

In addition to the above firms, there are many others trading from the different ports of England and Scotland to Australia and New Zealand.

The particular port of Australia to which the passage should be taken is a point demanding consideration.

Formerly—that is to say, some twelve or fourteen years ago—as many vessels sailed from England for Sydney as for Melbourne. After a time Melbourne seemed to absorb the direct trade, and nearly all the ships belonging to the great firms went to that port. Recently, however, New South Wales has been regaining her former influence, and some of the finest passenger ships are despatched direct to Sydney. As already mentioned, a good many vessels are also sent to Adelaide (South Australia), some to Brisbane and the other ports of Queensland, and a few to Hobart Town (Tasmania); while several great lines of vessels run to the various ports of New Zealand. The climate of each of these ports, and their suitability to the invalid, will be discussed in a future chapter; but, speaking generally, Melbourne will be found the most convenient destination for those who are sufficiently well to undertake a moderate amount of travelling on their arrival in Australia, because not only do many of the finest sailing vessels and nearly all the steamships sail direct to that port, but also because from thence, on account of its central situation, any other part of the colonies can be reached in a few days by local steamers.

Although a separate chapter has been devoted to the consideration of the homeward voyage, it may be mentioned here that all the steamers—including the auxiliary screws—now return from Australia by the Suez Canal; and the sailing vessels, with a few exceptions, by Cape Horn.

CHAPTER IV.

PRELIMINARY ARRANGEMENTS.

Securing a passage and engaging a berth—Personal inspection desirable—Hints on choosing a berth—Furnishing the cabin in sailing vessels—Articles of cabin furniture provided by the owners—Furniture to be provided by the passenger himself: bedding, folding-chair, lamp, bookshelf, carpet, bath, swing-tray, etc., etc.—Trunks and boxes—Travelling chest of drawers—Outfit of wearing apparel—Outfitters—Stores : medicines and sundries—Joining the ship—The ports of departure.

HAVING decided upon his route and time of departure, and chosen the line of vessels in which he will sail, the next thing for the intending passenger to do will be to secure his passage and choose his berth.

When the dock in which the ship is lying is sufficiently near to be easily accessible, it will be always much more satisfactory to see the ship before taking a passage, or, indeed, to compare several ships belonging to the same or rival lines.

This, however, is usually practicable only in the case of sailing vessels, which, remaining a considerable time in dock, afford ample opportunities for inspection. Steamers, on the other hand, are despatched so quickly, that it is often necessary to secure a passage in them before they arrive in dock.

The earlier a berth is selected the better, even in the case of sailing vessels, as the favourite passenger ships fill up very rapidly, and the best cabins are soon engaged.

Where a personal inspection cannot be made, the

owners or their agents will, on application, send full particulars of the ships, together with the regulations relating to passengers, and a plan of the cabins. The position of each vacant berth will thus be seen at a glance, those that are already engaged being usually marked off.

It is, of course, always best to act under the advice of some friend who has been to sea, or who is practically acquainted with ships; but where such assistance cannot be obtained, the following hints may be found useful.

In all ships that have poops, take if possible a poop cabin—*i.e.*, do not be induced to take one on the lower deck.

In steamers and on hot voyages, such as that to India, deck cabins (where they are to be had) will be found cooler and altogether more pleasant than those opening into the saloon, but on rough or cold voyages they are better avoided, at any rate by invalids. They are generally rather more expensive than the saloon cabins.

The dimensions of each cabin in feet and inches are generally marked on the plan, and you will see that the cabins vary more or less in size. *Cæteris paribus*, choose the largest in proportion to the number of berths in it.

Bear in mind that the nearer you approach the centre of the ship, the less motion there will be, and that the stern cabins, which in sailing ships are almost always larger than the others, are in *this* respect the least desirable. In steamers also the noise and vibration of the screw are much more unpleasantly felt than they are nearer the centre of the ship. The after-cabins are therefore seldom so much crowded as those more amidships. Those who are not easily disturbed by noises may feel inclined to take advantage of this fact.

The stern cabins in sailing vessels have one or two

other drawbacks: they are more liable to be "washed out" in rough weather (especially if they have large old-fashioned ports), and the noises of the rudder chains and of the waves are apt to disturb sleep. But as these are after all comparatively slight inconveniences, the greater size and cheerfulness, and the superior ventilation of the stern cabins in sailing ships will always recommend them, and they usually fetch a higher price than the others.

Avoid taking a cabin in the immediate neighbourhood of the steward's pantry, the store-room, or the bar, and—in steamers—of the engine-room, and get as near as possible to a skylight or other means of ventilation. It is customary to advise that the cabin should be taken on the windward side of the ship—that is, on that side on which the wind will most often blow during the voyage. This is no doubt of importance in steamers on the Indian and other hot voyages; but in sailing ships, owing to the frequency with which they change their position by tacking, there is but little difference between the two sides, except perhaps in the trade-wind regions.

In steamers, the number of berths in each cabin varies from two to four or even six; in auxiliary screws, each cabin contains usually either two or three berths, an additional payment of about fifteen per cent. securing the half-share. In sailing vessels, however, it is seldom that more than two passengers are put into each cabin; whilst by paying an additional fifty or sixty per cent. upon the passage money it is generally possible to secure the whole cabin.* Of course, when a ship does not fill up, it is often possible to secure the sole use of a cabin without additional payment.

* If the passenger is a confirmed invalid, and is not accompanied by friends, it will of course add immensely to his comfort if he can arrange to travel with a medical man, or, at any rate, if he can

In choosing a berth, do not, if you can help it, take one that is either over or under another berth, for both positions are undesirable, although unfortunately such an arrangement is, from the economy of space so obtained, a very frequent one on steamers. Choose, if possible, a cabin in which the berths are on different sides. Select a berth *opposite* a port, if you can, but not *under* one, or you may, when you least expect it, get "a sea" in, and be exposed for days afterwards to that crowning discomfort of sea life—wet bedding.*

Of two berths, one under the other, the upper is the more airy and comfortable when once you are in it, but for an invalid the necessary climbing involved is sometimes trying, especially in rough weather.

It is customary, when a berth is engaged, by letter or otherwise, to pay half the passage money (sometimes a less sum) as deposit, the balance being paid a few days before sailing, when you will receive a properly filled up contract ticket, which it is advisable to preserve carefully, as it is sometimes required for official purposes.

The next point for consideration is the fitting up of the cabin—that is, in those cases in which it has to be done by the passenger himself. In all steamers (I believe there are no exceptions) the cabin fittings and furniture, as well as bedding, bed-linen, and towels, are provided by the owners. The passenger has therefore nothing to do but

take with him an experienced male nurse or attendant, who would share his cabin and give him any attention he might require. Indeed, where a patient goes to sea seriously ill, such an arrangement is indispensable. It need not be said, however, that the expense is considerable.

* In steamers, the position of the berths frequently offers only a choice of evils, as one of the most usual arrangements is for two berths—one under the other—to be placed opposite the port, and one (generally called the sofa) just beneath it.

to walk on board with his baggage and take possession of his cabin. He will there find his berth—which to a landsman's eyes looks preposterously narrow—containing his bedding, ready prepared for occupation. There will also be a fixed washstand (with water laid on to a tap), to be used throughout the voyage jointly with the other occupants of the cabin. The furniture will be completed by a strip of carpet for the floor, a curtain at the head of the bed, a looking-glass, and a lamp, or some other means of lighting the cabin.

But in a sailing vessel, except in those lines where all cabin requisites are provided, things are very different. Some few years ago your passage money entitled you only to your share of a cabin with four bare walls. Now, most of the owners provide the following articles—viz., a fixed berth or sleeping-place, a looking-glass, a rack to contain a water-bottle and tumblers, and a fixed washstand with more or less complete fittings. I say advisedly more or less complete, for the washstand fittings provided in different ships vary greatly; and, trifling as such a matter may seem, it will be advisable, if possible, to ascertain before starting exactly what *is* provided, as it is exceedingly uncomfortable during a long voyage to find oneself without some necessary article, such as a wash-hand basin, a water-can, or a water-bottle; and, once afloat, it will be next to impossible to supply any such deficiency.*

The passenger who is bound on a voyage to Australia in a sailing vessel will find that, in addition to the fittings provided by the owners, it will be necessary to obtain for himself a good many articles of cabin furniture before he will be able to start upon his journey with any prospect of comfort.

The first thing to see to will be the *bedding*, which,

---

* In some ships, by extra payment, the passenger may be supplied with all cabin requisites, bedding, linen, etc.

although reduced to the narrowest dimensions by the width of the berth (2 ft. 6 in.), is an important consideration. I cannot too strongly recommend the purchase of a *horsehair* mattress, which, although dearer, is far more comfortable, cleanly, and wholesome than any other kind. A horsehair bolster, a pillow, blankets, and a good railway rug (to act as a coverlet) will also be required, together with the necessary bed-linen.*

A *folding chair* will be convenient, not only in the cabin, but also for use on deck. It should be as light and portable as possible.

A *lamp* of some sort will be required. Those usually sold are small spring lamps (to burn Price's candles) mounted on a swivel arrangement which, when secured to the wall of the cabin, always ensures an upright position. I have however found a small brass flat candlestick heavily weighted with lead quite as useful as, and less troublesome than, a lamp.

A small *bookshelf*, with a bar in front to prevent the books falling out, is very useful to hold the supply of literature which is almost indispensable during a long voyage.

A *strip of carpet* or a rug for the bedside is a luxury which can be dispensed with without much inconvenience, except, perhaps, during the colder parts of the voyage.

A *water-can* (unless provided by the ship) is a necessity. It should hold nearly a gallon, and should be of a "squat" shape, not liable to fall over.

A small *portable bath* of some kind will be found a great comfort. It must, however, be either a folding bath or quite a small one, as otherwise it will take up too much room in the cabin.

Where a convenient place can be found for hanging it,

* Sheets are by no means a necessity if a pyjama sleeping suit be worn.

a *swing-tray* is sometimes useful in a cabin. It consists merely of a round japanned tray about twelve inches in diameter, hung by cords or chains from the deck overhead. It is used for holding anything liable to spill (such as a glass of water) in rough weather.

A "*cabin pocket*" is amongst the most useful and indispensable of the articles for cabin use. It consists of a piece of holland or other material divided into compartments or pockets for the reception of brushes, combs, slippers, bottles, etc., etc. This arrangement is nailed against the cabin wall, and is effectual in preventing those erratic movements to which small loose articles are so liable on board ship.

When the cabin is sufficiently large, a small, firmly fixed *table* will be found most convenient during a long voyage. It can only be introduced, however, jointly with the other occupant of the cabin; and this is one of the many instances in which it will be seen at once that it is of great advantage either to travel with a friend or attendant, or, at any rate, if possible, to make the acquaintance of your future travelling companion before starting, as many articles of cabin furniture will do for joint use, and need not be provided in duplicate.

A *curtain for the door*, hung upon a semicircular rod of iron, is very useful, especially in hot weather, as it allows of the cabin door being left open during the night, greatly to the improvement of the ventilation.

A small curtain for the head of the bed may also be provided, if desired.

During a long voyage a good deal of wearing apparel will of course be required, and the form and size of the *trunks* or *boxes* in which it is to be taken will be a consideration. In all steamers the amount of personal baggage is strictly limited to a certain number of cubic feet, and the most convenient form of box for cabin use in steamers is the "overland" trunk. In the Peninsular and Oriental Company's steamers the size of the trunks is limited to 3 ft. × 1 ft. 3 in. × 1 ft. 3 in.; and although other companies allow them to be of a somewhat larger size, yet, where much travelling is to be undertaken, the smaller the trunks are the more convenient they will be found.

In a sailing vessel, however, in which the allowance of luggage is much more liberal than in steamers, and there are no restrictions (within reasonable limits) as to the size of the packages, *a travelling chest of drawers* will be found most convenient for cabin use. It consists of a small, strongly made chest of drawers, divided in the middle in such a way as to form two boxes of moderate size. The front of each portion is made to close with a cover when removing from place to place. Although very suitable for cabin use, it must be acknowledged that these two chests form rather clumsy and cumbersome packages for travelling on land. The convenience of the chest of drawers when in use at sea may be greatly increased by having a rim of wood (about an inch and a half deep) made to screw on to the top, round the edge. In this way a most useful table is made, upon which numbers of things may be placed without fear of their slipping off in rough weather.

Should ornamentation be desired, the addition of a few small *pictures* in gilt frames will make the cabin look bright and homelike.

Wearing Apparel.—With regard to the outfit of wearing apparel, it is possible only to speak generally, as it will vary greatly according to individual requirements and the voyage to be taken. The invalid should bear in mind that the English Channel is almost always cold, even in summer. In the Australian voyage, cold weather lasting several weeks is also always met with south of the Cape, and must be provided for, especially as it follows so closely upon the heat of the tropics. A thick warm suit of clothes should in every case be provided, as well as under-clothing to match; also a warm overcoat, and another of lighter material. For the warmer parts of the voyage, suits of thinner woollen materials, such as serge or flannel, are recommended; and one or two coats of China-silk or cashmere for cabin use in equatorial regions. There is generally so much humidity in the air at sea, that I should strongly advise all invalids to abjure linen shirts, and to wear only flannel—thick for cold and thin for warm latitudes. Under-waistcoats should, in my opinion, always be worn. Even in the warmest weather a thin India gauze under-waistcoat will generally be found more comfortable than none at all.

It is customary on board ship to wear white canvas shoes during the warmer weather, and these certainly have the advantage of requiring no blacking; but I should advise the invalid to take with him, in addition to thinner shoes, one or two pairs of thick strong boots, made as waterproof as possible with dubbing or grease, for use when, as is so often the case, the decks are wet and sloppy, either from the weather or from being washed.

While passing through the tropics, it is often found almost impossible to bear bedclothes of any kind over one. A sheet is even more uncomfortable than a blanket, and a cotton or linen night-dress is an abomination. For use under these circumstances, and indeed during the whole voyage, the traveller is strongly recommended to provide himself with one or more sleeping-suits of thin flannel, consisting of a shirt and a loose pair of drawers, or "pyjamas," made to tie round the waist. Bedclothes may then be boldly dispensed with, and the gain in point of comfort can only be appreciated by those who have tried both plans.

The best way of determining the amount of wearing apparel, linen, etc., to be taken, is to make a rough calculation based upon the probable length of the voyage and the number of articles generally used per week. It must be borne in mind that the services of a laundress are not obtainable on board ship, and although the sailors will sometimes wash clothes for the passengers, this cannot always be depended upon.*

All necessary articles, both for cabin use and personal outfit, may be obtained at any of the respectable outfitters that are to be found in the neighbourhood of Cornhill and Fenchurch Street, London. At some of these establishments an outfit for any purpose—from a voyage to the North Pole to an expedition to Central Africa—may be obtained at a few hours' notice.

Every British seaport of any importance has also usually one or more outfitting establishments, at which all the requisites for a voyage may be obtained.

In an appendix is given a list of the various articles that may be required for use during a long sea voyage. It is, however, intended more as a memorandum than as a statement of the actual requirements of *every* passenger, and the list should be reduced to the *smallest possible* dimensions that are compatible with comfort.

The outfitter usually undertakes to deliver on board ship and to place in the cabin all articles that are purchased of him; and he will also, if desired, do any fitting

---

* In the above hints as to wearing apparel at sea, no special reference has been made to ladies' dress: first, because it can be arranged on the same general principles that have been indicated; and, second, because, in the author's opinion, the discomforts of a long voyage in a sailing ship are, for an invalid lady, so much greater than for a man, as to render it very doubtful if such patients should be sent to sea at all.

up or fixing that may be necessary. Great care should be taken that everything that is likely to shift its position (such as chests, boxes, etc.) is properly secured; or in nautical language, "cleated and lashed"—*i.e.*, prevented from sliding by little blocks of wood (cleats) which are screwed to the deck; and lashed down to the deck by means of thin cord and screw-eyes.

Nothing is more unpleasant than on the first rough day to find all your cabin penates lying in a confused heap to leeward; and although the ship's carpenter may sometimes be prevailed upon to cleat your belongings, it is always better to get it done before sailing, either by the outfitter's man or a man of your own. Of course these remarks apply only to sailing vessels.

There are a few sundries in the way of stores with which an invalid may find it well to provide himself when starting on a long voyage: a few tins of preserved milk, some Liebig's extract of meat, a bottle or two of effervescing citrate of magnesia (so called), and some mild aperient medicine of whatever kind he is accustomed to take, will all be found useful. A small filter (a "pocket filter" answers very well), and some contrivance for heating water by means of spirits of wine may be added with advantage, as clear drinking water and hot water are both rather difficult to obtain on board ship. A small private stock of fresh fruit—especially oranges and lemons—will be found very grateful during the first few days of the voyage, particularly when suffering from sea-sickness.

All preparations being now completed, the cabin fitted up, and the baggage on board, nothing remains but to join the ship.

Many of the steamship companies grant facilities to

intending passengers in the shape of free railway passes from London to the port of departure, or else they issue tickets at reduced fares.

In some cases the passenger has the option of embarking at one of two ports. Thus passengers by the Orient line and other Australian steam lines may join generally either at Gravesend or Plymouth; while in the case of the Union Company the choice lies between Southampton and Plymouth; and in the case of Messrs. Donald, Currie and Co., between London and Dartmouth. Some of Messrs. Green's ships call at Plymouth. Where this option is given, it becomes a question whether to go on board at first or to choose the port that is farthest down Channel. In summer and in fine weather the run down Channel is often very pleasant, passing, as one does, so many familiar places along the coast. There is also time to settle down before the remainder of the passengers come on board; and the apprenticeship to sea-sickness, if it *must* be served, is partly, if not entirely, got through before making a final start. In the late autumn or winter, however, it is advisable that as much as possible of the Channel should be avoided, as the weather is then often cold and trying to invalids, and the passage, particularly in a sailing vessel, is often tedious, and not without risk.

CHAPTER V.

LIFE AT SEA.

The Australian voyage—Commencement of the voyage—Sea-sickness—Daily routine—General arrangement of the ship—Meals on board ship—Quality of the various articles of food in sailing vessels—Supply of water—Unavoidable defects of the dietary on long sea voyages—The quantities of provisions consumed during an Australian voyage—List of officers, crew, etc., of a large passenger ship—Mode of indicating the time : the "bells,"—Taking the noon " sights"—Agreement of passengers amongst themselves—Reading—Open-air games— Quoits— Cricket —" Bull-board "— Shooting sea-birds — Athletic sports—Dancing—Theatricals, concerts. etc.—Newspapers—Chess tournaments—Sailors' amusements—Crossing the line—" Burying the dead horse "—Sailors' songs—Speaking passing ships—Sending home letters—Excursions in the ship's boats.

AS it would be impossible within the limits of a work such as the present to give a detailed description of each voyage that has been mentioned, I have chosen one—the voyage to Australia by way of the Cape of Good Hope—to illustrate life on board ship, and to show the intending voyager, as faithfully as may be, what he has to expect in the way of comfort and discomfort, climate, food, amusement, and occupation, during his absence from his native shores.

The Australian voyage has been selected for several reasons. It is the one most frequently taken by invalids; it is the longest; and as all the latitudes which are traversed in the other voyages are sailed through on the way to Australia, the description of each region of the ocean may, *mutatis mutandis*, be applied to most other routes.

A sailing vessel has been chosen, because it gives, on the whole, a better illustration of true sea life than a steamer; but any material points of difference between the two classes of vessels will be mentioned as they arise.

We will suppose, then, that the reader, having sailed down the English Channel with fine weather and a fair wind, and having watched the last point of the familiar English coast as it vanished from the distant horizon, has now fairly entered upon his ocean voyage. The attention of all on board, hitherto engrossed by surrounding objects, will now be turned to the ship in which they are destined to spend so many days and weeks.

But it is probable that by this time the traveller, if not a good sailor, will have been aware of certain uncomfortable sensations which have forcibly reminded him of the fact that he is now no longer on dry land; and if this should be the unfortunate experience of the present reader, I cannot do better than refer him at once to the hints I have endeavoured to give in Chapter VII. upon the management of sea-sickness,—and, for the present, draw a curtain over his sufferings.

What with unavoidable " attention to private affairs," bad weather, and the confusion inseparable from the commencement of a long voyage, it is generally not until the Bay of Biscay has been passed that the passengers begin to settle down to regular habits, and the many gaps that have hitherto been seen on the benches down the sides of the saloon table begin to be filled up at mealtimes. At last, however, brighter skies and calmer weather tempt even the worst sailors from their cabins, and all begin to take more or less interest in their novel mode of life.

The daily routine on board a sailing vessel is always

pretty much as follows : About five o'clock in the morning you are probably awakened by that most noisy of operations, washing decks. If "holy-stoning" is also in vogue, the pounding, scraping and grinding noises which go on over your head will effectually banish sleep, unless you are a very determined sleeper indeed. .

At 8 o'clock the dressing-bell rings ; but in the warmer latitudes most of the passengers have been up long before that time, have had their bath, and are promenading on deck to encourage appetite, or are more quietly enjoying the cool and refreshing morning breeze. At 8.30 (in some ships 9 o'clock) the breakfast bell summons the passengers to a very substantial meal, to which they probably do good justice, as by this time their sea-appetite has most likely set in in earnest.

Lunch is at twelve o'clock ; this is the time also for taking the noon " sights," to determine the position of the ship and the progress she has made since the previous day. The result is usually chalked upon a board for the information of the passengers.

Dinner, which in most ships is at 4 o'clock, is another of the events of the day. Tea is at 7, and at 9 biscuits and hot and cold water for grog are put upon the table. At 10 o'clock the lamps in the saloon are put out, and all lights in the cabins have (nominally) to be extinguished by 10.30 p.m.*

For the benefit of such readers as have had no previous acquaintance with matters appertaining to the sea we will now look round the ship, and endeavour to get some idea of its general arrangements.

* In steamers the hours for meals vary considerably ; they are, however, generally later than in sailing ships. In the Union Co.'s vessels they are as follows :—Coffee in cabin, 6 a.m. ; breakfast, 9 a.m. ; luncheon, 12.30 p.m. ; dinner, 6 p.m.; tea, 8 p.m.

In most passenger sailing vessels the first-class saloon occupies the after part of the ship, extending from the stern nearly as far forwards as the mainmast. In poop ships the saloon and principal sleeping cabins are built above the main deck, and the raised deck that covers them is called the poop deck. In flush-deck ships the whole of the passenger accommodation is below the main deck. In most ships, the saloon, which is necessarily long, low, and narrow, runs "fore and aft," and has the sleeping cabins on either side. In a few vessels, however, it is still "athwart ships"—*i.e.*, transverse in direction. It is lighted from above by means of long skylights, and has a table down the centre, with fixed benches on either side. Above the table are swinging lamps, swing-trays, and racks for glasses and bottles.

The lower deck, which (in poop ships) communicates with the saloon by a short staircase, generally contains at its after part extra first-class cabins and the rooms of some of the officers; while farther forward, and partitioned off by a "bulkhead," is the second-class department, and farther forward again the third-class.

Returning to the upper deck by the "companion hatch," we find near the mainmast the galley in which the cooking for the whole ship is carried on, and done, too, with a rapidity and excellence which seem a mystery when one sees the very small space which the cook has at his disposal. Farther forward, in the bows of the ship, we see the forecastle, in which the sailors have their quarters; and near this is generally to be found the small deck-house inhabited by the cow, usually a great pet of the tars. On the top of the galley, in the long-boat, and in other apparently strange positions, may be noticed the pens, or rather cages, containing the sheep, pigs, geese, and other live stock.

The poop-deck above the saloon is kept exclusively

for the use of the officers and the first-class passengers. There the deck is scrubbed and scoured until it is specklessly white and clean, and the ropes are neatly coiled by the midshipmen, whose special domain it is.

All round the sides of the poop are the hen-coops, the tops of which serve as seats, and inside which are the fowls and ducks, whose melancholy fate it is either to be eaten, or to die a natural death before the end of the voyage; and who avenge themselves by smelling very unpleasantly in the hot weather, and (in the case of the cocks) by crowing vociferously at all hours of the night. Here—on the poop—congregate the passengers day after day during the long voyage, reclining in their chairs in all stages of laziness, or walking industriously backwards and forwards for exercise; and from hence they survey, as from a tower, the sea, the sky, and all that goes on in the ship, either on deck or aloft.

FOOD, which is a matter of importance to every one, is more especially of moment to the invalid. I will therefore endeavour to give some idea of the fare on board an average Australian passenger ship.

For the first week or two you might be inclined to wonder at the variety of dishes that appear at each meal, but after a time you find that it is a variety that repeats itself day after day, and which becomes at last rather wearisome.

The breakfast consists of broiled and cold ham, cold meat, grilled bones, rissoles, mutton cutlets, preserved fish of various kinds, potted meats, marmalade or preserves, tea, coffee, and cocoa. In many ships, hot rolls are provided every morning, and, by special desire, porridge is sometimes added to the bill of fare.

The luncheon varies in different ships. In some, only bread, cheese, butter and biscuits are put on the table, but in others cold meats, preserved salmon, Australian meats, etc., are provided.

Dinner commences with soup, followed by joints of mutton and salt beef, and sometimes joints of pork; fowls, ducks, and occasionally geese; made-dishes composed of mutton and preserved meats cooked in various ways; potatoes and preserved vegetables of various kinds. In Messrs. Green's and in Wigram's ships currie is always served as a separate course. Then come pastry and puddings, cheese, and finally a dessert, which for the first few weeks perhaps boasts some dishes of apples and pears, but towards the end of the voyage consists only of almonds and raisins, nuts, and similar dry fare.*

A few words may now be said as to the *quality* of the various articles of diet on board a sailing vessel, and their suitability for the invalid.

Water.—In former days, when the whole of the water for a long voyage had to be carried in casks or tanks, it was not only a scarce, but often a nauseous, or even an unwholesome, article on board ship. The allowance to each passenger was strictly limited to a few pints a day for all purposes. Even if the casks were in thoroughly

---

* In steamers, the bill of fare is much of the same description, although rather more ambitious, and comprising various articles of diet which cannot be supplied throughout a long voyage in a sailing vessel. The following breakfast and dinner *ménus* profess to be taken at random from the steward's bill of fare book in one of the Union Company's steamers. *Breakfast*, rump steak and onions, mutton chops, fried soles, hashed duck, grilled bones, minced beef, currie and rice, porridge, potatoes, cold ham, beef, and mutton. *Dinner*, soup; giblet,—fish; cod, and anchovy sauce—entrées; lapereaux sautée, haricot de mouton,—roast joints; geese and apple sauce, sirloin of beef and horseradish—boiled joints; legs of mutton and caper sauce—vegetables; baked and boiled potatoes, green peas, mashed turnips—beef-currie and rice—pastry; plum puddings, baked custard, sandwich pastry—dessert; assorted. Tea and coffee.

good order, the water in them usually underwent decomposition from the organic matter contained in it, and after a few weeks became offensive both to taste and smell. Occasionally, too, the water was contaminated, either from the casks being foul, from red-lead being used for the joints of the tanks, or from other causes. I have known a whole ship's company reduced to a state of emaciation from drinking poisonous water. At the present day things are very different. Nearly all the large passenger and emigrant ships are provided with an apparatus for distilling sea-water, called a " condenser." This is capable of producing several hundreds of gallons of fresh water daily; and although a large supply is also carried in tanks, it is seldom necessary to fall back upon this. The distilled water, although somewhat flat and vapid to the taste, is thoroughly pure and wholesome, and is supplied on a much more liberal scale than formerly. There is still, I believe, a nominal allowance to each passenger, but it is by no means strictly enforced.

Meat.—Fresh beef is of course a thing unknown, except for the first few days after leaving port. Mutton forms the staple diet, and fortunately English sheep thrive well at sea, and the mutton is generally fairly good, although in the warm weather it has necessarily to be eaten so soon after being killed, that it is often tough. Pork is, for the most part, excellent, as the pig, like the sheep, takes remarkably well to ship life. Pigs are generally only killed during the cooler parts of the voyage. Poultry, on the other hand, never seem to thrive at sea, and the skinniness, toughness, and want of flavour of the fowls and ducks is beyond belief. Those of them, however, that survive to the latter part of the voyage, escaping not only the butcher's hands, but also a high rate of mortality from natural causes, sometimes recover their condition and become more eatable. The geese are, as a rule, a shade better than the fowls and ducks.

Bread is usually fairly good, considering the circumstances under which it is made; but towards the end of the voyage the flour sometimes deteriorates, and often contains weevils; the same remark applies to pastry.

Potatoes are pretty good for the first month or two, but before the voyage is over they frequently become poor, and sometimes fail altogether. It is then necessary to fall back upon the stock of preserved potatoes, which, for a continuance, are neither very wholesome nor inviting.

Milk.—The cow, by habit, becomes so good a sailor that she will often give a full supply of milk during the whole voyage, but it sometimes happens that the artificial conditions under which she is placed tell after a time upon her constitution, and the supply fails. So long as there is plenty of good preserved milk, this is not of so great consequence, but if *that* also fails through the supply being inadequate, the want becomes a serious one, especially for children and invalids. For this reason the traveller has been advised to provide himself with a small private stock of preserved milk, which will be found a valuable supplement to that supplied by the ship.

Butter is seldom good. It is necessary thoroughly to salt it in order to preserve it for the voyage; and although the steward does his best to remedy this by having the butter well washed before use, it is never very inviting at any time, and in the hot weather is still less attractive.

Preserved Stores.—The art of preserving vegetables has been brought to so great a perfection that dishes of green peas, French beans, carrots, parsnips, etc., are often put upon the table, that could scarcely be distinguished from the freshly gathered vegetables. The same may be said of preserved fish, the tinned salmon being particularly good.

Wines, Spirits, etc.—Several years ago it was the custom in some of the lines of sailing vessels to include beer, wine, and spirits in the passage money, which was then rather higher than it is now. But the universal custom at present, both in sailing ships and steamers, is for the passenger to purchase these things for himself. They are supplied on board at fixed prices, which, although somewhat high, considering their quality, and the fact that they pay no duty, are not exorbitant. An account is delivered to each passenger by the head steward at the end of every week, and there is no doubt that, on the whole, this arrangement is far preferable to the old one.

It will be seen from the foregoing remarks that the great drawbacks to the dietary on board a sailing vessel are the want of fresh vegetables, fruits, salads, eggs, and butter, and the tendency of the stores to deteriorate towards the end of the voyage. In a steamer, the comparative shortness of the voyage, the usual provision of an ice-room, and the fact that it is generally necessary to call at some port to take in coal, all tend to make the fare better and more varied. In addition to this, the efforts of the commissariat department, which may be kept up to the mark for a month or six weeks, are apt to flag during a voyage of three or four months. At the same time it must be clearly understood that, although the fare is perhaps not so luxurious as in a steamer, there is nothing in the dietary of a sailing vessel that need prevent an invalid choosing the latter; or that would in any way prevent his deriving benefit from the voyage.

Before leaving this part of the subject it may not be uninteresting to the reader to know the quantities of the various stores that are required for a voyage to or from Australia. The subjoined list was given me by the captain of a favourite Australian ship, as the quantity laid in of each article named for the return voyage:—173 sheep, 30 pigs, 18 sucking-pigs, 720 fowls, 420 ducks, 144 geese, 1 cow;—flour, 12 tons; sugar, 2½ tons; butter, 1 ton; biscuits, 3 tons; preserved meat, 6,000 lb.; salt meat, 6,200 lb.; soup in tins, 1,200 lb.

There were on board 73 first-class, 37 second-class, and 25 third-class passengers, together with a crew of 62 all told, making a total of 197, including about 30 young children.

As a large passenger vessel is not only a ship, but also a floating hotel, it may be imagined that many and various officials are required both for its navigation and for its commissariat department. It may therefore be interesting to the intending passenger to be furnished with a list of the officers, crew, etc., of a first-class Australian ship of moderate size. The following will represent the average ship's company on board one of Messrs. Green's sailing vessels:—

Captain; first, second, third, and (sometimes) fourth officers; from four to eight midshipmen; surgeon; boatswain; carpenter; sailmaker; engineer; three or four quarter-masters; from twelve to sixteen able seamen; from two to four ordinary seamen; three or four boys. Chief steward; four to six cuddy servants; pantry-boy; second-class steward, third-class steward; midshipman's servant; captain's cook, ship's cook; baker; butcher, butcher's mate; storekeeper.

Amongst the novelties on board ship, one of the first to attract one's attention is the method of indicating the time. Every half-hour one of the midshipmen strikes "the bells," which by no means coincide with the striking of a clock. Thus, at half-past 8 in the morning, *one* bell is struck; at 9, *two* bells; at half-past 9, *three* bells, and so on up to 12 o'clock noon, when *eight bells* are struck.

They then begin again in the same order from one to eight. *Eight bells*, therefore, always indicates either 4, 8, or 12 o'clock, and is the signal for *changing watch*. But from 4 to 8 in the afternoon the order is a little different, because then the watches last only *two* hours instead of four, and are called the "dog watches." The order of the bells is then 1, 2, 3, 4; 1, 2, 3, 8. You will notice that the strokes are struck in pairs—*e.g.*, five bells are struck thus: 1, 2—3, 4—5.

One of the great events of the day, as before mentioned, is the taking of the noon "sights" for longitude. Most of the officers then turn out upon the poop, and with their sextants take frequent observations of the sun until he passes the meridian. These observations (in connection with others taken earlier in the morning for latitude) give the exact position of the ship at twelve o'clock, and, as a deduction, the distance she has sailed since noon on the previous day—or, as it is generally called, "the day's run."

The result is chalked on a board for the benefit of the passengers, and gives rise to much interest and speculation, bets being frequently made on the day's run. Even sweepstakes are sometimes got up amongst the passengers.

The noon "sights" also determine the actual time by the sun, and the ship's clock is therefore corrected at twelve o'clock each day. When travelling due east or west, the loss or gain in time each day is considerable. As the difference of time for each degree of longitude is about four minutes, and as a fast ship will often accomplish six degrees of easting when running before the strong westerly winds south of the Cape of Good Hope, the clock has sometimes to be put on as much as twenty-four minutes at a time.

If after leaving England a passenger keeps his watch going without correcting it, the difference of time becomes at length rather startling; but if he perseveres until he reaches the antipodes, it will, of course, have corrected itself, because the difference will then be twelve hours.

Any one starting upon a voyage, the monotony of which will for months be unbroken by letters, newspapers, or visits from friends, and in the course of which it is quite possible that not even a passing glimpse of land may be obtained, naturally asks himself what sources of amusement and occupation will be open to him, to prevent his falling a victim to that *ennui* which to some minds is almost as bad as, and indeed sometimes directly productive of, ill-health itself. But although, as a general rule, nothing very exciting is to be looked for on board ship, yet a well-balanced mind ought not, I think, to find a sea life insufferably dull. To those who have an eye for the wonders and beauties of Nature, objects of interest in sea and sky are daily and hourly presenting themselves; while, if the passengers themselves possess a fair amount of vivacity and enterprise, there will be no lack of amusement even within the limits of their little floating community.

And here it may be as well to refer very briefly to a matter of great difficulty and delicacy—viz., the agreement of passengers amongst themselves. Probably no mode of life has so great a tendency to bring into prominence whatever is weak or little in a character as the life on board ship. The conditions are all peculiar; and the want of usual occupations, the enforced association, and the tedium and monotony of the voyage, are all factors tending to destroy the balance of even the best regulated minds.

The late Canon Kingsley has, however, written much more forcibly on this point than I can hope to do. He says:[*]

[*] "At Last," by Charles Kingsley.

"We see in travel but the outside of people; and as we know nothing of their inner history, and little usually of their antecedents, the pictures we might sketch of them would be probably as untruthfully as rashly drawn. Crushed together too, perforce, against each other, people are apt on board ship to make little hasty confidences —to show unawares little weaknesses, which should be forgotten all round the moment they step on shore and return to something like a normal state of society. The wisest and most humane rule for a traveller towards his companions is to

> 'Be to their faults a little blind,
> Be to their virtues very kind,'

and to consider all that is said and done on board ship like what passes among the members of a club, as on the whole private and confidential."

Reserving for a future chapter some little description of such objects of interest at sea as are connected with Natural History, I will now endeavour to say a few words about those amusements and occupations which are available on board most passenger ships.

First and foremost comes reading, for which a long sea voyage presents unusual facilities. If each passenger provides himself with a few books, a fair variety may be obtained by circulating and exchanging the stock of each. This course, however, should not be taken with works that are of much value to the owner, as books have a great tendency mysteriously to disappear on board ship.

Those who expect to be able to *study* in the sense of reading hard will almost always be disappointed. There is something in a sea life that seems to be antagonistic to work of this kind, and it is generally seen that those who started with high resolves in this respect very soon subside into light literature or idleness. There are of course exceptions, but they are rare. The prevailing inability to study is, however, scarcely to be regretted in the case of invalids, who cannot do better than provide themselves with a supply of light literature, and direct all their energies towards deriving the greatest possible benefit from their voyage.

There are several open-air games which can be played on board ship, and which furnish a capital means of obtaining that exercise, the want of which is one of the drawbacks of being shut up within such narrow limits.

Of these, one of the most universal is a modification of the game of quoits. The quoits are made by the sailors, and consist of circles of stout rope about six inches in diameter. Each player has two quoits, and there are several ways of playing the game. One of the most usual is to throw from a given distance at a dot chalked on the deck, which takes the place of the peg in the original game. The two quoits that are nearest the mark each scores one, unless one of them is directly over the dot, in which case it scores three. A great point in the game as played on board ship is to attempt to drive an adversary's quoit from an advantageous position. It requires some little skill to allow properly for the force of the wind and the roll of the ship; and a good match between champion players always excites a great deal of interest. Other modifications of the game are—playing into circles with numbered divisions; endeavouring to throw the quoit over an upright wooden peg fixed in a stand; and (in rough weather) throwing the quoits into a bucket placed at some little distance from the player.

A good deal of exercise and considerable amusement may be obtained by playing cricket, with such modifications as are necessary to adapt it to a ship's deck. The single-wicket game is the one usually played, and the wicket is fixed on a wooden stand, but has loose bales. As the balls are necessarily very frequently lost overboard, they are made by the sailors of "spun yarn," and are supplied to the passengers at so much a dozen. The bats are generally either roughly made by the players themselves, or are supplied by the carpenter. Much amusement is caused by the strange localities into which the ball is sent, and by the difficulty of making the runs if there is much sea on at the time.

Another game sometimes played on board ship is called "bull-board." It consists of a sloping board marked off into nine divisions, all of which are numbered except the two upper corner ones, which have a bull's head painted upon them. The players are provided with flat pieces of lead covered with leather, and these they throw upon the board, standing at a distance of a few feet. Each player has four throws, and his score is reckoned according to the value of the squares upon which the leads pitch. Any lead, however, pitching upon either of the squares marked with a bull's head, deducts ten from the score. Leads lying upon a line do not count.

The number of sea-birds which, in some parts of the voyage, constantly follow the ship, prove a great inducement to passengers with sporting tastes to try the qualities of their guns and rifles. But as it is almost always impossible to obtain the birds that have been shot, this form of sport cannot but be regarded by most in the light of a cruel and useless destruction of life. For this reason some captains will not allow shot to be used,—permitting the guns to be loaded with bullets only, which, while furnishing a far better test of skill, do comparatively little execution. When a bird is hit, it is but seldom killed outright, and it is always sad to see it floating away astern with a broken wing or leg, to be pecked to death by other birds, or perhaps to linger on in agony for hours or days.

When once the passion for shooting has set in amongst the passengers who possess fire-arms, the perseverance with which they aim at everything, animate and inanimate, is truly surprising. Empty bottles or tins are thrown overboard, or are towed astern, to act as targets for rifles and revolvers. The motion of the ship and of the sea combined make it very difficult to hit these floating objects. I have seen a large target made from the head of a cask and suspended from the yard-arm, and as this follows the movements of the ship, it answers very fairly for rifle shooting.

In the evenings, when the weather is fine, the midshipmen and those whose tastes incline in that direction frequently indulge in athletic sports of various kinds, such as jumping, boxing, singlestick, as well as various strange games and feats of agility such as one sees only on board ship. Some of the more adventurous passengers are on such occasions tempted to make excursions in the rigging; but those who have not been aloft before must bear in mind that they are liable to be lashed to the rigging by the sailors until they have paid, or promised to pay, their "footing"—viz., the price of a bottle of rum.

On fine calm evenings, too, there is sometimes dancing on the poop, to the strains of a violin, piano, or any other musical instrument that may happen to be forthcoming; and the impromptu dance is perhaps kept up by the light of the tropical moon until a comparatively late hour.

But many of the amusements on board ship require

more organization than those which have been already enumerated; and the plan adopted with regard to these, where there are a sufficient number of passengers to render it practicable, is to convene a meeting soon after the commencement of the voyage, and to form an "amusement committee," which in its turn may appoint dramatic, literary, and musical sub-committees, to get up amateur theatricals, concerts, negro entertainments, mock trials, etc., and, in the case of the literary department, to start and keep up a newspaper or magazine. The latter, if well managed, and kept free from offensive personalities, causes great interest and amusement, and often brings out unexpected talent. The newspaper is generally issued weekly, and is, of course, in manuscript. If there are artists amongst the passengers, its interest is much increased by the addition of illustrations. At the end of the passage, the newspapers are frequently printed in the form of a pamphlet, and form a capital souvenir of the voyage.

Chess and draughts, always favourite games on board ship, are made of more general interest by being played in the form of a "tournament." The rules for chess tournaments vary, but the usual plan is for each member of the tournament to play three games with every other member, the players having been previously divided into classes, and handicapped according to their proficiency, the upper classes giving various pieces to the lower. The player who wins the greatest total number of games is of course the champion of the tournament. Where there are a good many players, the tournament lasts for several days, and becomes very interesting towards its close.

If there is any one on board who is competent to give instruction in foreign languages, and who does not mind the trouble, French or German classes may with much advantage be formed amongst the passengers. Capital progress is sometimes made in this way, as a feeling of rivalry springs up, which keeps the pupils up to their work at any rate for a time, although, like everything else entailing exertion either of body or mind, such classes are apt to die a natural death under the enervating influences of the warmer latitudes.

The introduction of spelling bees or of geographical or grammatical bees, though they are now obsolete on shore, will, if properly managed, make an agreeable variety in the amusements of a long voyage.

Card playing is of course a great resource on board ship, especially during those evenings when the state of the weather or of the temperature prevents the passengers being on deck. One or two whist parties are generally formed; while others play bézique, loo, cribbage, etc. Unfortunately, however, card playing but too frequently leads to gambling, and considerable sums of money that can but ill be spared often change hands during a voyage.

Another evil incidental to ship life is the practice of betting upon almost everything. Thus the day's run of the ship, the date of passing various points in the journey, the day and hour of arrival in port, as well as the various games that are played, all form excuses for bets and sweepstakes amongst those who find a difficulty in employing their time in a more sensible manner. Bets have even been made upon the order of appearance at the breakfast table of habitual late risers!

There are one or two time-honoured customs amongst sailors which furnish a good deal of amusement to the passengers.

One of these—the ancient drama attendant on crossing the line—is now very properly discouraged by most captains, on account of the ill-feeling that sometimes results from the rough horse-play indulged in on the occasion. It still, however, survives in a few old-fashioned merchant ships, and flourishes also in some of the ships of the Royal Navy. Quite recently in the *Bacchante*, which had on board their Royal Highnesses Prince Albert Victor and Prince George of Wales, the various ceremonies were gone through in very grand style indeed, and it is said that Prince Louis of Battenburgh was the first novice to submit himself to the barber's razor and the other rough attentions of Neptune and his suite.

Although " crossing the line" has been described numberless times, the following account from a lady's diary may prove interesting to any readers who may not happen to have seen these descriptions:—

"On Saturday, the 9th November, we crossed the line. It was a day of great festivity among the sailors, and from morning to night all kinds of amusements were carried on on board.

"They commenced on Friday night by Neptune's secretary coming on deck and delivering letters from ' His Majesty the King of the Seas' to our captain. One of the sailors was dressed up to represent the character, and it was most amusing to see the grave manner in which the skipper carried on a conversation with this individual. His inquiries for Neptune, his queen and family, were gone through with the utmost decorum, and he ended by saying, 'You must give my respects to His Majesty, and say that I shall be prepared to receive him on board tomorrow, and swear allegiance to him as Monarch of the Seas.' Then the secretary took his leave, and our letters were distributed.

"The next day, at the appointed time, Neptune, accompanied by his satellites, appeared on board. He certainly seemed more hair than anything else, but that no doubt was correct. The queen was too modern to be in character. She had a huge chignon of yellow tow, and was less careful in her deportment than might have been expected from a person in her dignified position. Their son was decidedly the best of the three. He looked really capital. He was painted a dark yellowish red, with all kinds of mystic emblems in black on his face and body. His only clothing was a brilliant striped cloth round his loins and a silver (?) crown on his head. Round these principal personages were grouped several droll characters, representing a doctor and barber, with their attendants.

"Neptune and his train came on the poop-deck, where they were received by the captain with all due honours. After this ceremony they went on the quarter-deck, and the barber, who had an enormous razor, shaved various passengers who had not before crossed the line. They were then put into the bath and had a good ducking. All this was carried on with perfect good humour, only willing victims being sacrificed. Then Neptune took his departure amidst great cheering.

"The afternoon was devoted to sports of various kinds —a prize of money being given to successful candidates. The most interesting was a race to the masthead and back, a prize of 10s. being given by the first mate. It was won by a Dutch sailor, who performed the feat in two minutes five seconds; this, the captain told us, was remarkably quick work.

"There was also a smoking race, a prize being awarded to the man who could get through a quarter of an ounce of tobacco in the shortest time. In the evening a grand concert was given, the captain having offered a prize for the best song. The quarter-deck was lighted up for the occasion, and some men blacked their faces and came out as Christy Minstrels. Their 'get up' was capital, and they gave us some really good songs. I expect that the glorious night we had, with the moon so bright that one could easily read by it, had much to do with the affair going off so well. So the day came to an end, and a very jolly day it was."

The ceremonies attendant on crossing the line are believed to be of very ancient origin indeed, and it is dimly conjectured that they may have some connection with the festive rites in honour of Neptune, performed by mariners on the occasion of a ship passing the Pillars of Hercules, from the Atlantic into the Mediterranean, or *vice versâ*. How the scene of the ceremonial came to be transferred from the boundary separating the two seas to that dividing the northern from the southern hemisphere baffles all conjecture, and is lost in the mists of the past.

The ceremony known as "burying the dead horse" is a curious one, and is still practised in a good many Australian ships. It takes place during the outward voyage, on the twenty-eighth day after departure from port, and seems to have a double signification. Sailors, before they join their ship, have an advance note given them for a month's wages. This they usually spend, so that the first month they may be said to be earning no wages. They therefore symbolise the first month's work by the *dead horse*, and speak of it as "working the dead horse." The second signification seems to have to do with the probable position of the ship at the end of the month, for by this time she is likely to be in the "horse latitudes" (calms of Cancer).*

The following is a description of the "burial of the dead horse" as it took place in one of Messrs. Wigram's ships:—

"In the morning we were called upon for contributions, and about £7 was collected. At tea-time a bell was rung, and a crier announced in different parts of the ship

* See page 107.

that the dead horse would be sold by auction at eight o'clock the same evening, prefacing his proclamation with 'Oyez! Oyez! Oyez!' and ending up with 'God save the Queen.'

"By eight o'clock all the passengers and officers were assembled on the poop, and the second and third-class passengers on the quarter-deck, making altogether quite a crowd. Presently we heard a dismal chant proceeding from the forecastle, consisting of a solo and chorus, one of the refrains being 'Poor old horse.' Gradually the sounds drew nearer, and a procession was revealed, headed by a groom with a halter and two policemen. A number of other characters in various costumes next appeared, drawing after them the effigy of a horse of very peculiar construction, but not by any means a dead one, to judge by his prancing legs. On his back was a man dressed in a white dress coat and a white hat, with his face blackened, and riding vigorously. Following were two men armed with sticks, with which from time to time they dealt resounding blows upon the hindquarters of the horse.

"After making the tour of the main deck, the procession stopped in front of the poop, and then the auctioneer (the cook), dressed in racecourse costume, took his stand upon a barrel, and, assisted by his two clerks, proceeded to sell the horse, after making a very humorous speech as to its merits and pedigree, symbolical throughout of the ship and the men's work. The passengers on the poop made successive bids up to £7 10*s*., at which price the horse was knocked down, the auctioneer using as a hammer a gigantic mallet.

"Then came the most curious part of the peformance. The horse *with the man on his back* was hauled bodily up from the deck to the main yard-arm, illuminated during his ascent by blue lights burnt on the yard. The appearance was most peculiar, as the ropes were not visible, and the horse and his rider seemed to be suspended in mid-air over the foaming sea, which looked very grand in the strange blue light. As soon as the yard-arm was reached, the rider detached the horse from the line, and it fell with a great splash into the seething water beneath. The man was then hauled down upon deck, with a blue light burning in his hand, and after hearty cheers for the captain, the officers, the ladies, and the Prince of Wales (whose birthday it was), the performance terminated."

Amongst the first things to attract the attention of a landsman will be the songs, or, as they are sometimes called, "chanties" of the sailors.

The men in most ships indulge in these songs on every possible occasion, but it is when hauling up the topsails after a gale, or when heaving up the anchor at starting upon the homeward voyage, that they sing with the greatest vigour. Many of the songs are said to be ancient, and to have been handed down from remote generations of sailors. They nearly all consist of a solo alternating with a chorus, which, being very short, and recurring between each line of the solo, serves to mark the point at which all the men pull together. To the uninitiated it seems as if there were a vast amount of singing in proportion to the work done. Many of the songs are in a minor key, and most of them are quaint and "taking," and when heard either amidst the roaring of a gale or in the stillness of night, they have a wild and impressive effect. The words of the "chanties" will seldom repay investigation, as they are often unfit for ears polite, and when not coarse, are generally nonsensical: not unfrequently they are more or less improvised for the occasion. Occasionally popular land songs are adopted by the sailors, but they never seem so suitable, nor do they "go" as well, as the original time-honoured ditties.

Next to the chance of seeing land, nothing excites more interest at sea than passing vessels.

The number of ships met with during a voyage to Australia varies greatly. I have heard of cases in which not a single sail has been seen between the English Channel and Port Phillip Heads. But these were quite exceptional instances, and usually a large number of vessels are passed, although not so many now as before the opening of the Suez Canal; for then the Atlantic was the great highway to India and China, as well as to Australia.

The greatest number of ships are usually met with in the tropics, where the tracks of outward-bound and homeward-bound vessels cross each other.

Although sighting a ship is at all times a matter of interest, it is in those localities where but few are seen, and where the loneliness of the ocean is most felt, that the greatest impression is produced. Whether the approaching vessel is outward or homeward bound (sometimes difficult to decide); what are her rig and tonnage; to what nationality she belongs; and whether she will come near enough to speak, are all questions which excite much discussion and surmise. As she approaches, all glasses are brought to bear upon her, and any sign of hoisting signals is carefully noted.

The order of signalling is as follows: First the ensign is hoisted—the etiquette being that the smaller vessel should take the initiative. This being interpreted means, " I belong to such a nation; what is *your* nationality ? " Then the other vessel hoists her ensign in reply. Of course, in the case of an English merchantman the ensign is the Union Jack without the St. George's cross, which is used only by men-of-war. The next proceeding is for the first ship to hoist her "number"—that is, a combination of flags that signifies her name. In the "Commercial Code of Signals," which is now almost universally in use, there is a flag for every letter of the alphabet, except x, y, z, and the vowels. Every captain is furnished with a list in which the combination of letters which constitutes each ship's number is placed opposite her name, together with her tonnage and other particulars. When the number has been responded to by the answering ship, the first ship hoists a combination of flags which stands for the port from which she has sailed; then another signifying the port to which she is bound; next the number of days out—which, when a ship has made a slow voyage, is sometimes reduced to smaller limits than are quite compatible with truth. After this, flags are hoisted which signify "all well on board," if such is the case, and, in the case of an outward-bound English ship, "Please report me at Lloyd's," if it is wished that tidings should reach the owners. Questions on other subjects are sometimes asked and answered—such as the kind of weather that has been experienced, the point at which the trade-winds have been picked up or lost, or the exact time by the ship's chronometers. The latter is communicated in a very ingenious manner, but the method would take too long to describe here.

Finally, the ensign is dipped three times as a parting salute, signifying "We wish you a pleasant voyage," and then each of the ships goes on her way. Of course, the whole of this routine is not gone through with every ship that is spoken; and indeed there is often time only to hoist the ensign or the number while passing; and some ships are churlish or lazy, and take no notice of signals.

But it is when meeting a homeward-bound ship in a

calm, after many weeks spent at sea, that the greatest excitement prevails amongst the passengers, because then there is a chance of sending letters home; although in these days of clipper-ships, which move at the rate of two or three knots an hour in the lightest airs, the opportunity occurs far less frequently than in former days.

As the two vessels almost imperceptibly near one another, every eye is strained to discover the nationality and probable destination of the approaching ship, and as soon as the slightest probability of sending letters by her is discerned, every passenger falls to writing letters with frantic haste, except perhaps such wiser spirits as have adopted the precaution of writing a sort of journal letter day by day, ready for such an opportunity.

A canvas bag, upon which the name of the ship has been painted, is usually provided for the reception of the letters, which, as they are written, are dropped into it until, at the last moment, the sail-maker sews it up securely. In the meantime a boat has been lowered, and is manned by a crew under the command of one of the officers of the ship. A present of some kind, such as potatoes or flour, is put into the boat, together with the latest newspapers from England, and finally the bag of letters is lowered into her, and she departs on her errand, eagerly watched by all on board. Presently the homeward-bound ship is reached, and the officer, together with any of the passengers who may have accompanied him, climb up her side and are lost to view, while the men remain in the boat and exchange ideas with the sailors who look down upon them from the bulwarks above. It is surprising how quickly, even when it is apparently almost a dead calm, the combined progression of the two vessels carries them away from each other; and when the visitors come over the side to regain their boat, they often find they have quite a long pull before them in order to reach their own ship. They usually bring with them a return present—generally some produce of the country from which the ship has sailed, such as preserves, pickles, etc. On their arrival they are surrounded by a crowd of eager questioners, all anxious to know full particulars with reference to the captain, crew, and internal arrangements of the vessel they have visited.

Ships' letters are posted unpaid at the port of arrival, whether it be in England or on the Continent, and are charged the ordinary rates of postage on delivery—not double, as in the case of other unpaid letters.

During a dead calm a good-natured skipper will sometimes allow one or more of the boats to be lowered, in order to permit the passengers to enjoy the novel sensation of looking at their floating home from the outside, while they exercise their muscles with a little rowing.

Sometimes, too, the younger men, on finding themselves at a considerable distance from the ship, indulge in a bath, although this is at all times a hazardous proceeding, especially in the tropics, where sharks abound. During a voyage to Australia the author once saw two sharks prowling about between the ship and a boat from which a party of young men were bathing, and it was with some difficulty that the absentees were apprised of their danger.

CHAPTER VI.

COURSE, CLIMATE, AND WEATHER.

Course of a sailing vessel bound for Australia—The "regions" of the ocean—Climate and weather experienced in the various portions of the Australian voyage—The English Channel—Bay of Biscay—Northern region of prevailing westerly winds—The calms of Cancer—Region of north-east trade-winds—The equatorial calms or "doldrums"—Equatorial rains—Region of south-east trade-winds—Calm-belt of Capricorn—The southern region of prevailing westerly winds—Course of sailing vessels between the longitude of the Cape and Australia—The "roaring forties"—Occasional gales—Rapid alteration of apparent time—Temperature—Reversal of the characteristics of the winds—Effects of the cold weather on invalids—Land sighted on outward voyage—Canary Islands—Cape Verd Islands—Tristan d'Acunha.

IF we examine the ordinary track of a sailing vessel bound for Australia,* we shall find that the general direction in which she shapes her course after leaving the English Channel is (speaking roughly) S.S.W. as far as the equator; from thence nearly S.E. as far as the meridian of the Cape of Good Hope; and from that point to Australia nearly due east.

During the first two portions of this course—viz., from the English Channel to the Cape—the vessel traverses districts of the ocean in which great and varied changes of climate and weather are experienced.

As regards the temperature, it may be stated in general terms that the heat increases until the equator is passed, and afterwards diminishes until the extreme southern limit of the voyage has been reached.

* *See* Map.

With regard to the weather, however, it will be found that different latitudes possess peculiarities of their own, which are marked with tolerable distinctness both in the northern and in the southern hemispheres.

In consequence of these peculiarities, the ocean has been divided by physical geographers into *regions*, the principal of which—taken in the order in which they are traversed—are (1) the northern region of prevailing westerly winds, (2) the calm-belt of Cancer, (3) the region of the north-east trade-winds, (4) the equatorial calm-belt, or "doldrums," (5) the south-east trade-wind region, (6) the calm-belt of Capricorn, and (7) the southern region of prevailing westerly winds.

It will not, of course, be expected that these regions present any sharply defined limits. They merge one into another almost imperceptibly, and they also change their position to a certain extent according to the season of the year. Still, on the whole, they possess in a marked degree the characteristics ascribed to them.

I will endeavour to give a brief general description of the climate and weather to be looked for in these various portions of the voyage, and their effects upon invalids.

As mentioned in a previous chapter, the weather usually experienced in the English Channel, and in fact in all the seas around our coasts, is exceedingly trying to invalids. In late autumn and winter, rain, cold winds, and even gales, are to be expected; and even in the summer months the weather is frequently cold, especially at night. Wind, weather, and temperature are all far more variable near land than quite out at sea; and while one day may be calm and warm, with bright sunshine, the next may be rough, cold, and rainy.

Hence the invalid leaving England in the autumn cannot be too careful during the first few days of the voyage. He should wear warm clothing, wrap up well when on deck, and avoid exposure to rain and night air.

The weather met with while passing the Bay of Biscay is but little better than that of the English Channel. Here heavy rolling seas are often experienced, together with strong winds and frequent rain. But on the whole the temperature is appreciably higher than it is off the coast of England.

As soon, however, as Cape Finisterre has been passed (which, with a favourable wind, will be on the third or fourth day after leaving Plymouth), more pleasant weather may be expected, and the passenger who, recovering from sea-sickness, goes on deck now for the first time, will be astonished at the changed aspect of affairs. The gray clouds and turbid sea of the Channel and the Bay of Biscay are replaced by a blue sky and bright blue waves, while the temperature has risen some $8°$ or $10°$, and the air is mild and balmy.

This kind of weather, interrupted by occasional showers, and accompanied by variable winds, sometimes strong and sometimes light, but for the most part from the west or south-west, continues until the ship has reached a latitude of about $30°$ to $35°$ N., when she enters a narrow belt of calms, the calms of Cancer; whereas hitherto since leaving the Channel she has been sailing in that region of the sea known as the *variables*, or the *region of prevailing westerly winds*.

This arbitrary division of the ocean extends from the arctic regions on the north to the calm-belt of Cancer on the south, and has received the designation by which it is known because in these latitudes the winds, although variable, are (taken all the year round) more or less westerly in direction in the proportion of *two* days to *one*.

The Calms of Cancer, which are entered at a latitude

of about 30° to 35° N., according to the season of the year, are otherwise called the "Horse Latitudes," "from the circumstance that vessels formerly bound from New England to the West Indies, with a deck-load of horses, were often so delayed in this calm-belt, that for want of water for their animals they were compelled to throw a portion of them overboard." *

The calm-belt of Cancer extends over about six degrees of latitude, and its position, changing with the season, is farthest north in the autumn and farthest south in the spring.

In the "horse latitudes," calms and light or baffling winds may be expected; but however vexatious the delay caused by these may be to the captain and officers of the ship, and to those of the passengers who are in a hurry to reach their destination, invalids and health-seekers will generally find the weather here very delightful, and will be able to sit about on deck all day without wraps, enjoying the calm sea and the bright sunshine. The thermometer, which in the English Channel indicated perhaps 45°, will here have risen to about 70°—a most enjoyable temperature, and one that suits all sufferers from chest complaints most admirably.

It must not be imagined that this region of the calms of Cancer is a district that is always clearly defined and mapped out by the characteristics of the weather experienced in it. Sometimes a ship may pass through it without experiencing any calms whatever, but as a general rule the weather in these latitudes will be such as has been described.

When the ship has reached a latitude of about 25° to 30° N., according to the time of year, the light variable winds begin to draw round to the north-east, and at last

* Maury.

freshen to a steady breeze from that quarter. The ship is now in the *region of the north-east trade-winds*, and every stitch of canvas is set so as to make the most of the favourable breeze.

It will soon be noticed by those who have not been to sea before that the trade-wind is altogether unlike any wind that they have experienced on land. It has no gusts or inequalities, but is one continuous and perfectly steady current of air, remaining at the same strength and in the same direction hour after hour and day after day, so that sometimes, even for days together, scarcely a sail has to be trimmed or a rope to be touched.

The appearance both of sea and sky in the trade-wind region is very characteristic. The sea, in place of the greasy or glassy surface which it exhibited in the calm-belts, is covered with crisp, curling waves, whose summits are crested with white foam, and the sky, although for the most part clear and blue, is dotted here and there with the small detached clouds which are almost peculiar to these regions.

I cannot do better than give Lieutenant Jansen's description of this region of the sea, as quoted by Maury. He says: "When . . . ships which have lingered in the calm-belt, run with the north-east trade, and direct their course for the Cape Verd Islands, then it seems as if they were in another world. The sombre skies and changeable—alternately chilly and sultry—weather of our latitudes are replaced by a regular temperature and good settled weather. Each one rejoices in the glorious heavens, in which none save the little trade-clouds are to be seen; which clouds in the trade-wind region make the sunset so enchanting. The dark-blue water, in which many and strange kinds of *echini* sport in the sunlight, and when seen at a distance make the sea appear like one vast field adorned with flowers; the regular swellings of the waves, with their silvery foam, through which the flying fishes flutter; the beautifully coloured dolphins; the diving schools of tunnies,—all these banish afar the monotony of the sea, awake the love of life in the youthful seaman, and attune his heart to goodness. Everything around him fixes his attention and increases his astonishment." *

Speaking roughly, the belt of the north-east trades occupies about twenty degrees of latitude, but its breadth and position vary in common with the other regions, all of which, as before mentioned, shift their places within certain limits, following the sun as he travels either to the north or the south of the equator.

Although the quarter from which the trade-wind blows may shift through several points of the compass, yet its general direction is always pretty much the same. As a rule, it blows steadily and constantly from its commencement to its termination, but it is sometimes interrupted by "flaws," and occasionally it is broken up by gales or hurricanes. Invalids usually greatly enjoy what has been called the "champagne atmosphere" of the trade-winds, and the steady breeze and the rapid rate of sailing are pleasant and invigorating to all. The temperature is singularly equable, the daily range of the thermometer being only 3° or 4° in the twenty-four hours. At the same time there is always a certain amount of chilliness about these winds, even though the actual temperature may be higher than it was in the calms. This is no doubt partly owing to the rapid movement of the air, but it is also due in a great measure to the large amount of moisture contained in it. The reason of this dampness will at once be evident when we consider that the trade winds are the great evaporating winds, carrying moisture to all parts of the earth. The depth of water evaporated

* Maury's "Physical Geography of the Sea."

from the surface of the sea by the north-east and south-east trade-winds has been variously computed at from eight to sixteen feet during the year!

It is probably owing to the presence of this large amount of moisture in a current of air constantly in motion, that the trade-wind regions do not, as a rule, suit those who suffer from rheumatism, neuralgia, or sciatica. The rheumatism, however, is seldom of an acute type, and neuralgia, though painful at the time, will generally pass off as soon as the trade-wind region has been left behind.

The Belt of Equatorial Calms.—A few degrees to the north of the equator (about $10°$ N. in November) we enter the equatorial calms, or "doldrums," of evil reputation. From my own experience, however, I am inclined to think that the discomforts of this part of the voyage have been much exaggerated.

The sea and sky here have a very different appearance to that which they presented in the trade-wind regions. Calms and light airs prevail, and the sea is either of a deep glassy blue under a scorching sun, or black as ink under a leaden sky. The dense clouds that so often obscure the heavens in this region have caused it sometimes to be called the "equatorial cloud ring." From these massive clouds, from time to time, deluges of rain descend with a violence unknown in more temperate climes. Nor are they always passing showers, for sometimes they will continue with a steady downpour for twenty-four hours at a time, or even longer.

Though both rain and clouds fulfil a most important part in tempering the heat of these equatorial regions, still they certainly have their discomforts for voyagers; for everything becomes saturated with moisture, and the atmosphere, steamy and oppressive, acts as a constant vapour-bath.

The sense of heat that is experienced is out of all proportion to the actual temperature, for the thermometer very rarely rises higher than 83°—the highest shade-reading on deck that I have ever seen in a sailing vessel being 85°. In a steamer, however, the temperature will sometimes reach 89° or 90°, owing no doubt in part to the heat of the furnaces. The heat in the cabins is of course higher by several degrees than it is on deck, and this is particularly the case in steamers and in iron vessels.

As these temperatures are scarcely higher than those experienced during hot summers in England, we must conclude that the oppressiveness of the equatorial calms is due, not only to the very large amount of humidity in the atmosphere, checking the evaporation of sensible and insensible perspiration, but also to the state of electrical disturbance that constantly exists in these latitudes. The feeling is, in fact, less one of actual heat than of a constant dampness, owing to the perspiration, which flows freely on the slighest exertion, not being carried off by the air, as it would be in a dryer atmosphere. When on deck, and sitting perfectly still, it is possible to keep moderately cool; for even in the most complete calm the rolling of the vessel and the flapping of the sails produce a movement of the air which is very refreshing. But it is when driven below by the tropical rains or the necessities of eating or sleeping that the greatest discomfort is experienced.

Absolute calms are, however, rare; and, owing to their improved construction, it is but seldom that ships now-a days lose their steerage-way. In airs so light that formerly the helm would have been lashed and the vessel left to her own devices, she will now move ahead at the rate of two or three knots an hour, often, apparently, only by the flapping of the sails. Even with daily runs of only fifty or sixty miles, this part of the voyage, however unpleasant it may be at the time, seldom, at the present day, lasts more than three or four days, or a week at the outside, whereas formerly it was not unusual for a ship to be becalmed in the "doldrums" for two or three weeks.

Although the oppressive weather of these latitudes must always be more or less trying to invalids, yet they generally get through it fairly, and seldom suffer permanent harm from it. As for those who are well, although they may lose weight a little, and complain a great deal, yet their general health usually remains remarkably good; while those who suffer from rheumatism or derangements of the liver frequently derive considerable benefit from the profuse perspirations induced by this natural vapour-bath.

The tropical downpours of tepid fresh water often tempt both passengers and crew to indulge in a shower-bath of nature's own providing, and as many as fifty or sixty people may sometimes be seen skylarking about the decks at these times, clad in the most airy costumes in lieu of bathing-dresses. Invalids had, however, better refrain from following this example.

The sailors collect the plentiful fresh water, and indulge in grand washing operations, and sometimes the rain-water which flows down from the forecastle or the poop is collected to the extent of many hundreds of gallons, and transferred to the ship's tanks.

After the requisite number of melting days and nights have been endured in passing through the doldrums, a squall of wind and rain, often accompanied by thunder and lightning, ushers in a pleasanter state of affairs. The variable airs, drawing round to the south-east, freshen into the eagerly expected *south-east trade-winds*. The gloomy canopy of clouds rolls away, revealing the characteristic trade-wind sky, with its small clouds, which vanish as you look at them; and under the influence of a cool and refreshing breeze, and the rapid movement of the ship, every one shakes off the languor of the equatorial calms.

The south-east trades are usually met with a little to the north of the equator. They are, as a rule, steadier, stronger, and of greater extent than the north-east trades. While the latter occupy a belt of only from fifteen to twenty degrees of latitude, the former extend over from twenty to twenty-five degrees.

A glance at the map will show that the south-east trades are not so favourable in direction for an outward-bound ship as the north-east trades are; and a vessel is frequently compelled to sail a good deal to the west of her true course in order to avail herself of them to the full extent. The plan usually adopted is to sail as close to the wind as is consistent with keeping the sails full.

But, although to a certain extent head-winds, the south-east trades are so steady and strong, that fine runs are made each day, and the captain strains every effort to make the most of them, and is exceedingly sorry when they come to an end.

The sky and sea present much the same aspect in both trade-wind regions. The same small detached clouds, bright skies, and crisp, curling waves are seen in both, but squalls accompanied by thunder and lightning are perhaps more frequent in the south-east than in the north-east trades. Both very often begin and end with these squalls.

The Calm-belt of Capricorn.—In the latitude of about 25° S. the outward-bound ship enters the regions of light variable airs and calms known as the calms of Capricorn. The weather here is much the same as in the corresponding belt of Cancer in the northern hemisphere, except that, on the whole, it is cooler. For the invalid who is suffering from chest disease, and who likes warmth without oppressiveness, this will be found one of the most delightful portions of the voyage, the average temperature being from 68° to 70°.

Like the "horse latitudes" in the northern hemisphere, this calm-belt has not by any means well-defined limits, and sometimes the ship will pass through it without a check; but in the majority of instances a few days of calms and light airs will be experienced in this neighbourhood.

Having reached a latitude of from 30° to 35° S., the ship enters the *southern region of prevailing westerly winds*. This arbitrary division of the ocean extends from the southern limits of the calms of Capricorn to the Polar seas, and a vessel proceeding to Australia will remain in it during the whole of the latter half of the voyage.

At first the winds are often light and variable; but as the ship pursues her south-easterly course, and gets well to the south of the Cape of Good Hope, she meets with those strong breezes which have been called "the brave west winds of the southern hemisphere."

As the ship sails southward, the weather becomes colder and more bracing every day, until, when the extreme southern limits of her course have been reached, the temperature is almost that of winter in England.

In this part of the voyage the aspect of the sea is far more familiar than in the tropical latitudes, and often reminds one of the foaming waves around our own shores, especially as in this locality they are sometimes green, particularly when seen by transmitted light.

The principles of "great-circle sailing" have caused the captains of vessels to take a much more southerly route than they did before their discovery. They now sail as low as 45° or 50° S.;* and this they do for two reasons;

---

* Some of the "invalid" ships preserve a more northerly course, in order to avoid the rough and cold weather experienced farther south.

first, because by taking this route the actual distance to Australia is materially lessened; and secondly, because, as a rule, the further south they go, the stronger are the prevailing westerly winds.

A favourite latitude for running down the easting is about 46° S., and here all the characteristics of the "roaring forties," as they have been called, are abundantly exhibited. Maury thus describes this part of the ocean: "The billows there lift themselves up in long ridges with deep hollows between them. They run high and fast, tossing their white caps aloft in the air, looking like the green hills of a rolling prairie capped with snow, and chasing each other in sport. Still their march is stately, and their roll majestic. The scenery among them is grand, and the Australian-bound trader, after doubling the Cape of Good Hope, finds herself followed for weeks at a time by these magnificent rolling swells driven and lashed by the 'brave west winds' furiously."

This kind of weather, accompanied by strong winds, generally more or less westerly in direction, together with a cold temperature, continues with scarcely any interruption until the vessel, approaching the Australian shores, runs somewhat suddenly into warmer and calmer weather.

It may be readily imagined that winds so boisterous and long-continued not unfrequently freshen into gales of considerable violence. As, however, the barometer usually gives due notice of their approach, every preparation can be made in good time; and their direction being generally favourable to the ship's course, she can run before them with as much sail set as it is wise to carry.

Sailors say of the gales experienced in these latitudes, that "if they are rough they are honest," and they seem greatly to prefer them to the sudden cyclones and hurricanes in other parts of the world, which often give comparatively little notice of their approach, and veer so rapidly in direction, that a ship is sometimes "taken aback" without any warning.

The gales off the Cape almost repay by their grandeur any inconvenience to which one may be subjected by them. When they last, as they sometimes do, for two or three days at a time the waves become grand beyond all description; and during the day-time, at least, when able to remain on deck to watch the magnificent spectacle of the vast towering waves, and to admire the wonderful manner in which the ship rides over them as they come sweeping onwards as if to crush her, the beholder is filled with a sense of exhilaration and delight that must be experienced in order to be understood.

It must be acknowledged, however, that during the night, or when the weather is so bad as to compel one to remain below, a gale is by no means a pleasant matter. The extraordinary and unexpected movements of the ship, the roaring of the wind and the sea, and the dashing of the waves against the ship's sides, not only tend to banish sleep, but also render it difficult to employ oneself in any way. The cabins, too, are made gloomy and dark by the closing of the dead-lights, and meals are only accomplished under considerable difficulties and in an incomplete manner.

All things considered, those who have once experienced a violent gale seldom wish to see another, and few are sorry if, as not unfrequently happens, the voyage is accomplished without encountering a single storm of any magnitude.

Although it is but rarely that other ships are met with in the more southern latitudes, yet these seas are by no means deserted, for they are tenanted by numberless seabirds, from the tiny Mother Cary's chicken to the stately albatross, as well as by schools of porpoises and numerous whales of various kinds.

The reversal of the seasons in the southern hemisphere is, at first, somewhat perplexing. The voyager who leaves England in the late autumn will find, as he travels southwards, that the days do not at first draw out as rapidly as he might have expected. Indeed, as long as he is north of the line he will notice but little difference—the reason being that the sun is travelling southwards as well as the ship, and that the movement of the one almost compensates that of the other. But no sooner has the equator been passed, than the days begin to lengthen with a rapidity that would astonish us if we did not remember that in the southern hemisphere the 21st of December is the *longest* instead of the shortest day. A Christmas spent in the South Atlantic seems, therefore, particularly strange to an inhabitant of the northern hemisphere; for although the weather may be as cold as it usually is at Christmas-time in England, yet the days will be as long as they are with us at midsummer.

As before mentioned, the changes in the apparent time are very marked while running down the easting between the Cape and Australia; for as the winds are strong and favourable, and the degrees of longitude are narrow so far south, it is no unusual thing for a ship to run five or six degrees a day for several days in succession, causing a difference in the clock of from twenty to twenty-five minutes each day. While to the *west* of the meridian of Greenwich the ship's clock will, of course, be *slow* as compared with Greenwich time; but to the *east* of that meridian it will be *fast*.

The mean temperature experienced in the region of prevailing westerly winds (in a latitude of about 45° S.) is seldom higher than from 45° to 47°, even in the summer months; and it will be at once seen that this is much colder weather than that met with in a corresponding latitude of the northern hemisphere, where the mean temperature would be some ten degrees higher. In point of fact, the whole of the southern hemisphere is colder than the northern, and midsummer south of the Cape is nearly as cold as midwinter at the same latitude in the Atlantic.

When days are in the southern hemisphere it is the *north* wind that is the warm and rainy wind, and the south wind that is cold and dry; also the north-west wind is more frequent than the south-west—just the reverse in every respect of what is the case to the north of the line. A moment's reflection will suffice to explain this. The north wind comes from the hot moist equatorial regions, whereas the south wind comes from the Polar seas.

Between the Cape and Australia the prevailing winds, though generally more or less westerly, frequently veer from north-west to south-west, blowing usually for a few consecutive days from each of these quarters, and the difference in the weather produced by the polar and equatorial currents respectively is most marked. With the latter the weather is 5° or 6° warmer than with the former, but on the other hand the north-west wind is almost always accompanied by rain.

The transition from the heat of the tropics to the cold bracing weather of the " roaring forties" is, as may be imagined, not only great, but also comparatively sudden; and it will be asked, " What effect does this change of temperature produce upon the invalids ? " A favourable answer can, I think, be given to this question. Nervous invalids, as well as those suffering from a tendency to pulmonary disease, usually improve more during this part of the voyage than in any other; and at this time a marked increase of weight takes place, owing no doubt in a great measure to the improved appetite and vigour of digestion that result from the bracing climate of these southern latitudes.

The coldness of the weather not only necessitates the wearing of very warm clothing, but also renders vigorous exercise both pleasant and desirable. In sailing vessels it is not always customary to warm either the saloon or the cabins by artificial means, and with the thermometer at 45° the passengers are sometimes glad to wrap themselves in their great-coats and railway rugs even when sitting below. Long hours in bed become the rule, and when on deck, both invalids and those in robust health are glad to tramp up and down for hours at a time in order to keep themselves warm; and, as may be imagined, the keen sea air and the vigorous exercise combined, tend to produce an enormous appetite.

During the four or five weeks that this kind of weather continues, I have known some of the younger invalids gain more than a stone in weight, and the improvement in their health and appearance has been perfectly astonishing.

Colds are very seldom caught in these latitudes (they are much more frequent in the tropics), and with moderate care the most delicate may be on deck for many hours in the course of the day.

Those who suffer from bronchitis are usually more affected by the cold than other pulmonary invalids, but even they almost always improve in their general health, although the cold may have a somewhat irritating effect upon the bronchial mucous membrane.

The following extract from a diary kept during a voyage to Australia, made in company with a very large number of invalids, may serve to illustrate the effects of the climate of these southern regions:—

"The passengers, now near the end of their three months' voyage, present, with scarcely an exception, an appearance of rude—I may almost say full-blown—health that is quite ludicrous. Their faces are red and tanned and fat; and as for their bodies, it seems a marvel how in some cases their garments retain their buttons, so great is the strain upon them! Several 'invalids' have left off waistcoats, being unable to make them meet, and one young fellow *says* that he measures eight inches more round the body than when he started. The improvement in the appearance of the ladies is quite as marked as in the case of the opposite sex. The costumes of all are as amusing as possible. On every side are seen nondescript and shapeless hats and caps, shabby and threadbare coats, torn unmentionables much bedaubed with tar, and sadly in want of patching, boots burst out at the sides, or tattered canvas shoes. The ladies' dresses in some cases retain scarcely a vestige of their original colour, their hats are collapsed and shapeless, and some, who still have a lingering desire to preserve the delicacy of their hands, wear the most wonderful old gloves that can be conceived. As I watch the motley throng promenading the deck, I cannot help thinking what a sensation we should produce if we were all transported just as we are into Regent Street or the 'Row' at the most fashionable hour of the day."

LAND SIGHTED ON THE OUTWARD VOYAGE.—Nothing is so eagerly looked for, after the first week or two spent at sea, as land—even if it be only a passing glimpse of some island or barren rock lying near the ship's course. On the outward passage to Australia it not unfrequently happens that land is never sighted at all, from the commencement of the voyage to its termination. Sometimes, on the other hand, land is seen five or six times, or even oftener.

After leaving Plymouth, if the wind is contrary, it is not unusual to obtain frequent glimpses of the Cornish coast, or of the coast of France, while beating out of the Channel.

Then comes a long stretch of ocean, which may possibly, though not very probably, be broken at the end of ten days or a fortnight by a distant view of Madeira.

The next land likely to be seen will be one or more of the Canary Islands—Ferro or Palma, the two most westerly of the group, being those that are most frequently sighted by outward-bound ships; but occasionally the Peak of Teneriffe, which under favourable circumstances is said to be visible at a distance of seventy or eighty miles, may be seen towering into the sky. The names of the Canary Islands are Grand Canary, Teneriffe, Fortaventura, Lanzarote, Palma, Gomera, Ferro, and some others of smaller size. They are all of volcanic origin. They produce fruits of all kinds, and in great profusion; tobacco, cotton, silk, sugar, etc. Barilla wine and brandy are manufactured by the natives for exportation. The climate of the islands is delightful. The seat of government is at Santa Cruz, Teneriffe. The islands belong to Spain. The population of the group is 283,859.

The Cape Verds, which are situated off the extreme west point of the African continent, are perhaps the oftenest sighted of any of the groups of islands lying near the outward track of sailing vessels; and as they consist for the most part of high mountainous land of volcanic origin, they come into view at a considerable distance. S. Antonio, the most westerly of the group, is the one most frequently seen by sailing ships, but steamers generally pass to the east of the islands, between them and the African coast. The Cape Verd group comprises Santiago, Fogo, Brava, Mayo, Boavista, Sal, St. Nicholas, St. Lucia, St. Vincent, and St. Antonio. They are all mountainous and rugged. Fogo, the loftiest, has an active volcano 9,150 ft. high. Fruit is tolerably abundant in all the islands, and they also possess a particular breed of asses and mules, which are exported to the West Indies. The islands belong to Portugal. Population of the group, 76,000.

The Islands of Ascension and St. Helena are out of the usual track of outward-bound ships; but if driven much to the west by the S.E. trades, the solitary island of Trinidad may possibly be sighted, in lat. 20° 30′ S., long. 29° 10′ W. It is a mere barren rock, inhabited by myriads of sea-birds, especially Soland geese. The Portuguese at one time attempted to establish a penal settlement there, but it was soon found unsuitable for the purpose. This Trinidad must not be confounded with the larger island of the same name belonging to the West Indian group.

A distant view is sometimes obtained of another barren island of the South Atlantic—viz., Tristan d'Acunha, which lies in lat. 37° 6′ S., long. 77° 2′ E., and is surmounted by a dome-shaped volcanic mountain 6,400 ft. high. The island is one of a group of three—the names of the others being Nightingale Island and Inaccessible Island—the latter being so named from the difficulty of landing except in the calmest weather. At the beginning of the present century a few Scotch and American families settled in Tristan d'Acunha, but its isolated position and stormy climate have been against its prosperity as a settlement. The population now numbers little more than 100, but the Society for the Propagation of the Gospel in Foreign Parts have recently sent out a missionary. The islands nominally belong to Great Britain.

From this point the track of an outward-bound sailing ship lies through a long waste of ocean, which stretches as far as the shores of Australia, almost without a break in its vast expanse. The Crozet Islands lie to the south of the usual course, and the only land at all likely to be seen after passing the Cape of Good Hope will be the two small volcanic islands of St. Paul and Amsterdam, in lat. 39° 52′ S., long. 77° 48′ E.; but it is usually thought expedient to give these a tolerably wide berth.

The first point of the Australian continent usually sighted by vessels bound for Melbourne is Cape Otway, at the western entrance of Bass' Strait.

CHAPTER VII.

MANAGEMENT OF THE HEALTH AT SEA.

The treatment of sea-sickness—Regulation of the diet—Exercise—Bathing—Ventilation of the cabin—Closet arrangements—Management of the health in the tropics—Sleeping on deck—Tropical colds—Ulcerated sore-throat—"Prickly heat"—*Languor tropicus*—Necessity of fresh air for invalids.

ONE of the earliest troubles of those unaccustomed to the sea will, of course, be *sea-sickness*. I will therefore endeavour to offer a few practical suggestions that may prove of service to those who become victims to this much-dreaded complaint.

First of all, the invalid must not fall into the error of looking upon sea-sickness as an unmitigated evil: on the contrary, it should rather be regarded as being, within moderate limits, decidedly beneficial, and an admirable preparation for receiving the full benefits of the sea voyage. Dr. Faber's experience in this respect entirely coincides with my own. He says, "On a long voyage sea-sickness has not in the eyes of the passengers that paramount and terrible importance it has on a short passage across the English Channel or German Ocean; in the former case most of them submit patiently to it as an inevitable tribute to the grim rule of Neptune, which being once paid makes the pleasure of sea life only the more enjoyable, as a convalescent is most sensible to the charms of health." Most unpleasant it doubtless always must be, but it is very seldom prejudicial to health, and even in those happily rare cases where people of unusual susceptibility (almost invariably ladies) suffer more or less from sea-sickness during the whole voyage, the constitution is seldom injuriously affected, and a week or two on land will restore the patient to more than usual health. Generally, however, sea-sickness only lasts from one to four or five days, although unusually rough weather will sometimes cause a slight return even late on in the voyage.

The following hints may be useful to sufferers:—

Try to bear the discomfort patiently, as a necessary and unavoidable evil, and dismiss from your mind the idea that the ship's surgeon possesses any specific for its cure. Ice bags to the spine, chloroform, chloral hydrate, nitrate of amyl, and all the numberless remedies that have been proposed, have been weighed in the balance of experience, and found wanting. Some of them, like opiates, may relieve for a time, but they interfere with the natural course of the complaint, and do more harm than good in the long run.

During the first violence of the attack the best thing to do is to retire to your berth and keep as quiet as possible. Do not encourage unnecessary retching, but on the contrary endeavour to control it by the exercise of the will. More can be done in this way than you may imagine. Get as much sleep as possible; but above all do not go too long without food. However much it may excite loathing at first, persevere in taking a little nourishment at intervals, if it be only a morsel of dry biscuit. When the stomach is much exhausted by sickness, small quantities of stimulants, especially in an effervescing form, will be found of great service. The best stimulants to take are brandy in *very small* quantities, well diluted with soda-water, or dry champagne either alone or mixed with soda-water. When ice can be obtained, it may, with very great advantage, be either taken with the fluids, or allowed to dissolve in the mouth in small quantities at a time.

When the stomach is beginning to recover its tone, beef-tea perfectly free from fat (a difficult thing to obtain at sea), or better still, a solution of the Liebig's extract with which you have provided yourself, will be found most useful, especially if well seasoned with cayenne pepper. In fact, cayenne pepper appears at all times to exert a very beneficial effect upon the weakened mucous membrane of the stomach, and I have often seen strong cayenne lozenges more useful in allaying that uncomfortable feeling of nausea which sea-sickness leaves behind it, than almost any other remedy.*

But, above all, directly you feel able to do so, if the weather be favourable, make your way on deck, and remain in the open air as much as possible. Those who have sufficient determination to do this always make a much more rapid recovery than those who remain in their cabins. According to one theory, sea-sickness is caused by the brain failing to understand the movements of the waves. If this should be true (which is however very doubtful), it would follow that there is much more opportunity for studying and comprehending the complex movements of the sea on deck than below. But whatever the *modus operandi*, the fact remains that the open air is wonderfully beneficial, and advantage should be taken of the first symptoms of returning energy and the first interval of fine weather to go on deck.

Finally, do not be discouraged if, for some mornings after the actual sickness has subsided, you feel much nausea and discomfort on first attempting to rise. Summon your resolution, get up, face breakfast boldly, and

* Dr. Faber recommends oxalate of cerium in two-grain doses every three or four hours for the treatment of this form of sea-sickness.

go on deck, feeling sure that in a few days this last vestige of your enemy will have disappeared.

Sea-sickness generally leaves behind it a good deal of constipation, and a few doses of some mild aperient medicine will usually be necessary in order to complete the cure.

For the encouragement of invalids it may be mentioned that consumptive patients are generally not so subject to sea-sickness as people in good health; but even when most affected by it, its action seems as a rule to be beneficial rather than otherwise, and I have never known serious results, such as hæmorrhage, follow even the most severe attacks. Thin people usually suffer less than stout people, and Australians are not so susceptible as Englishmen.

Diet.—After the sea-sickness has subsided, a ravenous appetite will most probably set in, caused partly by the sea air and partly by the improvement in the digestive functions brought about by the sickness. This craving for food should not be indulged to its full extent, but should be kept well under restraint. The diet should also be chosen judiciously, with due regard to the kind of food that has been found to agree best on shore. Do not fall into the error of supposing that everything will agree with you because you are at sea. The digestion may be improved, but it will not lose its own peculiar idiosyncrasies. For instance, to some weak digestions pork always acts almost like an irritant poison; and even in the case of those with whom it agrees well as an occasional article of diet it can seldom be taken for several days in succession with impunity. I have seen quite an epidemic of indigestion occur on board ship when, after nothing but mutton had been put upon the table for a considerable time, a pig has been killed, and fresh pork in many inviting forms has been added to the bill of fare. In fact, indigestion is often very rife amongst the passengers, especially towards the close of the voyage. This is no doubt partly due to the character of the dietary and want of exercise; but it is believed that the reversal of day and night in the southern hemisphere may have something to do with it—the digestive organs being unable at once to adapt themselves to the change.

Vary your diet as much as is practicable, and bear in mind that as the fresh vegetables and fruit so important to the maintenance of health cannot be obtained at sea, it is necessary to supply their place with the preserved vegetables, which are usually pretty freely supplied, and which form the best substitute that can be had.

With regard to stimulants, you will find, as a rule, that you will require less at sea than on shore, probably because the amount of exercise taken is so much less. If accustomed to beer, it may be taken in moderation during the cooler portions of the voyage; but as the bottled beers supplied on board ship are usually much more potent than ordinary draught ales and porter, they should be taken much more sparingly. In the tropics, claret will be found by far the best beverage, and when diluted with lemonade or soda-water, it is very useful in allaying the distressing thirst that is so often experienced during the hotter portions of the voyage.

All rules for the management of the diet at sea may be thus summarised. Be more moderate both in eating and drinking than you would be on shore.

Exercise.—One of the most serious drawbacks to the life on board ship, for those in health as well as for invalids, is the absence of any inducement to take sufficient exercise for the due maintenance of health. In the warm latitudes particularly, the temptation to sit still all day enjoying the luxuries of idleness is very great. The voracious appetite which most people have when at sea is, however, in itself a sufficient reason why this disinclination to exertion should not be indulged. It is true that the constant motion of the ship, especially in rough weather, gives the muscles a sort of passive exercise; but this is not sufficient; and however wearisome it may at first seem to pace systematically up and down the short limits of the poop or quarter-deck, I cannot too strongly urge perseverance in this respect. Set aside, each day, certain hours for exercise, and adhere to them whenever the weather is sufficiently fine. Walk for a certain time proportioned to your strength. By common consent the hour just before dinner seems to be fixed upon in most ships as the favourite time for promenading the decks, and this is a very good hour for one instalment of exercise; but it will always be better to take a second walk—in the evening during the hot weather, and in the forenoon during the cooler weather.

A good many miles may in this way be traversed in the course of the day, and the actual distance may, for curiosity's sake, be easily calculated by ascertaining the length of the deck, and counting the number of turns taken. Passengers generally promenade in pairs, and sometimes the deck becomes quite crowded with walkers, especially in calm weather.

In the case of young men, the walking exercise may sometimes with advantage be supplemented by gentle and moderate practice with the dumb-bells, etc. The best time for this is in the morning, after the bath. Dumb-bells should, however, always be used in moderation by invalids, and never to the extent of producing muscular fatigue. I do not recommend invalids, especially those who suffer from delicacy of the chest, to join in those violent athletic sports that are in vogue amongst the midshipmen and junior officers of most ships; neither should they indulge too freely in excursions aloft amongst the rigging. I have seen serious results follow over-violent exertion of this kind.

Bathing.—Most modern ships are provided with bath-rooms for the use of the passengers, but in old ships they are seldom found except in the "quarter-galleries" of the stern cabins, where there are rudimentary shower-baths, which, however, seldom act properly, and when they do, are only of use to the occupants of these cabins. Even in those ships which are best found in this respect the demand for baths in the hot weather generally far exceeds the supply. Some of the male passengers, therefore, usually go up when the decks are being washed, at five or six o'clock in the morning, and have recourse to the "wash-deck tub," or are played upon by the hose, or have buckets of water thrown upon them by the sailors.

This is, of course, too violent a form of bathing to be indulged in by those in delicate health, and I am inclined to think that total immersion even in an ordinary cold bath is often too great a shock for consumptive invalids. It has therefore been recommended, when speaking of the outfit, that, where practicable, a small bath should be provided by the passenger himself, for use in his own cabin. If desired to do so, the cuddy-servants will bring down one or more buckets of sea-water every morning, and in this way the safe and invigorating luxury of a sponge bath can be indulged in at your own time. After rubbing dry, it will be found of great advantage to employ brisk friction with horsehair gloves or a hard flesh-brush for about ten minutes. This not only acts most bene-ficially upon the skin, but also removes any saline par-ticles that may have been left behind by the sea-water, and which will otherwise produce a very unpleasant feeling of stickiness in hot weather.

In the tropics it will often be found desirable, in addition to the morning bath, to sponge the body, especially the chest and back, with *fresh* water (if it can be obtained) just before retiring to rest at night. A small quantity is sufficient for this purpose; and if there is a tendency to profuse perspiration during sleep, a little vinegar may with great advantage be added to the water.

Ventilation of the Cabin, etc.—The number of cubic feet of air contained in an ordinary sleeping cabin on board ship would, unless constantly renewed, be quite inadequate to the requirements of healthy respiration, even for one person. It will therefore be noticed that ventilators are freely introduced in those sides of the cabin which adjoin the saloon. But although these may be sufficient to ensure a renewal of the air during the cooler weather, such will not be the case in the tropics. Here it will be found that unless a constant current of air passes *through* the cabin it will soon become close and uncomfortable, and the health will be liable to suffer. Fortunately, during this part of the voyage the weather is usually sufficiently calm to allow of the ports being kept almost constantly open, especially in the case of the upper cabins in poop ships; and in this way the atmosphere of the cabin may be kept fairly pure by the current of air passing between the window and the ventilators.

Do not be afraid of sleeping with the port open when the weather is warm,—the night air will do far less harm than a vitiated atmosphere,—but at the same time avoid sleeping in a thorough draught. The head can easily be protected by means of a curtain, and the port need only be sufficiently open to ensure ventilation without too much draught.

Sometimes, however, owing to bad weather, it will be necessary to keep the ports closed; and this is one of the most trying things that can happen while in the tropics. It is now that a curtain for the doorway will be found of the greatest advantage. By this means the cabin door may be left open even at night, and as the saloon skylights are only closed during very bad weather indeed, the sleeping-cabins receive the benefit of whatever fresh air enters the saloon.

Whenever the officers advise or order the ports to be closed, the passenger should on no account be tempted to re-open them until permission is given to do so, for the inconveniences of getting a sea into the cabin are far greater than the temporary deprivation of fresh air. The berths are often partly under the ports; and if once the bedding becomes wet with salt water, it is most difficult to get it dry again. Added to this, if the cabin itself becomes thoroughly soaked by a sea, it takes many days, in the steamy regions of the tropics, before it dries again, and in the meantime it is pervaded by a damp, mouldy atmosphere which is not only unpleasant, but unwholesome.

In Government emigrant ships the undesirableness of washing the decks when the air is loaded with moisture is fully recognized, and they are ordered either to be dry-rubbed instead of being washed, or if washed, are to be carefully dried by means of hot sand and stoves specially provided for the purpose. In passenger vessels, however, these precautions are much neglected; and very often the stewards take advantage of a tropical downpour (which, though it loads the atmosphere with moisture, provides them with rain-water) to wash, not only the saloon decks, but also those of the various cabins. For my own part, I have always raised a vigorous protest against this proceeding as regarded my own cabin, and have insisted upon the washing being deferred to a bright and dry day.

The dampness of a ship's cabin, even under favourable circumstances, is shown by the condition of all leather articles at the end of a voyage. Portmanteaux, boots, and gloves become mouldly or mildewed, unless they are kept in tin or other damp-proof cases, and so excluded from the air. It may be mentioned, however, that (except in the case of gloves) leather does not suffer in any way from a coating of mould, which, when cleaned off at the end of the voyage, leaves the surface quite uninjured. Kid gloves should always be kept in tin boxes. Woollen clothes sometimes suffer from the damp. They should be taken out and dried in the sun two or three times during the voyage.

It must not be imagined, however, that the dampness of a cabin on board ship is as serious a matter as a damp room on shore would be. Owing perhaps to some peculiarity of the sea climate, it seldom produces colds or other ailments, and, in a properly ventilated passenger ship, it is generally unpleasant rather than injurious. At the same time, it is desirable to keep all immediate personal surroundings as dry as possible; and for this purpose, at intervals during the whole voyage, but more particularly during the hot weather, the cabin servant should be desired to take the whole of the bedding on deck for the purpose of thoroughly drying and airing it in the sun. This is a matter that should be carefully looked to, especially by invalids.

During a long voyage there will of course be a considerable accumulation of soiled linen, and as this must necessarily be kept in the cabin, it should be carefully looked to, especially in hot weather. The best way of dealing with it is to hang up the various articles of clothing—if possible, in a current of air—for an hour or two before putting them away. They should then be rolled up as tightly as possible before placing them in the soiled clothes-bag, the contents of which should be disinfected from time to time by sprinkling with carbolic acid.

The arrangement of the *closets* on board most sailing vessels is far from satisfactory. It is customary for each saloon cabin to contain an open closet, with water laid on from the deck tanks. The stern cabins are the only exceptions. In these the closet is generally in the quarter-gallery, which, being enclosed, and having a separate ventilation, forms a far preferable arrangement. In the more modern ships, general closets are provided for the male passengers, and when this is the case the closets in the cabins should on no account be used by them except in the case of illness. In hot weather especially, the cabin closets are apt to become offensive, unless they are used with great care. They are usually freely supplied with water from the tanks on the poop, and advantage should be taken of this to flush them thoroughly once or twice a day. Chloride of lime (so called), or better still, carbolic acid powder, should also be freely used. A large quantity of these disinfectants is put on board every passenger ship, and they can be obtained on application to the surgeon. In some new sailing vessels an enclosed closet with separate ventilation is attached to each cabin; while in steamers there is generally one closet to each group of two or three cabins. Deck closets are, however, in my opinion, preferable to all others for the use of male passengers.

The Tropics.—While speaking of bathing, ventilation, and other matters, I have already incidentally touched upon several points which may with advantage be borne in mind by the invalid while passing through the tropics, but there still remain a few special hints which may be found of service.

With regard to clothing, as it has been elsewhere remarked, it is at all times better to be over-clothed when at sea than under-clothed. In the tropics this is particularly the case; for tropical colds are not only severe, but easily caught; and although they do not usually leave behind them any permanent ill effects, yet, partaking as they do of the nature of influenza, they are very weakening at the time. I cannot too strongly urge the importance of wearing *woollen* clothing, however thin, during the hot weather; it is not only far more wholesome than linen, but also *actually cooler*. For the day-time, a thin woollen gauze under-waistcoat, a flannel shirt, and thin woollen trousers, should be worn; the rest of the costume may be of any description that is most conducive to comfort. The nights, which, being spent in the cabin, are by far the most trying portion of the twenty-four hours, may be rendered much more bearable by allowing nothing but woollen materials to come in contact with the body. Sheets should be entirely discarded during the warmer portions of the voyage. A horsehair mattress, with a blanket laid smoothly upon it, will be found the most comfortable couch; and if provided with the thin flannel sleeping shirt and loose pyjamas, which have been previously recommended, all other covering may be dispensed with. Only those who have tried this way of sleeping in hot weather know how far preferable it is to any other. Even the linen covering of the pillow is uncomfortable, and a piece of thin Indian matting may with advantage be placed between it and the head. It is as well to keep a thin woollen covering, such as a shawl, at hand, in case of feeling chilly towards morning.

The fresh yet genial air of the tropical nights presents many inducements towards *sleeping on deck;* and sometimes a dozen or more prostrate forms may be seen dotted about, lying on matresses and wrapped in railway rugs. To those in robust health this way of sleeping is a great luxury, as I know of no sensation more pleasurable than on waking in the middle of a bright tropical night to feel the pure cool air fanning one's cheek, to see the stars glittering overhead, and to listen to the lazy flap of the sails against the rigging, until all is lost again in the oblivion of sleep. But, even for the robust, sleeping on deck has its drawbacks; for sometimes a tropical squall comes on, and then the sleepers present an absurd spectacle when, aroused by the pattering rain, they stagger off with their mattresses to take refuge in the saloon or in their own cabins. Even when undisturbed by squalls, all deck sleepers are aroused betimes by the sailors, who come without ceremony to wash the decks at about five o'clock in the morning. All this is very well for those in strong health, but invalids, especially those with any affection of the chest, must on no account allow themselves to be tempted to sleep on deck. The heavy dew, and the possibility of being soaked by passing showers, etc., are in themselves sufficient reasons against doing so, without reckoning the liability to disturbance from all kinds of causes.

Sometimes a whole colony of sleepers may be seen established upon the saloon table under the open skylights; but except in extreme cases of suffering from heat all these irregularities are best avoided by the invalid, who, with an open port and door, will generally find his own cabin bearable, and more conducive to sound and undisturbed sleep than any other locality.

There are several little ailments which in the tropics sometimes make their appearance in almost an epidemic form. One of these is the tropical cold before alluded to, and which seems to be a kind of influenza. It is generally confined to the mucous membrane of the nose and throat, but is sometimes accompanied by a troublesome cough. It usually subsides at the end of two or three days, and is best treated by means of diaphoretics and salines.

A kind of ulcerated sore throat, which looks a good deal worse than it is, sometimes makes its appearance. It arises from relaxation, and a few doses of the solution of perchloride of iron, together with one or two local applications of the same to the tonsils and the back of the throat, will generally effect a complete cure.

An eruption of the skin peculiar to warm climates, and popularly known as "prickly heat," may make its appearance, especially amongst the children. It is a very troublesome affection, accompanied by intense itching, and in severe cases it produces a crop of suppurating heads resembling small boils. Effervescing salines, such as the so-called citrate of magnesia, will be found of service internally, while externally a lotion of glycerine and water may be used; or olive oil applied with a feather will sometimes relieve the itching.

The peculiar debility and digestive disturbance produced in some constitutions by the damp heat of the tropics has been called by Dr. Faber *languor tropicus*. It is generally very successfully treated by a simple tonic such as sulphuric acid, given with a bitter infusion or a few grains of quinine.

In conclusion, I cannot too strongly urge upon invalids the importance of being as much as possible in the open air, if they wish to derive full benefit from their voyage. The air on deck is pure and health-giving; that of the saloon and cabins always more or less vitiated, and seldom so good as in a well-arranged house on shore. Hence, except for the necessities of eating and sleeping, all the time should be spent out of the cabins. If there is any kind of shelter on deck, such as a smoking-room or deck-house, even rainy or rough weather should not drive an invalid below. In the colder parts of the voyage he should clothe himself warmly, and remain on deck as many hours as possible, keeping up the circulation by frequent exercise. In some cases, however, it will be well to avoid the night air in the cold weather.

When compelled to remain below, every possible means should be taken to keep the cabin fresh and well ventilated, and it should always be remembered that too much air is better than too little.

CHAPTER VIII.

OBJECTS OF INTEREST AT SEA.

Colour of the sea—Composition of sea water—Waves—The southern constellations—Auroras—Shooting-stars and meteors—Lunar coronas and haloes—Waterspouts—Sunsets at sea—Vertical sun—Living creatures of the sea—Whales—The Greenland whale—Finbacks—The sperm whale—Food of whales—The enemies of the whale—Dolphins and porpoises—Sharks—Pilot-fish—Catching a shark—Saw-fish and sword-fish—The bonito—Barracouta—Flying-fish—Turtles—Lower forms of marine life—Capturing crustacea, jelly fish, etc.—"Portuguese man-of-war"—Mode of obtaining microscopical objects—The phosphorescence of the sea—Sea-birds—Mother Cary's chicken—Soland goose—The albatross—Sea-birds south of the Cape; their number and variety—Cape hen—Mutton bird—Boatswain bird—Whale bird.

IN endeavouring to give a brief account of some of the objects of interest in sea, sky, and air, met with during a voyage to Australia, no attempt will be made to enter into anything like minute scientific details, which would be not only beyond the powers of the writer, but also foreign to the scope of this little work. All that will be attempted is to describe such things as are usually seen, just as they would strike a non-scientific observer, who yet is interested in what comes under his notice.

One of the first things external to the ship that is likely to arrest the attention of any one taking a voyage for the first time is *the colour of the sea*.

As soon as the ship has left the English Channel the muddy-green hue of shallow water begins to be exchanged for the clear blue tint of the deeper seas; but it is not until the Bay of Biscay has been passed that the true colour of the ocean is to be seen in perfection.

So much has been written on this subject, that it would be an impertinence to attempt anything like a description here. Suffice it to say that those who have seen that glorious blue as it appears in bright sunshine under a cloudless sky will feel inclined to regard the seas around our shores (although beautiful in their own way) as bearing much the same relation to the deep ocean as the waters of a pond bear to those of a mountain lake.

But the colour of the sea is constantly changing, from many causes. The mere reflexion of the clouds will turn it from the brightest blue to a dark indigo tint or an almost inky blackness; while the presence of ripples or waves also greatly modifies its hue.

It appears, however, that when viewed in a mass, pure sea water possesses in itself a clear blue colour, quite irrespective of the reflexion of the sky; and in some cases the mingling of the prevailing yellow tints of the sandy beds of shallow seas with this natural blue of the ocean may tend to cause the green colour of shoal water.

In addition to this the colour is affected; especially near land, by the admixture of chalk, sand, and other suspended matter; also in some cases, even far out at sea, the presence of animalculæ or minute algæ will, in certain localities, produce a white, brown, red, or yellow discoloration of the ocean for many miles in extent.

Recent researches by Professor Tyndall have tended to establish the above fact. In a series of observations taken by him between Gibraltar and Spithead, he found that the colour of the sea was largely dependent upon the particles of solid matter held in suspension. Careful examination of samples of water taken at various parts of the voyage proved that those portions of the sea which presented a yellow-green colour contained the most suspended matter, whereas a deep black-indigo colour indicated the greatest purity.

There can be no doubt, however, that the purity or otherwise of the water is by no means the only condition affecting its colour. The amount of sunshine or of cloud, the colour of the sky and the character of the light reflected from it, the angle at which the light enters the water, the clearness or density of the atmosphere; all these exert a most important modifying influence upon the apparent colour of the sea—the same district of the ocean sometimes passing through every gradation of tint, from brightest azure to inky blackness, or, in more shoal waters, from emerald green to deepest olive, according to the amount and character of the light falling upon it in the course of a single day.

One of the first signs of approaching land or of getting into shoal water is a change in the colour of the sea. It loses its clear transparent blue, and becomes of a dark olive-green hue, which changes to a lighter green as the water gets shallower, until it assumes the appearance familiar to us on our own coasts. One is sometimes surprised when far out at sea, and perhaps several hundreds of miles from land, to see the colour of the ocean suddenly change from its characteristic blue to dark green. But on reference to a good chart we shall find that we are sailing over sandbanks or reefs, which, although perhaps a hundred or even two hundred fathoms below the surface, are yet sufficiently near to account for this alteration.

The water of the ocean is almost always brilliantly clear, and any light-coloured or bright object that is dropped overboard in full sunshine becomes converted, as it sinks, into brightest silver, with a bluish-green tinge, and, gradually diminishing to a shimmering speck, is lost by distance rather than by obscuration.

Every one knows that the sea is salt; but it may occur

to some of my readers to inquire to what the saltness of the water is due. That it is not all due to the presence of common salt may be easily proved; for if we taste a few drops of sea water, we shall find there is a super-added bitterness, quite distinct from the simple saltness of ordinary brine.

If 1,000 ounces of sea water are taken, say from the English Channel, and evaporated to dryness, we shall find that no less than $35\frac{1}{4}$ ounces of solid matter will remain behind in a crystalline form. The crystals are made up of various salts—by far the largest proportion being sodium chloride (common salt); the next largest, magnesium chloride, and the third largest, magnesium sulphate (Epsom salts). The peculiar nauseous bitterness of sea water is mainly owing to the presence of the two latter ingredients. The exact proportion of the various salts is given in the following table:—

100 grains of sea water contain—

Water	964,745
Sodium chloride	27,059
Magnesium chloride	3,666
Magnesium sulphate	2,296
Calcium sulphate	1,406
Potassium chloride	0,766
Calcium carbonate	0,033
Magnesium bromide	0,029
Traces of iodine and ammoniacal salt .	1,000,000

The ocean is by no means uniformly salt in every part, although the proportions of its saline constituents are tolerably constant. In land-locked arms of the sea, such as the Persian Gulf and the Red Sea, especially if subjected to the action of a fierce tropical sun, the water is found to be perceptibly salter than the open ocean. This is owing, no doubt, to the enormous evaporation that goes on from the surface of the sea, and which, in these localities, is unchecked by the free circulation of ocean currents, and by the large compensating rainfall of other tropical regions. In the neighbourhood of melting ice, on the other hand, as in the arctic and antarctic regions, the sea is less salt; also near the mouths of large rivers, such as the Amazon, whose enormous volume of fresh water displaces or mingles with the water of the Atlantic over an area of many hundreds of square miles. There is a story current amongst sailors which illustrates this. It is said that a ship whose crew had undergone great sufferings, from their supply of fresh water having failed during a long voyage, signalled their urgent need to a passing vessel. The prompt reply was, " Let down a bucket;" the fact being, that without suspecting it, the thirsty crew, though far out of sight of land, were opposite the estuary of one of the great rivers of South America, and were surrounded by water that was sufficiently fresh for drinking purposes.

The appearance of the *waves* in the Atlantic or Pacific Oceans is altogether different to what it is near land. The short chopping waves of narrow seas are exchanged for a long sweeping swell, which is always apparent, even in the calmest weather. The waves follow each other in regular succession, and are of great length, covering the sea with vast parallels separated by very broad and (in calm weather) shallow troughs. The distance from crest to crest of the Atlantic waves seems to average from about sixty to a hundred feet.

The height of the waves during a storm is often very considerable, but the current notions on this subject are exaggerated. To speak of the waves as running "mountains high" is, of course, absurd, unless regarded as a poetical figure. It is very difficult to form a correct estimate of their height, but from personal observation on several occasions I should judge that from twenty-five to thirty feet from the trough to the crest is the extreme limit, even in violent and continuous gales off Cape Horn or the Cape of Good Hope. By some observers, however, the maximum is placed higher, and I believe that Dr. Scoresby mentions having seen waves which attained a height of forty-three feet from trough to crest.

In order to raise waves of the *largest* dimensions, it is necessary that the wind should blow with violence from the same quarter for many consecutive hours; yet it is surprising to see how soon the sea will become turbulent when a brisk gale suddenly succeeds even the calmest weather. Two or three hours are sometimes quite sufficient to change the whole aspect of the sea from a dead calm to the wildest storm scene.

The disturbance of the sea is more than superficial: during very violent storms it is believed to affect the ocean to a depth of several hundred feet. The lowest depths of the sea, however, probably preserve a state of perpetual calm.

The apparent velocity of the waves is often very considerable: in violent gales it has been computed at thirty miles an hour or more. But it will be noticed that the waves exercise little if any *propulsive* force upon floating objects; they seem to pass under a ship, for instance, without affecting its direction or even speed to any considerable extent. This is owing to the peculiar character of the wave-motion, into any explanation of which it will be unnecessary to enter here.

Those who have a taste for astronomy will watch with much interest for the appearance of the *southern constellations* as they rise above the horizon, and reveal themselves more fully, night after night, as the ship sails southwards. Nearly every one seems to be disappointed with the first sight of the much-talked-of Southern Cross. The stars of which it is composed are large and brilliant, it is true, but they are few, and not very symmetrically arranged, and indeed the whole constellation in shape more resembles an unevenly made boy's kite than a cross. Our own *Ursa Major* is, according to the opinion of many competent authorities, a far finer constellation than the Southern Cross.

But there are compensations for any disappointment with regard to the constellations of the southern hemisphere; for the stars there often shine with a brilliancy such as is seldom if ever to be seen in our own latitudes, and the planets will sometimes cast a long wake of light across the sea, almost equal to that of the moon at its first quarter.

Then there is the *Milky Way*, which presents great peculiarities in the southern hemisphere. It is not only split or divided for part of its length (it has a general resemblance in shape to a pair of trousers), but it also presents detached patches of nebulæ, like small luminous clouds, which are known as the Clouds of Magellan. The main portion of the milky way is also perforated by black patches perfectly devoid (to the naked eye) of stars. These spaces, which by contrast with the surrounding luminous nebulæ, appear intensely dark, are called by sailors the "coal bags," and have a very curious appearance.

Occasionally very fine *Auroras* are seen at sea. One that was witnessed by the writer in lat. 43° 12′ S., long. 67° 24′ E., was thus described at the time: "First there was a great glare over the southern heavens. Then from a point on the horizon which formed the centre of this glare there darted beautiful radiating bands of light of various changeable colours—blue, pink, red, yellow, and white. Besides these radiating lines there were concentric rainbow-like bands of light, but much fainter than the vertical ones. Every now and then all the bands suddenly shone out much more brightly and distinctly, as if by the drawing up of a gauze curtain."

Generally one or more *eclipses* or other astronomical phenomena are to be seen during a voyage, under conditions which are very favourable as regards clearness of atmosphere and comparative absence of cloud. An eclipse of the sun is very impressive at sea: the light thrown upon the waves is strange and unearthly, and if it should happen that a storm is raging at the time, the scene is altogether one that is not likely to be soon forgotten.

Shooting-stars and *meteors* are of frequent occurrence, and are often exceedingly beautiful. A meteor that I saw some years ago, when near the equator, gave a light equal to that of the moon at its full. The apparent size of the body was about half that of the moon, and it had a long spreading tail of the most lovely hues—red, purple, and blue. The arc through which it travelled could not have been less than $100°$, and during its transit the body changed from blue to white and from white to blue again. Its passage through the sky was attended by a loud whizzing noise.

Lunar coronas and *haloes* are of frequent occurrence, and often of large size; and I must not forget to mention a curious appearance which is sometimes seen at sea, resembling a fragment of a rainbow set on end upon the horizon, and which is called by sailors a "sun-dog" or "rain-dog."

Waterspouts are not very frequently seen on the Australian voyage, and, however interesting they may be from a scientific point of view, their absence is scarcely to be regretted, as they are sometimes dangerous to ships. During most voyages, however, at least one or more will be seen, although sometimes the view is a distant one.

Waterspouts would seem to be caused by an eddy of

wind resembling a minute cyclone, and rotating with such extreme velocity as to suck up a column of water from the surface of the sea. The column of water thus raised is sometimes several hundred feet in height. It is smallest in the middle, and enlarged above and below, resembling two cones united at the apex. The upper cone consists of dense aqueous vapour, the lower of water. They are seldom of long duration, lasting usually only from a few minutes to half an hour at the longest. Their movements are very irregular; sometimes they advance with considerable rapidity, while occasionally they remain almost stationary. They are met with most frequently near the coast and in tropical regions.

Nothing will excite more admiration than the magnificent *sunsets* which are often to be seen at sea. In some latitudes and in certain months of the year they are much finer than in others, and evening after evening for many successive days the passengers congregate at the side of the ship to watch the setting sun and the western heavens.

The sunset clouds in the tropics often assume the most fantastic forms, producing effects resembling long processions of strange figures—men and beasts—with huge birds and flying dragons hovering over them. Sometimes they give the appearance of great plains of gold, or of seas studded with islands, or vast mountain ranges.

But it is the colours that are most extraordinary. Every tint that can be imagined is to be seen—from palest grey to darkest indigo or inky black; from pink to deep lurid crimson; and from lightest gold to deepest orange. A very curious pale apple-green tint is also frequently present in tropical sunsets. For the comfort of those who are not fond of early rising, it may be mentioned that sunrise at sea is seldom so grand as sunset.

Either north or south of the equator, according to the

time of year (or very rarely on the equator itself), a point will be passed at which the sun will be exactly vertical at noon, and when he will throw *no shadow* from upright objects. It is quite possible, at that time, for the shadow of a slim man to be entirely included within that of his hat, if it has a tolerably broad brim.

As in England we of course never have any approach to a vertical sun, this phenomenon is worth noting.

Returning to the sea itself, I will now endeavour to give what must necessarily be a very brief and imperfect sketch of such of its living objects of interest as will meet the eye of an ordinary observer during most voyages to Australia.

WHALES.—When once fairly out at sea, it is seldom that more than a day or two will pass without the cry of "Whale!" causing a general rush of passengers to the side of the ship.

But it must not be imagined that all whales are alike. On the contrary, the term "whale" is so wide in its application, and includes so many different creatures, that it will be as well to say a very few words as to some of the principal species and their general peculiarities.

The whale family (*Cetaceans*) as a whole are distinguished from the fishes in many important particulars. Their organization is much more perfect. They bring forth living young; breathe by means of lungs instead of gills; have a double heart; and possess warm blood, the temperature of which is kept up by a skin of great thickness and an enormous layer of fat or "blubber" from one or two feet in depth. They are also furnished with a "blowhole" in the upper part of the head, which corresponds with the nostrils of terrestrial animals, and which is either single or double, according to the species.

The tail is also set on horizontally, instead of vertically, as in the case of the fishes.

The cetaceans are divided into two great classes—viz., those that have teeth, and those that have a fringe of whalebone instead of teeth. The latter—the *whalebone whales*—are again divided into "smooth-backs" and "fin-backs."

Amongst the smooth-backs is included the Greenland whale (*Balæna mysticetus*), which is not only the largest of the whales, but also the greatest of all animals, attaining sometimes a length of sixty to seventy feet and a girth of some forty feet. The whale of the southern hemisphere, which corresponds to the Greenland whale of the north, is considerably smaller, but in other respects very similar. Its scientific name is *Balæna antarctica*. Neither this nor the Greenland whale is believed to pass the equator, the two species remaining quite separate.

The fin-backs, which are at once distinguished by the large vertical fin rising from the back, are considerably smaller, as a rule, than the smooth-backs, although still huge creatures. They are the kinds most usually seen on the Australian voyage, especially in the North Atlantic, and are not nearly so valuable to fishermen as either the Greenland or the sperm-whale. All whalebone whales have *two* blowholes on the top of the head.

The whales with teeth include the *sperm-whale* (which is almost as large as the Greenland whale, and very valuable), and many smaller species, amongst which may be mentioned two that might scarcely be supposed to belong to the family of whales—viz., the dolphin and the porpoise. The whales with teeth have only *one* blowhole.

The apparatus with which the jaws of the whalebone whales are provided in lieu of teeth is most admirably adapted for securing the creatures upon which they feed.

It consists of an enormous number (400 or 500) of laminæ of whalebone, placed side by side at a distance of less than an inch apart, and forming a gigantic fringe pendent from both sides of the upper jaw.

As these whales subsist almost entirely upon the small molluscous animals with which, in the localities frequented by the cetaceans, the sea swarms in countless myriads, their mode of feeding is rendered exceedingly simple. They merely move slowly along near the surface of the sea with their enormous mouths open to receive their prey. At intervals they close their jaws and eject the water through the whalebone laminæ, which, acting as a sieve, strain off the molluscs which have found their way into this huge trap.

The various species of whales that are provided with teeth feed, as may be imagined, upon larger animals than the whalebone whales. The food of the sperm-whale consists mostly of cuttle-fish of various kinds; while many of the smaller cetaceans, as the grampus, are exceedingly voracious, and attack fishes of large sizes.

The view obtained of these monsters of the deep from the deck of a ship is usually only a very transient one. An immense black rounded mass, surmounted, in the case of the fin-backs, with an enormous vertical fin, is seen tumbling in haste away from the ship's side. Indeed, the peculiar tumbling, rolling movement of the cetaceans is very characteristic, and cannot be mistaken when once it has been seen. When startled by the approach of a ship, the whale usually dives into the depths of the sea, and only appears again at a considerable distance, where he can be seen spouting and rolling his great black back above the waves for a few moments before again disappearing from view. Occasionally, however, when swimming in a direction parallel to a ship that is not perceived by them, whales may be seen to much better advantage.

In this way I was enabled on one occasion to watch for some time three whales—a "bull" and a "cow," accompanied by their "calf"—which swam close to the ship for a considerable distance, rolling about and disporting themselves without taking the slightest notice of us. The two full-grown whales were of enormous dimensions —at least forty to fifty feet in length.

As long as they are above water, whales continue to spout at frequent intervals. The column, which is ejected to a height often of seven or eight feet, appears to consist of fine spray rather than of water. In fact, it is probable that the air and water are mixed together much in the same way as in a "spray producer." *

In calm weather the sea is often observed to be covered with greasy-looking tracks of a peculiar appearance and of great length, extending as far as the eye can reach, and intersecting each other in many directions. These marks are a sign that cetaceans of some kind are about, and sometimes a large number of whales, constituting what is called a "school," may be seen spouting in all directions.

Although, as a rule, these monsters make haste to get out of the way of an approaching vessel, yet cases have been known in which a ship has been violently struck by the tail of an irate whale,—an event by no means to be desired. A year or two ago a steamer was struck in this way, and the blow broke one of the blades of the screw propeller, and disabled the ship. Soon afterwards a dead whale was seen floating in the same locality with a large

* Professor Flower has lately pointed out that, according to recent rescarches, the whale in blowing merely discharges from the lungs air loaded with watery vapour. I find some difficulty in reconciling this view with the fact that even in tropical regions, where the temperature of the air is but little below that of the whale's body, the column ejected from the blowhole is quite visible *immediately* it quits the orifice, and remains opaque to a height of several feet.

gash in its side, the inference being that in striking the ship it had itself received a mortal wound from the propeller.

The whale, big and powerful as he is, has enemies, the principal one being the thresher-fish, the sword-fish, the saw-fish, and the Greenland shark; all of which, though greatly inferior in size to their gigantic adversary, frequently overcome him in combat. The thresher-fish or sea-fox attacks the whale by threshing him with his tail, and, his superior activity enabling him to avoid being struck in return, he often succeeds in killing the whale by his persistent castigation. The whale endeavours to escape from his enemy by diving to the depths of the sea. whither it is supposed that the thresher cannot follow him. I was once fortunate enough to witness a contest of this kind. The thresher constantly leaped out of the sea, and descended with tremendous violence upon the whale, which struggled and lashed the waves with impotent fury until the sea was covered with foam. For some reason (which the captain suggested might be the presence of a sword-fish) the whale did not sound, and the combat continued at the surface until the combatants passed out of sight beyond the horizon.

The threshers and the sword-fish are said systematically to hunt the whale in company—the former attacking him on the surface of the sea, and the latter at the same time stabbing him from below; but this seems to be somewhat problematical. There is no doubt, however, that both the sword-fish and the saw-fish are persistent enemies of the cetaceæ, for whom their powerful weapons make them formidable foes.

All these creatures, as well as the various sharks—but specially the Greenland variety—feed upon the whale when dead; hence, no doubt, arise their efforts for his destruction.

Whales are troubled with parasites of various kinds. Old whales are sometimes found almost covered with barnacles and masses of seaweed; and a peculiar kind of louse of gigantic proportions infests their skin to such an extent as in some cases to cause large sores, and to attract numbers of birds which alight upon the back of the whale to devour these parasites.

Dolphins and Porpoises.—Few days pass at sea without there being seen a troop of active creatures rushing along by the side of the ship, leaping from wave to wave, and apparently enjoying themselves immensely. These are invariably called porpoises by the sailors, but according to scientific writers it would appear that they are in reality the dolphins of mythological celebrity (*Delphinus Delphis*).

A good deal of confusion seems to exist with regard to the distinction between the dolphin and the porpoise; but it would seem that the true porpoise (*Delphinus phocæna*) is smaller than the dolphin, being indeed the least of all the cetaceans, and attaining only a maximum length of some five feet. It frequents the estuaries of rivers, calm bays, and sea-shores generally, rather than the open sea. The dolphin, on the contrary, prefers the wide expanse of the ocean, and travels in companies or "schools" of from two or three to fifty or more.

Of all the denizens of the sea, dolphins appear to be the most playful, and they seem to have a special liking for following or swimming beside a ship, especially when she is sailing at a good speed. It is then a beautiful sight to watch them rushing through the water with such velocity that they seem to be covered with a silver film, while now and again they leap from wave to wave, following in each other's wake with a peculiar movement of their rounded backs that irresistibly reminds one of a boy's game of leapfrog. Occasionally one of the company, more active than the rest, turns a complete somersault; and on one occasion I saw a dolphin that appeared to be quite a professor of the acrobatic art, for he repeatedly leaped high out of the water, and turned *three* complete somersaults whilst in the air!

When in a calm sea a large number of dolphins are seen near the horizon indulging in their peculiar habit of rolling their rounded backs out of the water at regular intervals along an extended line, it is easy to understand how the notion of a monstrous sea-serpent may have taken its rise; for the appearance presented bears a really striking resemblance to the convolutions of an enormous snake.

In the cold latitudes of the southern hemisphere the dolphins (or porpoises as they are always called on board ship) present quite a different appearance to those of the warmer northern seas. They are smaller in size, and are pied with large patches of bluish-white, which give them a very peculiar appearance. These dolphins are, if anything, even more lively than their northern brethren.

The sailors often try to spear the dolphin from the bows of the ship with a kind of harpoon, and occasionally succeed in doing so; but it seems a pity that such a happy-looking creature should have its existence cut short, especially as its body is almost useless for food. Sometimes, indeed, its flesh is eaten; but those who have partaken of it say that it bears a strong resemblance to fine sponge saturated with train oil!

The dolphin and the porpoise closely resemble in their general formation the larger cetaceans. They have the same smooth, tough skin and rounded form, as well as the horizontal tail, to which, no doubt, their peculiar rolling movements in swimming and leaping are greatly due. Their mode of progression is in fact altogether different from that of the fishes; for whereas the latter swim by means of a series of lateral movements, the cetaceans obtain their impetus by doubling their flexible tail under them and forcibly extending it.

FISHES.—Although the sea, even in its remotest regions, doubtless swarms with fishes of every imaginable species, yet it is a fact that in an ordinary ocean voyage, such as that to Australia, the different *kinds* that will be seen might almost be counted on the fingers, although the number of individuals belonging to one species (as in the case of the flying-fish) is, in some cases, innumerable. There are some few kinds of fishes, however, that will seldom fail to be met with in the course of every voyage, and some little account of these may be of general interest.

Sharks.—Of all the members of the great family of fishes, these have probably gained the worst name. Sailors regard them with an almost superstitious hatred, and neglect no opportunity of capturing them if they are seen prowling about a ship; and although some of the "yarns" that are told with reference to their ferocity are probably somewhat exaggerated, yet enough that is authentic remains to prove that the shark is indeed one of the most dangerous of the inhabitants of the sea, and by no means a desirable bathing companion. Where sharks abound—as they do, for instance, in Sydney harbour—it is necessary to construct bathing-places that are enclosed with palisades for the protection of the bathers. Fortunately, our own shores are very rarely visited by any of the more formidable kinds of these unwelcome guests.

Of all the different species of sharks, the largest, strongest, and most ferocious is the white shark (*Squalus carcharias*), and this is the kind that is most frequently caught at sea. Those that are generally taken are from ten to fifteen feet in length, but sometimes these monsters attain a length of twenty-five or even thirty feet from the snout to the tip of the tail.

The appearance of the white shark is sufficiently repulsive. It is of a bluish-green colour on the upper surface of the body, and dull white beneath. Although its general outline is elongated, there is a peculiar rounded appearance about not only the body itself, but also the fins and tail, that gives it somewhat the look of being made of thick leather stuffed with some soft material, and which greatly adds to the unpleasantness of its aspect. The eyes are small and dull; and the enormous mouth, which is shaped somewhat like the letter U, is placed far back under the snout, so that it is easy to see why the shark cannot snap at anything above him without turning on his back. The jaws are furnished with a multitude of sharp triangular teeth, arranged in rows and slanting backwards: these can be raised or depressed at will.

The *Blue Shark*, which is also sometimes caught at sea, is both smaller and more slender than the white shark. It is darker in colour on the back, somewhat more symmetrical in form, and altogether less repulsive in appearance, than its larger relative.

The larger sharks are usually attended by from one to six or eight pilot-fish (*Naucrates ductor*), lovely creatures belonging to the mackerel family, and of about the same size as the common mackerel. They are most beautifully marked with transverse bands of brightest azure blue, alternating with deep black or indigo blue. They appear to hold much the same position towards the shark that the jackal is supposed to do to the lion. From personal observation I can testify that the pilot-fish appear to call the attention of their master to any food that he may not have noticed, and that they appear much disconcerted when he is hooked and hauled on board ship. They are no doubt actuated by interested motives, and probably appropriate the smaller fragments of any prey destroyed by the shark, which would have been beyond their own powers of attack, but at the same time they evidently preserve most friendly relations with their huge companion.

A number of small parasitical fish, an inch or two in length, are often found attached to the lips of a shark, and are called by the sailors "suckers."

As catching a shark is one of the few excitements of sea life, perhaps the following account (written many years since) of the first capture witnessed by the writer may not be altogether out of place:—

"But our attention was soon withdrawn from the ship we had been watching by a new excitement. For some one who was looking over the side cried out, ' A shark ! ' whereupon all rushed to the gunwale. I shall never forget the impression made upon me by that first sight of the monster, about whose ferocity and cruelty we had just been conversing. There he lay, long and grim, floating near the surface of the clear water, which, as the bright sunshine fell upon it, beautified his ugly form with sparkling emerald tints. Hovering and darting about his head were six pilot-fish—creatures of exquisite beauty, bright with transverse bars of gem-like azure blue and deepest indigo. A shark-line was already hanging from the stern. It consisted of an enormous hook attached to a short length of chain, which was made fast to an inch and a half rope—in fact, the mainbrace of the ship. The hook was baited with two or three pounds of fat pork. After the shark had once or twice dived downwards until he became a mere faint shimmering silver speck far down in the clear depths of the sea, the attendant pilot-fish appeared to become aware of the savoury morsel upon the hook; they became greatly excited, swam round the bait, sniffed at it, and then darted back as if to communicate with their master, who at once appeared to place himself under their guidance, and having turned over first to look at the morsel (the eyes being on the under surface of the head), turned over a second time and snapped at it. Thereupon the captain, who was presiding at the line, gave a vigorous pull, and the monster was hooked through the upper lip. He took it all very quietly at first, and allowed himself to be dragged half out of the water without remonstrance. As, however, the hook would not bear the entire weight of the shark, we attempted to pass a noose over his body; but this not being to his taste, he gave himself one vigorous shake, which had the effect of tearing out the hook through the whole thickness of the lip, and setting him free. Much to our chagrin, he dropped back into the sea, and quietly swam away as if nothing had happened: but those who were learned in such matters declared that he would soon be back again; for such is the greediness and stupidity of these creatures, that they never profit by their experiences, however painful they may be. Sure enough, in about ten minutes back he came, and being allowed this time more effectually to take the bait, he was hooked right through the jaw, and was again hauled up. A noose was passed round the middle of his body and a second round his tail, and so by the united efforts of some twenty men he was hoisted on board. Then, amidst the howls and execrations of the sailors, he was dragged off the poop forward to the forecastle, where the carpenter cut off his tail with his axe, and the butcher plunged his knife into the spinal marrow, in order to despatch him, every one standing clear in the meantime, as a blow from the tail of even a small shark is sufficient to break a man's leg, and this monster was some fifteen feet in length. When the tail is severed from the body, a shark is rendered harmless in this respect, on account of the principal muscular attachments being severed; but it is still necessary to be very cautious with regard to the jaws, which will continue to snap savagely at anything placed near them, even after the trunk has undergone the greatest mutilation. In this case, so great was the tenacity of life, that, even after the head had been severed from the body, with a view to preserving the jaws, and the backbone had been entirely removed, to be subsequently made into a walking-stick, the mutilated carcase continued to flounder about for a considerable time, and the heart, that was placed in my hands for examination, continued to pulsate strongly for fully twenty minutes; and even when cut up for examination at the end of that time, each fragment showed signs of vigorous muscular action. In the meantime the pilot-fish, having lost their master, evinced their faithfulness so his memory by following close to the ship for many hours after the decease of the shark."

The flesh of the shark, although to most tastes exceedingly coarse and unsavoury, is sometimes eaten by the sailors, who are glad of anything to vary the monotony of their usual diet.

The saw-fish (*Squalus pristis*) and the sword-fish (*Xiphias gladius*) are both closely related to the sharks, and are occasionally seen during a voyage to Australia, especially in the tropical calms. The saw-fish, whose upper jaw is prolonged into the peculiar snout of some three feet in length that is to be found amongst most collections of curiosities, has his weapon furnished on each side with projecting teeth, whereas the weapon of the sword-fish is smooth and considerably shorter. On the other hand, the sword-fish sometimes attains a length of twenty feet, whereas the saw-fish seldom exceeds twelve or fourteen feet. Both these creatures attack the whale, to whom their powerful weapons render them formidable adversaries.

Another fish met with far out at sea is the bonito (*Thynnus pellamys*), called sometimes by the sailors the "skipjack." This, like its near relative the tunny, is a member of the mackerel family, and is one of the greatest enemies of the flying-fish. It is thick and rounded in outline, and attains a length of about thirty inches. The bonito is an active fish, and has a habit of swimming about the bows of a ship, keeping up with the vessel for many hours at a time, even when she is sailing at a very considerable speed. The sailors often endeavour to spear the bonito, as its flesh is much appreciated by them, although it is rather coarse, and sometimes poisonous, producing a kind of erysipelas of the face and head. This effect, which is occasionally produced by several other kinds of fish, is probably due to some peculiarity in the food upon which they have subsisted.

At the end of a voyage to Melbourne, when sailing through Bass' Strait, great shoals of large fish, called there "barracouta," are usually met with. In its general appearance the barracouta somewhat resembles a pike, but it is longer in proportion to its thickness, and much more graceful in shape. Its colours are splendid, comprising iridescent tints of green, blue, silver, and pink, which change to a slight extent at death. The average length of the barracouta is about three feet. If the ship happens to be going along at the rate of six or eight knots an hour, these fish can generally be caught in immense numbers by means of lines towed astern. A large hook may be used, baited with red cloth or red feathers, and this is the most effectual way of capturing them; but the sailors often use only a piece of mahogany or teak, about three inches long, with a sharp spike projecting from it with an upward curve. Mahogany, feathers, or red cloth, are all one to the barracouta; he rushes after the bait as it is towed swiftly along on the surface of the sea, and swallows it greedily. He will sometimes manage to escape from the unbarbed spike, but a hook catches him effectually. I have seen as many as forty or fifty of these fish caught in a couple of hours by three lines. The barracouta is good eating; its flesh is white and firm, but, to the taste of some, rather coarse and dry. The sailors, however, as well as the passengers, greatly appreciate this variety in their diet, and the fish are usually caught in sufficient numbers for all hands to have a good feast of them.

The barracouta is met with on many shores. In the West Indies it is plentiful; but when caught off some of the islands it is poisonous, whilst if taken near others it is wholesome. At the Cape of Good Hope and at St. Helena it constitutes a most important article of diet, but in both those places it is known by the uneuphonious title of the "snook."

Any portion of wreck or other timber that is met with in the warmer latitudes, and which has been floating for some time, will, if examined, be found not only covered with barnacles, but also, in many cases, surrounded by a number of fish of a dingy brown colour, and resembling in shape a carp or bream. These fish, which average about five pounds in weight, are called by the sailors "old wives," or "old maids," and unlike the majority of deep sea fish, they are really remarkably good and delicate eating. So well is this understood, that the captain of a sailing vessel will in calm weather occasionally send a boat's crew to investigate any floating timber and to spear the fish. A number of sea-birds may generally be seen hovering over any drifting object of this kind—attracted, no doubt, by the barnacles, fish, and other living creatures that are congregated around it.

As soon as the ship has entered the tropical regions of the sea, the *flying-fish* begin to make their appearance. They must exist in enormous numbers, for sometimes for many successive days they may be seen constantly rising and darting away from the ship in shoals of many hundreds at a time. Those who watch them carefully will, I think, be led to the conclusion that there are two species or varieties of flying-fish usually associated together. One of them, excepting the back, which is light blue, is of a uniform silvery-white colour all over, including the " wings," which are very delicate and transparent. This kind is about the size of a herring, always seems to rise in shoals, and does not fly more than from twenty to fifty yards. The other variety is a good deal larger, being about the size of a mackerel, which fish it also somewhat resembles in colour, except that the under part is of a purer and brighter white, while the " wings," which are of course only largely developed pectoral fins, are of a reddish-brown colour. This species is capable of supporting itself in the air for a distance of from a hundred and fifty to two hundred yards; and it would seem that the only reason why it cannot take even a longer flight is because the fin-wings become dry and stiff, their rapid vibration evaporating the moisture from their surface.

It has been affirmed by some writers that the flying-fish does not in reality fly at all, but that its passage through the air is merely the result of an impetus obtained before quitting the sea. I think, however, that the majority of those who carefully watch the flight of these creatures will be inclined to agree with Charles Kingsley, that this can scarcely be the case. The fact that the fish frequently rises and falls during its passage through the air, and also that it is capable of altering the direction of its flight without touching the water, would alone negative this supposition; whilst the rapid and bird-like vibrations of the " wings," and the distance traversed, seem to mark the movement as a genuine flight There can be little doubt that the wonderful power of leaving their native element has been given to this family of fishes to enable them to escape from their enemies, the principal of which are the bonito and the albacore, which prey upon them in enormous numbers. If carefully watched when they rise in shoals, it will generally be seen either that some larger fish is in pursuit of them, or that the roll of the vessel has alarmed them.

At night, flying-fish are attracted by any artificial light, and they will sometimes fly on board a ship. Sailors occasionally catch them by spreading a sail, supported horizontally on poles, near the surface of the sea, and placing a lighted lantern above it. In this way a good many may be taken ; and it must not be forgotten that, as an article of food, they are quite a delicacy, closely resembling a whiting in flavour.

The region of flying-fish in the Atlantic appears to extend a greater distance to the south of the equator than to the north. In the northern hemisphere they are seldom seen until the tropics have been well entered, whereas in the southern hemisphere I have met with them around the Australian shores, and even near the southern coast of Tasmania.

Most of the fishes that have been hitherto mentioned may probably be seen by any one with a moderate amount of observation during an ordinary voyage to Australia, but there are many others (such as the sun-fish, the porcupine fish, etc., etc.), which are of great interest, but which, as they are more rarely seen, need not be described here.

I must not, however, omit to mention the occasional appearance of shoals of innumerable tiny fishes (probably the small fry of some larger kind), which, although not remarkable in themselves, yet present, in a calm sea, a very beautiful spectacle.

One of these shoals is thus described in an old journal: "Just before sunset we observed a large number of what appeared to be particles of shining silver rising out of the water, and falling again with tiny splashes. They proved to be innumerable small fish of about the size of whitebait. They had brown backs; and when they floated quietly in a dense shoal near the surface of the sea, they presented the appearance of a great mass of seaweed; but when they leaped from the water, which they all seemed to do simultaneously, bringing the pure white under surface of their bodies into view, they produced the beautiful effect of a shower of silver particles."

On another occasion, when the same thing was seen at night in the tropics, the effect was even more striking— each tiny fish as it fell producing a brilliant spark of phosphorescent light.

A considerable number of *turtles* are met with in the neighbourhood of the island of Madeira and the adjacent seas; and as calms and light winds are very frequently experienced in this locality, opportunities occur not only for seeing, but also for catching these creatures. They may be seen floating lazily and apparently asleep on the surface of the sea, nothing being visible but their little black heads and a very small portion of the rounded shell of the back. When a boat is despatched to catch turtles, the crew endeavour to approach the creature without waking or startling it, because if alarmed it immediately sinks and is lost. The rowers therefore exercise the greatest caution, and abstain from rowing altogether when within a couple of boat's lengths of the turtle, allowing the boat to glide up to their unsuspecting victim by its own impetus; the steering under these circumstances being a matter of some delicacy. The member of the party who is to catch the turtle stands in the bows of the boat, and when near enough pounces upon it, and seizing it by one of its flippers, lifts it into the boat before it has time to recover from its astonishment. Several turtles are often taken in this way during one short trip; and the poor creatures present a sufficiently grotesque appearance, as they lie helplessly on their backs in the bottom of the boat, craning their long necks and flapping themselves with their fore flippers.

The turtles taken off Madeira are generally small, not exceeding fifty or sixty pounds in weight; but they are specimens, though small ones, of the true green turtle (*Testudo midas*), which often attains a length of seven or eight feet, and a weight of nine hundred or even a thousand pounds.

It must be confessed that these small turtles are somewhat deficient in the green fat dear to aldermanic palates. At any rate, the turtle soup manufactured at sea is not a great success.

There are many points in connection with the anatomy and habits of the turtle which are of very great interest, but space will not allow of their being all touched upon here. It will be sufficient to mention that the horny covering (or *carapace*) of the turtles and tortoises is not a shell, as might be supposed, but a sort of external skeleton formed by the amalgamation of the vertebræ, ribs, and breast-bone. This bony case has openings through which the head, legs, and tail protrude, and is covered externally with those large plates or scales which give the turtle tribe their peculiar tesselated appearance. These scales are most finely developed in the species from which the tortoiseshell of commerce is obtained (the *Testudo imbricata*), from whose back the plates are torn while the unfortunate reptile is still alive.

The turtle, being a cold-blooded animal, is unable to hatch its own eggs. It therefore deposits them, many hundreds at a time, in holes in the sand, where the heat of the sun hatches out such of them as escape the depredations of birds and beasts.

But it is in the lower forms of animal life that the sea most abounds, and presents a field for observation and research such as can probably be found in no other domain of nature. Some slight idea of the teeming millions of living creatures in the sea can be formed when we remember that deep sea soundings have revealed the fact that the bed of the vast North Atlantic Ocean (as well as other seas) is formed of a thick layer of microscopic shells (*Foraminifera*, etc.), which formed the habitations of animals that have lived and died at the surface of the sea. And this is only one of the numberless tribes that inhabit the ocean!

Maury, in his "Physical Geography of the Sea," thus refers to this subject: "The ocean teems with life, we know. Of the four elements of the old philosophers—fire, earth, air, and water—perhaps the sea most of all abounds with living creatures. The space occupied on the surface of our planet by the different families of animals and their remains is inversely as the size of the individual. The smaller the animal the greater the space occupied by his remains. Though not invariably the case, yet this rule to a certain extent is true, and will therefore answer our present purposes, which are simply those of illustration. Take the elephant and his remains, or a microscopic animal and his, and compare them. The contrast as to space occupied is as striking as that of the coral reef or island with the dimensions of the whale. The graveyard that would hold the corallines is larger than the graveyard that would hold the elephants."

After reading such an estimate as the foregoing of the wealth of animal life contained in the ocean, even an ordinary observer can scarcely help regarding it with increased interest, while those who have a taste for marine zoology or microscopic research will look forward to their voyage without any fear of *ennui*.

Unfortunately there is some little difficulty in prosecuting the study of the larger forms of marine life, because it is only in calm weather, and when the ship is sailing quite slowly, that it is possible to tow the larger nets required for their capture; while in a steamer it will never be practicable to do so, on account of the speed at which she moves.

As for microscopic organisms, however, there is scarcely a pailful of water pumped up from the sea but will yield, when filtered, a rich harvest of objects for examination.

For obtaining crustacea, molluscs, jelly-fish, etc., of moderate size, the following will be found a useful kind of net:—A strong wooden hoop, about twelve or fifteen inches in diameter (a child's hoop answers very well), acts as a framework for a net of the same shape as an ordinary landing net, and of about the same depth. The net should, however, be very fine—its meshes not being more than about three-sixteenths of an inch square. If rectangular netting of sufficient fineness cannot be obtained, the ordinary bobbin net of the shops may be used, although this is much more likely to be destroyed and torn. The net should be made as waterproof as possible by means of boiled linseed oil or tar. To the circumference of the hoop four pieces of line, about a yard long, should be attached at equal distances, and these joined together and fastened to a stout cord of thirty or forty yards in length. One side of the hoop is weighted with a piece of lead about two pounds in weight. If this arrangement is put overboard and towed astern when the ship is sailing at not more than about three or four knots an hour, it preserves a vertical position, with about half its diameter submerged, and collects from that part of the surface of the sea over which it is drawn any object that is not so small as to pass through its meshes.

In this way, with a little perseverance, numberless objects of interest may be obtained—crustacea, molluscs, marine annelids, jelly-fish and polyps, in infinite variety and of strangest forms; and as this vast storehouse of animal life has even now been but imperfectly investigated, there is always the probability of meeting with something that has hitherto been altogether unknown to science.

Of all these creatures of the ocean, I will only pause to speak of one, which is brought so prominently under the observation of all voyagers in calm tropical seas, that even those who are least interested in such matters generally, can scarcely fail to be struck with it. I refer to the "Portuguese man-of-war" (*Physalia caravella*), perhaps the most beautiful of all the cœlenterata. It is most generally met with in the equatorial calms, and when seen floating upon the blue tropical sea, with its semi-transparent, sail-like air vessel, bright with pink and azure blue, glistening in the sunlight and turning with every breath of air, it indeed forms a lovely object.

It is by no means difficult to obtain one of these floating gems, either by means of the net described above, or even with a bucket attached to a line; and it will then be found that only half the beauties of the creature have been revealed above the surface of the water. All that has hitherto been seen is the air vessel, formed of a thin iridescent membrane, surmounted by a brilliant carmine comb or crest. But it will now be discovered that from its under surface hang clusters of tentacles, which are of the most vivid blue and violet colour, and which, when fully elongated, extend, in a large specimen, to a length of five or six yards. These are the "fishing lines" with which the physalia angles for its prey; and beware how you touch them, for they will inflict a sting far exceeding in severity that of the most virulent nettle; and in some cases, where a large portion of the surface of the body has been exposed to the grasp of the tentacles, serious results have been known to ensue. With these weapons the "Portuguese man-of-war" is able to paralyse the resistance of creatures considerably larger than itself, such as the flying-fish, or even the bonito. The physaliæ vary in size from less than an inch to eight inches or more. These dimensions apply, of course, to the air vessel.

Numberless interesting objects for microscopical examination may, as before suggested, be obtained by simply filtering through fine muslin or filtering paper the sea water that is drawn up by the deck pumps. But as the openings of the pipes that supply the pumps are several feet below the water-line, it is necessary, in order to obtain animalculæ from the surface of the sea, to bale up the water by means of a bucket, or, which is far better, to use nets constructed on the same principle as those that have been recommended for the larger medusæ, etc., but very much smaller in size, and covered with fine linen or flannel instead of netting.

These small nets (which are preferably made upon an oblong wooden framework), can be employed when the ship is sailing at a considerably greater speed than that at which it is possible to use the larger ones.

The phosphorescence of the sea is so closely linked with the lower forms of organic life, that a few words on this subject will not be out of place here. As a general rule, it is in the tropics that the most striking displays of this remarkable phenomenon are to be observed; but this is not always the case, for in the more temperate seas, and around our own shores, the phosphorescence is occasionally truly magnificent.

Perhaps the grandest aspect under which this spectacle can be witnessed is when, on a dark night, a ship is sailing rapidly through a boisterous sea charged with phosphorescent matter. The crest of each wave as it curls over and breaks into foam is brightly luminous; cascades of pale liquid fire seem to be thrown from the bows of the ship; while her wake is converted into a broad path of light, widening as it recedes, until lost in the horizon.

But scarcely less lovely are the appearances sometimes presented when the ship is lying becalmed in the tropics, with her sails flapping as she rolls heavily in the long Atlantic swell. Each ripple caused by her movements produces vivid sparks and coruscations of light, generally silver or pale blue, but sometimes fiery red; and round the rudder, where the water swirls and eddies most, the scintillations are the brightest. As we look attentively downwards into the depths of the sea, we shall also see floating by from time to time the forms of the various jelly-fish and other organisms that we have noticed in the daytime, each faintly outlined in its own phosphorescence. Nor is it only these lower forms of life that are luminous. Large and small fish may sometimes be seen with their shapes marked out in pale blue light. When off the Cape of Good Hope, we saw one night a swarm of tiny fish which played about near the rudder of the ship. Each fish was clearly visible in its own phosphorescent light, while every now and then one of them, leaping out of the sea, made a bright silver star on its surface as it fell. Presently the shoal became singularly active and excited, darting about and leaping in every direction. The cause was soon manifest: five or six large fish (probably bonito, and also luminous) were seen gliding and turning amongst the small fry, until in a few minutes they had devoured the whole. Once, too, when boating at night in Sydney harbour, three or four sharks accompanied the boat for a considerable distance—the outline of each being clearly visible by its own luminosity.

Mrs. Brassey, in her interesting book, "Sunshine and Storm in the East," thus describes the phosphorescence of the sea as seen in the Mediterranean: "The most beautiful phenomenon of this sort . . . seen on this voyage, was off Lisbon, on a rough night, when the sea was like molten gold lit up to such a depth that thousands of fish could be seen darting away like comets on all sides."

The nature and causes of the phosphorescence of the sea are even now far from being thoroughly understood. One point, however, appears to have been clearly established—viz., that phosphorescence is in every case due to the presence of organic matter, either living or dead. Many different living organisms possess the property of luminosity, and nearly all belong to the lower forms of life. Most are minute, some microscopic, but a few are of considerable size, as the Venus' belt (*Cestum Veneris*) and the pyrosomas. In our own seas the phosphorescence is believed to be principally due to a minute infusorial animalcule—the *Noctiluca miliaris*, which is barely visible to the naked eye. Some fishes also are *constantly* luminous, as the sun-fish, while others possess this property at times; but it is doubtful whether, in some cases at least, the luminosity may not be due to the presence of minute phosphorescent animalculæ either adherent to their surface or present in the water through which they are moving.

But it is not in the animal kingdom only that this property exists: some algæ also possess it; and lastly, decaying organic matter will sometimes emit phosophorescence, either when present in a mass or diffused in minute particles through the water.

SEA-BIRDS.—A few words about sea-birds will conclude this brief sketch of the living objects of interest seen at sea. During the whole of the voyage from England to Australia it is seldom that a day will elapse without the presence of one or more species of sea-birds enlivening the solitude of the ocean.

The most universal of all is perhaps the "Mother Cary's chicken," or stormy petrel (*Procellaria pelagica*). This pretty little ocean-bird, which somewhat resembles the swallow in its size, colour, and to a certain extent in its flight, may be seen in every kind of weather flitting about near the stern of the ship. It flies close to the surface of the sea, often dipping its feet in the water; but I do not remember ever to have seen it resting upon the sea, although perhaps it does so at night. In the roughest weather it flutters about in the troughs of the great waves, where it seems to be but little influenced by the fury of the winds; while on the other hand it appears to be quite as much at home when skimming over the glassy surface of the calm tropical seas.

When examined closely, the Mother Cary's chicken is found to possess delicate little black feet, which are webbed like those of other aquatic birds, and a short hooked beak, with somewhat tubular nostrils, from which it has the power of ejecting an offensive oil when alarmed. Passengers sometimes endeavour to catch the stormy petrel and other small birds by the simple expedient of allowing a long piece of black thread with a small button at the end to fly astern of the ship. The little bird, in its constant flitting to and fro, sometimes entangles its wings in the thread, and is easily drawn on board. The sailors have a superstitious dislike to the capture of the Mother Cary's chicken, and if a violent gale were to arise soon after one had been destroyed, they might feel somewhat inclined to make a Jonah of its captor.

In northern latitudes, and while passing the Bay of Biscay and the coast of Spain, various kinds of sea-gulls are met with; but as most of them are familiar visitors to our own shores, any description will be unnecessary here.

As the tropics are approached, these gradually disappear, and the ubiquitous Mother Cary's chicken remains almost the solitary representative of the sea-birds. When passing, however, comparatively near land, a visit is occasionally received from land-birds of various kinds, and these are sometimes met with at a distance of a hundred miles or more from the nearest shore.

When in the neighbourhood of solitary islands, such as Ascension, large flocks of the gannet, or *Soland goose*, frequently make their appearance, and may be recognized by their white wings banded with black near the tip, and by their mode of flight, which is quite different from that of most sea-birds. The Soland goose, at any rate, while young, is useful for food, and enormous numbers of the birds are bred upon the Bass Rock in the Frith of Forth. Some of these find their way into the Edinburgh markets.

It is, however, when the ship has passed through the tropics, and has entered the cooler latitudes of the southern hemisphere, that the greatest number of sea-birds are to be seen.

Now for the first time the stately albatross (*Diomedea exulans*)—the largest of all the sea-birds—makes its appearance, and seldom fails to impress the beholder, by its indescribably graceful and majestic flight even more than by its size. Whether poising itself in mid-air with extended wings, or swooping along with the swiftness of an arrow, everything appears to be done without the slightest effort. An albatross may sometimes be watched for five or ten minutes at a time without detecting any movement whatever of the wings, although it may at the time be gliding along with great rapidity. Its mode of flight, in fact, in common with that of some others of the larger sea-birds, always appears a mystery.

When seen on the wing, it can scarcely be credited that the size of the albatross is as great as it proves to be. The average width from tip to tip of the extended wings is from nine to twelve feet,—these are quite ordinary measurements,—but birds have frequently been taken measuring fourteen feet; and there is an albatross in the museum at Sydney, the width of whose wings is seventeen feet!

The younger birds are quite dark in colour, almost approaching black; while the very old birds, especially in the colder latitudes, are almost pure white. The birds of medium age have white bodies, with wings and tail banded more or less with black or dark grey.

The albatross belongs exclusively to the southern hemisphere,—it cannot cross the equator; and although the Zoological Society have, I believe, offered a large premium for a living specimen, all attempts to bring the birds through the tropics have hitherto failed, on account of their being killed by the hot weather.

For many days in succession the albatross will follow in the wake of a ship, pouncing down upon whatever is thrown overboard of an edible nature. It is by no means a particular feeder, and is also, it is to be feared, somewhat ferocious, as the following story that was told the writer by an eye-witness will testify. While in the southern latitudes, a sailor was unfortunate enough to fall overboard when the ship was sailing at a considerable speed. He managed, however, to get hold of some fishing-lines that were towing astern, and would have been rescued, but several albatrosses swooped down upon him, and tearing at his eyes and face, caused him to lose his hold, and perish before the eyes of his comrades.

Although usually seen on the wing, the albatross not unfrequently settles on the sea; and sometimes a flock of six or eight may be seen swimming about, like so many enormous geese, quarrelling over some choice morsel of offal.

The albatross is caught by means of a hook baited with fat pork, and prevented from sinking by pieces of cork attached to the line immediately above it. The bait is towed astern, and when a bird approaches, the line is paid out rapidly, so as to give the piece of pork the appearance of merely floating. It is almost impossible to do this effectually when the ship is sailing at a speed of more than five or six knots, and even under the most favourable circumstances the birds often evince a wonderful power of discrimination between the bait and anything else eatable. Occasionally, however, when "on the feed" (which is usually early in the morning), they may be captured with the utmost ease, and I have seen as many as fourteen taken with two lines in half an hour. So voracious were the birds on that occasion, that they quarrelled and fought for the bait, making a most peculiar cackling noise as they endeavoured to drive each other away from it. As soon as one was caught, two or three others swam after him as he was drawn up, pecking at him and evincing great indignation at what, no doubt, seemed to them a monopoly of the food. An albatross, when placed on deck, is unable to take flight, owing to the great length of its wings and the comparative shortness of its legs. Seen under these circumstances, it seems sadly out of its element, and has a somewhat clumsy, awkward look, very different to the majestic appearance that it presents when on the wing. No sooner is an albatross brought on board than it ejects the contents of its stomach,—a phenomenon not uncommon with sea-birds when alarmed. It may be as well to mention that the most merciful method of killing an albatross—and, in fact, all birds—is to pierce the upper part of the spinal cord, at the point where it leaves the skull, by means of a long sharp instrument, such as a sailmaker's needle. If this is done properly (a lateral movement should be given to the needle in order to divide the cord), death is instantaneous, and the skin of the bird is uninjured by the puncture.

The breast of the albatross, which, besides the larger feathers, is covered with a thick layer of fine down of snowy whiteness, is prized for making ladies' muffs and trimmings. The small wing-bones are used for pipe stems, and formerly commanded a good price, while the feet, skull, etc., are prized as curiosities; so that there is some little excuse for capturing this monarch of the sea-birds.

But it is down in the "roaring forties," between the Cape of Good Hope and Australia, that the sea-birds flock around the ship in greater numbers and varieties than during any other portion of the voyage.

In a book like the present it would be impossible even briefly to describe each kind with any approach to scientific accuracy. I shall therefore only attempt to enumerate the principal varieties, giving the familiar names by which they are known to sailors.

Next in size to the albatross is the *Mollymoke*, which closely resembles its larger relative, but may be distinguished from it by a band of black, which extends across the back between the wings.

Then there is a most diabolical-looking bird known to seafaring men by the unsavoury title of the "Stink-pot," or *Cape hen*. It is of a uniform dark ashen grey, almost approaching black, and has great staring yellow eyes.

The bird known as the *Sea-auk*, also a sooty bird, is a good deal like the preceding, but has white spots on the wings, and is of a somewhat different shape.

The *Mutton bird*, a good deal smaller than any of the preceding, has a brownish back and white breast. It is very fair eating, and abounds on the coasts of Australia, where it is sometimes sold in the markets.

Next in size is the *Cape pigeon* or Cape dove, perhaps the most beautiful of all the sea-birds. It has white wings, spotted with black and grey in a manner which reminds one of the markings of a butterfly, to which it also bears some resemblance in its graceful fluttering mode of flight.

The *Boatswain bird* is very pretty and graceful, and has long tail feathers like our sea swallow.

Then there are the *Whale birds*,—not much larger than a swallow,—of a delicate silver-grey colour on the back and upper surface of the wings, and pure white beneath. These are often seen in flocks of two or three hundred, hovering over the sea, and are supposed to indicate the presence of whales.

Last and least in size of all are the everlasting Mother Cary's chickens, which here abound in greater numbers than ever.

All these varieties of birds may not unfrequently be seen in the course of one day, and they give to the sea an appearance of life and animation which it would not otherwise possess in these cold and cheerless regions.

Those of my readers who wish more fully to study the

natural history of the ocean will find no difficulty in providing themselves with standard works on the subject. Amongst these, "The Sea and its Living Wonders," by Dr. Hartwig—a book to which I am indebted for some of the information given in the present chapter—can be confidently recommended as an amusing and instructive companion on a long voyage.

CHAPTER IX.

END OF THE VOYAGE—FUTURE PLANS.

Approaching the Australian coast—Cape Otway—Bass' Strait—Port Phillip Heads—The "Rip"—Port Phillip harbour—Sandridge—Warehousing cabin furniture—Melbourne hotels—Deciding on length of stay in the colonies.

NO one who has not himself passed through the experience can realize the feelings with which those who have been "cribbed, cabined, and confined" within the narrow limits of a ship, and have seen little but sea and sky and an occasional passing vessel for weeks or months at a stretch, look forward to the first sight of land when near the termination of a long voyage. For those who are visiting a distant country for the first time, there will be, in addition to the prospect of standing once more upon *terra firma*, the delightful expectation of beholding much that is new and interesting; while those who are returning to the colonies after a visit to the "old country" will be looking forward to rejoining friends and relations, and revisiting familiar scenes. Under such circumstances as these, it is scarcely to be wondered at that an under-current of excitement pervades the ship during the last few days of the voyage, and that the routine, which during so many weeks has been preserved in unbroken regularity, suddenly comes to an end with the first sight of land. Meals are neglected, and the passengers pass the whole of their time on deck, watching the shores, which seem strangely beautiful to eyes wearied with the monotony of rolling waves.

Unfortunately the passenger to Australia, whose destination is Melbourne, will not see the country for the first time under its most favourable aspect, and will receive very different first impressions of the scenery of the coast to what he would have done had he sailed direct to Sydney or Hobart Town.

Approaching the Australian shores obliquely from the south-west, the captains of Melbourne traders usually aim at sighting land for the first time in the neighbourhood of Cape Otway, at the entrance to Bass' Strait. The cape itself, which is a headland of no great height, has on its summit a lighthouse and also a signal station, from whence the arrival of ships is telegraphed on to Melbourne. The neighbouring coast is by no means striking. In some places there are low-lying sand-hills; in others the land is more elevated, and covered with trees and dingy vegetation down to the water's edge. If it is towards the end of summer (January or February), bush-fires will very often be raging along the coast, as well as inland, filling the air, even far out to sea, with dense columns of murky smoke.

From Cape Otway to Port Phillip Heads is a distance of sixty miles, and the run through Bass' Strait between these points may, with a favourable wind, be made in five or six hours.

However tame the coast-line may be on the north side of the Strait, there is nevertheless much in this part of the voyage to amuse those who have been long at sea. The vicinity of land, the coasting vessels and steamers, the new kinds of birds, the floating masses of seaweed, the fishing for barracouta, are all novel and interesting.

When near "the Heads," as the two points of land on either side of the narrow entrance to the harbour of Port Phillip are called, the pilot usually comes on board; and as his is probably the first unfamiliar face that has been seen since leaving England, he is looked at with much interest and curiosity. He is plied with questions as to the latest news from England and the colonies; and if, as is generally the case, he has brought with him a few newspapers, these are most eagerly devoured.

"The Heads" themselves are sandy, low-lying necks of land, about a mile apart, with a lighthouse upon each. In a small bay near one of them is the pretty little watering-place Queenscliff, which looks quite English, with its pier and rows of white houses. Here the health officer comes on board to inspect the sanitary condition of the ship.

In some states of the wind and tide there is a curious commotion of the sea in the entrance to the harbour. This is known as the "Rip," and sometimes so great is the turmoil of the waves in this narrow strait, that it is necessary to close the deadlights while a ship is passing through it. Inside the Heads the sea is comparatively smooth; but it is difficult to realise that the vessel has entered a closed harbour, for the inner low-lying shores slope away on either hand until hidden by the horizon, and in front lies an apparently unbounded sea.

This magnificent land-locked harbour is, in fact, nearly forty miles across, and the passage from the Heads to Melbourne may, if the wind be so light or unfavourable as to make it necessary to employ a steam-tug, occupy the greater part of a day. A considerable portion of this broad harbour is so filled up with sand as to be too shallow for the passage of large vessels, but there are certain navigable channels which are marked out by numerous buoys and fixed and floating lights.

English vessels are usually berthed at Sandridge, one of the maritime suburbs of Melbourne; and while approaching the pier a capital bird's-eye view of the city and its surroundings may be obtained.

As far as the eye can reach is a low sandy bay, whose shores are for the most part lined with buildings, sometimes scattered, sometimes collected into groups; while here and there denser masses of dwellings mark the position of the more important towns and villages.

Just opposite Sandridge, on the west shore of the bay, is Williamstown; then come a number of scattered houses and villas, straggling along the water's edge, and beyond these a denser mass of buildings canopied with smoke and dust—this is Melbourne. Then, more thinly frayed out along the shores of the bay on the right, are the suburbs of Yarra, Sandridge, and Brighton; and further yet, other little watering-places down the coast as far as the eye can reach. In the foreground the shore consists mostly of low barren sand-hills, with here and there a little stunted vegetation. The background is formed by low barren-looking hills on the horizon. Altogether, it cannot fail to strike the observer that nature has done but little to beautify the site of one of the most wonderful cities of modern times.

Sandridge is connected with Melbourne by a short line of railway, about two miles in length; and, while travelling upon it, an Englishman visiting Australia for the first time cannot fail to be forcibly impressed with the paucity of labour in the colonies. Railway porters are scarce, and they seem to have an idea that the passenger should himself deposit his luggage in the van. In fact, porterage of all kinds is very expensive, and a man will charge five shillings for conveying a barrow-load of baggage from the ship to the station at Sandridge, a distance of two or three hundred yards.

It may be as well to remark, in passing, that the passenger who intends returning to England from Melbourne, and who does not care to be encumbered with his heavy luggage, may warehouse it for a few shillings a week at one of the outfitters' establishments that adjoin the entrance to the pier at Sandridge.*

Melbourne boasts several first-rate hotels. The two principal ones are Menzies' and Scott's. The former is a quiet family hotel, the latter rather more a bachelor's house, and situated in a more busy part of the city. In both, the cuisine, attendance, and wines are excellent, and will bear favourable comparison with the best English and Continental hotels. They are, however, rather more expensive than European hotels, the average rate of living being from ten to fifteen shillings a day, exclusive of wines. Besides these there are several other very good hotels, which are rather less expensive. There are also many boarding-houses in Melbourne, as there are, in fact, throughout the colonies. In these the terms for board and lodging vary from twenty-five to fifty shillings per week.

Our invalid (who, we will hope, has derived great benefit from the voyage) having established himself at the hotel of his selection, where, no doubt, he will do full justice to the unwonted shore delicacies, thanks to the voracious appetite he has brought with him from the sea, will now have leisure to form plans for his sojourn in the colonies.

One of the first points for his consideration will be his *length of stay on shore;* and this is a question of more importance than might at first sight appear.

As I have started with the assumption that the reader is desirous of trying the remedial effects of the climate of the ocean itself, and that he has not taken the voyage merely with the object of testing the Australian climate, I shall for the present confine myself strictly to the

* If the passenger intends to return in the same ship, the captain will sometimes allow the luggage to remain on board.

consideration of the subject from the former point of view.

There are two objects to be borne in mind in regulating the length of stay on shore. These are: *first*, not to stay long enough to lose the benefit that has resulted from the voyage; and, *second*, to remain sufficiently long to make a thorough break between the outward and the homeward voyage, and to gain the full benefit which *for a time* is sure to result from change of air and diet.

In several cases that have come under my own knowledge in which a sea-voyage has seemed to fail in its remedial effects, I am inclined to think that the failure has been largely due to remaining too long in the colonies, and leading a careless life whilst there. The invalid arrives in Australia feeling better for his voyage, and finds a warm climate that appears to suit him much better than that which he has left. He is tempted to remain, and perhaps finds some occupation, or resides on a station "up country." Here he lives more roughly, and takes more violent exercise than he was accustomed to do at home. He also neglects precautions that now seem superfluous, and perhaps led away by examples that are unfortunately only too frequent in the colonies, he at times indulges more freely than he ought in stimulants. After a while all this tells upon him, and he finds he is losing ground, and finally takes his passage back to England, but only after more mischief has been done than the homeward voyage is able to rectify. Of course this does not apply to all cases, but it fairly represents the history of many.

But on the other hand it will greatly aid the curative effects of the sea voyage to remain sufficiently long on shore to ensure a thorough change. An unbroken residence on the sea of more than about three months is not desirable, on account of the monotony of the diet, as well as for other reasons, and far greater benefit will be derived from the homeward voyage if it is preceded by a residence on shore of judicious length and in a well-chosen locality.

There is yet another point to be taken into consideration in arranging the time that is to be spent in the colonies —viz., the season at which the invalid will reach England at the termination of the return voyage. The best time to aim at is the late spring or early summer—namely, the end of May or the beginning of June. If the return is made sooner, the cold winds which so often prevail in the British Islands in the early spring will be found most trying after the warm weather of the tropics.

It is, of course, impossible to lay down any absolute rule in such matters, but, speaking generally, the stay in the colonies should not be less than six weeks, nor longer than three months, if it is desired to give a sea-voyage a thoroughly fair trial.

During the stay on shore the diet should be as varied as possible, and plenty of fruit, vegetables, eggs, milk, etc., should be taken, so as to make the change of diet from that on board ship as marked as it can be.

The question as to the place or places to be chosen for residence while in the Australian colonies is of equal importance with that of the length of stay. This subject will be fully considered in another chapter.

CHAPTER X.

THE HOMEWARD VOYAGE.

Various homeward routes—Steamship routes—Sailing routes—The voyage round Cape Horn—Homeward route round the Cape of Good Hope—Limited choice of ships for this route—Its advantages for invalids—Length of passage—Course, climate, and weather—South Indian Ocean—Mauritius hurricanes—Course round the African coast—Calling at Cape Town—Course after leaving the Cape—A day at St. Helena—Island of Ascension—The Azores—Passing ships—Sunsets in the Indian Ocean—Marine zoology—Sargasso Sea.

BEFORE deciding with reference to the homeward voyage from Australia, there will be several points to be taken into consideration by those who are travelling in search of health.

There will in the first place be several routes from which to choose:—

1. That of the Peninsular and Oriental, and other lines of steamers returning by way of India and the Suez Canal. 2. The Pacific route, by way of San Francisco or Panama. 3. The old sailing route round Cape Horn. 4. That of such sailing vessels as return to England by way of the Cape of Good Hope.

With reference to the first two routes there is but little to be said in addition to what has already been mentioned in a former chapter, when speaking of the outward voyage. Neither the Indian nor the Pacific voyage is very suitable for those whose primary object is to gain health, although both present great facilities for seeing a good deal of the world in a comparatively short space of time, and both possess considerable attractions for those who are in search of amusement.

The Peninsular and Oriental steamers sail from *Sydney*, calling at Melbourne, Adelaide, and King George's Sound.

The various other lines of Australian steamers—such as the "Orient" line, which at first returned to England by the Cape of Good Hope, now adopt the Indian route for the homeward voyage, the passage through the Suez Canal being not only more convenient for coaling, but also much quicker than the return Cape route, with its light and contrary winds.

The Pacific mail steamers also sail from *Sydney*, and call at New Zealand ports and at Honolulu on their way to San Francisco.

The homeward voyage by way of Cape Horn was until recently almost the only one in vogue for sailing ships; and even now by far the greater number of vessels return to England by that route, on account of the prevailing winds being so much stronger and more favourable than when returning by the Cape of Good Hope; thus shortening the voyage by two or three weeks.

Homeward-bound ships bear down at once into the region of prevailing westerly winds, and taking a south-westerly course, pass Cape Horn at a parallel of about 55° to 60°.

Enough has been said with regard to the weather in the "roaring forties" to render it apparent that ten degrees nearer the pole even rougher seas, more boisterous winds, and a bitterly cold climate are to be expected. In truth, the South Pacific off Cape Horn is as dismal a region of the ocean as can well be imagined. Although in the summer months (January, February, and March) there is plenty of daylight, there is then the danger of falling in with icebergs, which, however beautiful they may be as a spectacle, are scarcely to be desired as sailing companions. In winter, on the other hand, the ice is usually fast frozen, and is comparatively seldom encountered; but then the days are dull and dreary and very short, lasting, in the depth of winter, only five or six hours. At all times of the year, those who sail round Cape Horn must look for cold weather, with a temperature sometimes below freezing, heavy seas, rough winds, snow, and frequent storms. Sailors say of the gales off Cape Horn that "though they are rough they are honest," but to the majority of landsmen they will be far from pleasant.

On the whole, then, invalids, especially those who are suffering from any chest delicacy, can scarcely be advised to make their return voyage round Cape Horn, although it must be acknowledged that in some few cases the cold bracing weather appears to act beneficially.

There now remains only the homeward voyage by way of the Cape of Good Hope to be considered; and as this is the most suitable route of all for the majority of invalids, it will be more fully described than either of the others.

Unfortunately the choice of ships for this passage is extremely limited, especially now that the steam-lines have adopted the Suez Canal route. This would be of less consequence if there were a considerable number of sailing vessels from which to select; but such is not the case.

Nearly every ship that sails from Sydney, from Brisbane, or from the ports of New Zealand, returns to England round Cape Horn. The great majority of vessels from Melbourne also adopt this route; but there are three or four fine ships which sail from the latter port early in the year, and which, for the convenience of invalids, make the homeward voyage by way of the Cape of Good Hope.* In the earlier months of the year, too, some few of the ships from Adelaide also sail by this route, South Australia being of course nearer the Cape, by some hundreds of miles, than the more eastern ports of Australia. If the invalid can secure a berth in one of these ships (preferably from Melbourne) he should not fail to do so, particularly if he has made the outward voyage in a sailing vessel, and has derived benefit from it. He is acquainted with the mode of life on board a sailing ship, and knows both its comforts and discomforts, whereas a voyage in a steamer might not suit him, and might counteract some of the good that has already been gained.

The same remark applies to the various other routes—they are untried. The voyage round Cape Horn is cold, rough, and cheerless; and the Indian and Pacific routes not only compel the passenger to travel in a steamer, but are in themselves hot, relaxing, and in all respects unsuitable for invalids suffering from chest delicacy; whereas the homeward voyage by the Cape is, as regards climate, almost perfection.

The colonial newspapers contain advertisements of the sailings of the various homeward-bound ships, and every facility is given for inspecting those vessels that are lying in the harbours.

As full directions have already been given with reference to choosing and furnishing a cabin, and as by this time the traveller will have no doubt gained sufficient experience for his own guidance, it will be unnecessary to say anything more on these subjects. It may be mentioned, however, that both in Melbourne and Sydney there are outfitters who supply anything that may be required for the voyage back to England.

* See page 61, *et seq.*

The homeward voyage by the Cape of Good Hope being the only one that can with confidence be recommended to invalids—especially to those suffering from chest delicacy—will call for a detailed description as regards course, climate, temperature, etc.; and those who will follow the account of the weather given here and in the chapter on "Marine Meteorology" cannot fail to acknowledge that for any one in delicate health this passage is a thoroughly suitable one.

Owing to the light and often baffling winds which ships usually experience in that part of the South Indian Ocean through which they must sail between Australia and the Cape of Good Hope, vessels adopting this route are considerably longer on the homeward than on the outward voyage, during which they were able to take advantage of the strong, favourable westerly winds of the South Atlantic.

The average length of the voyage, even in the case of a fast-sailing ship, is seldom less than from eighty-five to a hundred days. Occasionally, however, the passage extends over a hundred and twenty days, or even longer.

The tedium of this route is much diminished by the fact that ships generally call at the Cape, and in some cases at St. Helena also.

Course, Climate, and Weather.—The course of a sailing vessel returning to England by the Cape of Good Hope will, until the Cape has been passed, lie through a very different region of the ocean to that in which the outward voyage was made.

After leaving Melbourne (if the departure has been from that port), instead of sailing down into the "roaring forties," the ship will steer a course almost due west, and passing close to the south coast of Australia, will sail through the South Indian Ocean, in a latitude of from

30° to 35° S. A glance at the chart will show that the track which the ship will thus follow on her way to the Cape lies just on the southern boundary of the south-east trade-wind region, or else in the calm-belt of Capricorn, between the south-east trades and the region of prevailing westerly winds. This route is chosen in order to avoid the contrary westerly winds and rough weather met with farther south, and also to endeavour to obtain some of the advantages of the favourable trade-winds without going so far north as to deviate materially from the direct course and approach the hurricane region. Captains, however, differ in their practice in this respect—some following the course that has been indicated, while others proceed at once well to the north, in order to get into the trade-wind region, and sail to the south again when approaching the coast of Africa.

While still near the coast of Australia, the temperature, as is usually the case when in the immediate neighbourhood of land, is somewhat variable and the weather uncertain. Gales are not unfrequent, but in summer they are generally short. After getting well out to sea, however, the weather becomes settled and fine; and day after day during the six weeks or more that are occupied by a sailing vessel in the passage between Melbourne and the Cape the remark, "warm, calm, and bright," is made in the log with almost unbroken regularity. With a temperature of from 65° to 72° in the shade, with a calm sea, a bright clear sky, and light, yet refreshing winds, this part of the voyage is indeed most delightful to all, but more especially to those invalids who are suffering from chest complaints, and upon whose respiratory organs the clear, pure, warm air of the South Indian Ocean exerts a most soothing and beneficial effect. But notwithstanding the enjoyment to be derived from this delightful weather, it is to be doubted if it is as invigorating to those who have strong lungs as the rougher, colder, and more bracing climate of ten degrees farther south.

The pleasant weather of the South Indian Ocean is, however, occasionally interrupted. Squalls of rain, accompanied by thunder and lightning, are sometimes experienced; and although the ship's course is too far south to encounter the violent hurricanes of the North Indian Ocean, yet, when in the neighbourhood of the Island of Mauritius, cyclones of limited area are sometimes to be expected. These, though usually of short duration, are violent while they last, and are characterised by a rapid shifting of the wind. In fact, these storms form almost the only interruption to the fine weather of the homeward route by the Cape of Good Hope; but with a good ship and a careful captain, they will, if they occur, seldom prove a source of danger, while it is quite possible that the voyage may be accomplished, especially during some months of the year, without meeting with anything of the kind.

If, as is usually the case, it is intended to call at Cape Town on the homeward passage, a straight course will be steered for the south coast of Africa, which will usually be sighted for the first time somewhere in the neighbourhood of Algoa Bay, after which land will be almost constantly visible until Table Bay is reached. But even when it is not intended to touch at the Cape, ships going home by this route keep as close to the African coast as possible, in order to avail themselves of the Agulhas current, which is sometimes so strong as to bear the vessel to the west at the rate of three or four knots an hour without the help of her sails.

A stay of two or three days at Cape Town not only affords a most agreeable relief to the monotony of the long homeward voyage, but also tends greatly to improve the health of the passengers by allowing of a thorough change of air and diet, and giving opportunities for obtaining exercise, the want of which is so much felt at sea. Fruit abounds at the Cape, and not only can a supply of the less perishable kinds—such as pears, apples, and bananas—be obtained, but also a good stock of fresh vegetables, poultry, etc., can be laid in for the use of the passengers.

A short description of South Africa and its climate will be given in another chapter.

After leaving the Cape, the ship, sailing to the north-west, will soon meet with the south-east trades, and her course will take her close to St. Helena, where sometimes the captain will give his passengers an opportunity of exploring that interesting island. From thence the vessel will sail through those various regions of the ocean that have been already described, until she reaches the north-east trades, when she will be close-hauled to the wind, and will often have to pass considerably to the west of her outward track. After sailing through the belt of light winds to the north of the trades, she will enter the region of prevailing westerly winds, which will carry her more or less quickly to the English Channel, near the mouth of which, however, she will frequently be baffled in the spring of the year by easterly winds.

Such is a general sketch of the homeward voyage. More detailed information as to the temperature and weather that are to be expected will be found in the chapter upon meteorology, where the observations taken during a voyage from Australia to England are given in full. It will be seen that the voyage was a long one, and as the instruments were placed under tolerably favourable conditions, the observations may be regarded as fairly correct, and as furnishing a good picture of the weather of the various regions of the ocean through which the vessel passed.

It now only remains to say a few words with reference to the special objects of interest that are met with on the homeward voyage.

Land sighted on the Homeward Voyage.—Between Australia and the Cape of Good Hope, no glimpse of land is likely to be obtained. The solitary Islands of St. Paul and Amsterdam lie several degrees to the south of the usual track of homeward-bound vessels, whereas the southern point of Madagascar, on the other hand, lies considerably to the north. After losing sight of the Australian shores, therefore, it is probable that the next view of land will (in the case of vessels bound for Cape Town) be obtained somewhere in the neighbourhood of East London, or between that port and Algoa Bay, on the south-east coast of the African continent. From thence the course lies for the most part within a short distance of land, and passes over the great sand-bank known as the *Agulhas Bank*.

The colour of the sea is here dark green, and soundings are to be obtained at a depth of from forty to a hundred fathoms. The Agulhas Bank swarms with codfish of large size; but the depth of water is, as a rule, too great for successful fishing. In the shallower parts of the bank the fish may be taken by dozens; but where the depth is from fifty to sixty fathoms, the only chance of obtaining any is to attach properly baited hooks to the heavy leads with which soundings are taken. Any lighter weight would probably fail to reach the bottom, on account of the current sweeping it away, even if the ship had no way upon her.

Between East London and Cape Town the course of a sailing vessel will generally lie too far from the coast to enable those on board to do more than make out the general features of the country, which will be seen to be undulating, with high flat-topped mountains inland, and bluff sandy cliffs towards the sea.

There are lighthouses at several points along the coast—viz., on Bird Island and Cape Recife (the two boundaries of Algoa Bay), on Cape Agulhas, and on the *true* Cape of Good Hope, which is several miles to the east of Cape Town.

The entrance to Table Bay itself is singularly bold and striking. Table Mountain, the Lion Mountain, the Devil's Peak, and more distant ranges, form a magnificent background to the town spread out at their feet. A short description of Cape Town will be found in a future chapter.

After leaving the Cape, the first land likely to be sighted will be *St. Helena*; and as it is possible that the ship may call there, a few words with reference to the island may not be out of place.

Occupying a solitary position in the South Atlantic ocean, in lat. 15° 55′ S. and long. 5° 40′ W., St. Helena is 850 miles distant from the nearest land. It is ten and a half miles long and six and a half broad, presents an area of about forty-seven square miles, and has a population of between six and seven thousand inhabitants. It is, of course, best known as having served as a place of captivity for Napoleon Buonaparte between the years 1815 and 1821.

Jamestown, the capital of the island, is situated in a bay on the north side, and is protected from the force of the south-east trade-winds by the high land that rises behind it. The town nestles in a beautiful gorge between two lofty mountains, and its white buildings straggle inland along the valley for a mile or more. Each point of advantage and the top of every hill bristles with fortifications.

Close to the town, on the right, a mountain rises almost perpendicularly to a considerable elevation, and up its precipitous side is constructed the celebrated flight of seven hundred and one steps known as "Jacob's Ladder."

Jamestown boasts one small inn, which is dignified by the name of the "Commercial Hotel," but its accommodation and food are of the roughest description.

Of course, every one who goes to St. Helena visits Napoleon's former tomb, as well as Longwood, the house in which he lived during the time he was in the island. Longwood is situated on high ground seven miles from Jamestown, and it is usual to hire a carriage or saddle-horse for the journey. The road lies steeply up-hill for nearly the whole distance, and is cut in zigzags along the mountain-sides. Soon after leaving the town, a magnificent view of the valley in which it is situated is obtained. Looking down from this elevated position, many of the larger houses belonging to the principal people of the island are to be seen. They are surrounded by extensive gardens, the vegetation of which grows in rank and tropical luxuriance, while, high above all, the feathery crowns of magnificent palm trees tower into the air.

On either side of the valley the hills rise precipitously, their sides clothed, in some places, with the brightest emerald green, and in others with the blossoms of thousands of scarlet geraniums which grow wild in the greatest profusion. Here and there are seen enormous aloes of various kinds and cactuses of strange form; while occasionally a canary flitting from tree to tree, or perched upon a branch, singing in happy freedom, reminds the stranger that he is in tropical regions.

Longwood, Napoleon's former residence, is interesting only from its historical associations. It is a poor building, one storey high, perched upon one of the highest points in the island, and exposed to the full blast of the trade-wind: the country immediately surrounding it is bleak and desolate. Napoleon's temporary tomb, on the other hand, is much lower down in the valley, and is situated in a very lovely spot. The tomb itself consists only of a rough slab of stone surrounded by clumsy iron railings.

The inhabitants of St. Helena are principally half-castes of every shade of colour. Most of them are intelligent, and nearly all speak English fluently. Although St. Helena is situated so near the equator, yet the heat is tempered by the constant current of the trade-wind, and its climate is a very salubrious one. Epidemic diseases and fevers are almost unknown there, the only illness peculiar to the place being a form of influenza, which is very prevalent at some seasons of the year. As is the case in all islands, the climate is a humid one; but it seems admirably to suit the health of the troops stationed there, and the island is used as a health station by Her Majesty's ships engaged on the west coast of Africa.

After leaving St. Helena, the next land that is likely to be sighted will be the *Island of Ascension*, another of the solitary islands of the South Atlantic. It is situated in lat. 7° 55' S. and long. 14° 25' W.; and as the greater part of the island consists of elevated land, rising in many places to a height of nearly 3,000 feet above the level of the sea, it is visible for a considerable distance. The nearest land is St. Helena, 820 miles to the south-east. The island of Ascension is a mere volcanic rock, and has an area of only about thirty-five square miles. The principal anchorage is at Georgetown, on the north-west side. The island, which belongs to England, is used as a depôt for the Royal Marines, of whom the population, to the number of about 600, principally consists. As there are no streams or springs in the island, the inhabitants are entirely dependent for their supply of fresh water upon the rain (which is stored in tanks), or upon artificial condensation. Turtle are found in large quantities at Ascension, and fish abound round its shores. It swarms with sea-birds, the eggs of which form an article of export. The castor-oil plant and the pepper plant flourish in the island.

The north-east trades will probably take the ship considerably to the west of the Cape Verd Islands and the Canaries, so that it is not likely that either of these groups will be sighted; but the *Azores*, which lie almost directly in the track of homeward-bound vessels, are very frequently seen. The Azores, or Western Islands, are a cluster of nine islands in the North Atlantic, situated between 37° and 40° N. lat., and 25° and 30° W. long. The names of the islands are St. Maria, St. Michael, Terceira, St. George, Gracioso, Fayal, Pico, Flores, and Corvo. They belong to Portugal, and produce large quantities of fruit, especially oranges and lemons. St. Michael is the largest of the group, but the governor resides at Angra, in Terceira. The total population of the islands is about 214,000.

Unless very contrary winds should be encountered, it is not likely that, after passing the Azores, land will be sighted until the English coast comes into view, somewhere in the neighbourhood of Start Point (the most southerly portion of Devonshire), which is generally looked upon as the point of departure of outward-bound, and the point of arrival of homeward-bound ships.

Of other objects of interest that are special to the homeward voyage, it will only be necessary to mention the following:—

Passing Ships.—Between Australia and the Cape of

Good Hope passing ships are rare. Those that are met with will most likely be either Chinese or Indian traders, which, after passing well to the south of the Cape, in order to take advantage of the westerly winds, are now bearing up into the south-east trades ; or else small vessels bound from the Mauritius to the Australian ports with a cargo of sugar.

After leaving the Cape, the passing ships met with by a homeward-bound vessel will be much more numerous, especially in the tropics, where the usual tracks of the outward-bound and homeward-bound ships intersect each other. In the equatorial calms and the "horse-latitudes," it is not at all unusual for an opportunity to occur of boarding one or more outward-bound vessels, from which a welcome supply of English newspapers may often be obtained.

Sunsets in the Indian Ocean.—Of all the regions of the sea traversed during a voyage to Australia and back, the South Indian Ocean is that in which the most gorgeous sunsets are to be seen. Sometimes they are magnificent beyond description, and afford delight to all on board, evening after evening for weeks together. As the hour of sunset approaches, the side of the ship that faces the west is thronged with gazers, who assemble to watch the sun as he sinks below the horizon in a blaze of splendour such as is seldom to be seen except at sea and in these latitudes.

Marine Zoology.—The South Indian Ocean swarms with animal life, and the calm weather and light winds usually met with whilst passing through it present facilities for fishing for the wonders of the deep, such as can scarcely be enjoyed during any other part of the voyage. Armed with nets of various sizes, and, if possible, with a microscope, the passenger who delights in natural history need never suffer from *ennui* during this part of the voyage; while the lovely weather that generally prevails renders this kind of open-air occupation particularly enjoyable.

The Sargasso Sea.—This name has been given to an arbitrary division of the North Atlantic Ocean lying between about 20° and 35° N. latitude, and extending from the neighbourhood of the West Indian Islands on the west, across the Atlantic towards the African coast as far as 65° W. on the east. It is bounded by the great currents of the Gulf Stream, which, dividing into two portions, enclose in their midst a vast area of sea almost free from any currents except such as are caused by the winds. This great tract of ocean contains enormous quantities of a floating seaweed commonly known as the Gulf-weed, but the scientific name of which is *Sargassum bacciferum*.

Although the Sargasso Sea is, theoretically, supposed to extend almost as far east as the Cape Verd Islands, yet it is seldom that the gulf-weed is met with during the outward voyage. Homeward-bound ships, however, if driven to the west of their course by the north-east trades, often pass through large quantities of the weed. It is sometimes so thick as to appreciably diminish the speed of ships, and is occasionally so massed together as almost to present an appearance of solidity.

Naturalists consider that the gulf-weed of the Sargasso Sea is an instance of the greatest aggregation of one species of vegetation to be found in Nature. Certainly those who, day after day, have sailed through vast plains of it, extending as far as the eye can reach, would easily believe such to be the case.

The weed itself, which can readily be obtained from the

"chains" of a ship by means of a boat-hook, is peculiar in structure, and differs in appearance from most other sea-weeds. It divides dichotomously, and the terminal branches are covered with the small berry-like fruit from which it derives its name. Not only is the Sargassum bacciferum interesting in itself, but it also swarms with animal life, and will afford to the naturalist a rich harvest of specimens for examination. Molluscs, crustacea, sertularias, and numerous other forms of animal life are to be found in countless multitudes in these floating forests, which also form a refuge for shoals of fishes; and these in their turn attract the sea-birds which prey upon them.

CHAPTER XI.

AUSTRALIA: ITS CLIMATE, CITIES, AND HEALTH RESORTS.

Discovery—Population, area, etc.—The aborigines—Rivers—Mountains—Government—Industries and productions—Droughts and floods—Mineral wealth—Exports—Railways—The Climate of Australia generally ; modifying influences—Climate of Victoria—Climate of South Australia—Climate of New South Wales—Climate of Queensland—Climate of Tasmania—Influence of the Australian climate on disease—Melbourne—Climate of Melbourne—Hot winds—Ballarat—Sandhurst—Geelong—Victoria unsuitable for invalids in summer—Selection of a suitable climate—Tasmania as a summer residence—Crossing Bass' Strait—Launceston—Hobart Town—Climate of Hobart Town—Fruit in Tasmania—From Hobart Town to Sydney—Beauty of Sydney Harbour—Sydney—Climate of Sydney—Health resorts of the interior—Queensland—Brisbane—Darling Downs—Adelaide—Climate of Adelaide.

AUSTRALIA, the vast island-continent of the southern hemisphere, appears to have been discovered soon after the year 1600, either by Dutch, Spanish, or French navigators who visited its northern shores; but maps of a still earlier date exist, in which land is indicated to the south of the Indian Archipelago.

In 1642, Tasman, a Dutchman, discovered the island of Van Diemen's Land, which has since been called Tasmania; and in 1770, Captain Cook sighted the mainland in the neighbourhood of Cape Howe, and sailing along the eastern coast, first landed in Botany Bay, and afterwards planted the British flag near Cape York.

In 1787, the first batch of emigrants from England, consisting chiefly of convicts and their military guard, and numbering altogether about 1,000 persons, landed at Botany Bay, after a voyage of eight months.

Australia measures from north to south nearly 2,000 miles, and from east to west about 2,400 miles; its area is computed at upwards of 3,000,000 square miles, and though it is equal in size to nearly four-fifths of the continent of Europe, its total population is only 2,500,000. The distance from England to the nearest point of its coast is in round numbers 11,000 miles.

The whole of the Australian continent, together with some adjacent islands, belongs to Great Britain, and it has been divided into six colonies, including that of the neighbouring island of Tasmania. Although the whole of the coasts have been surveyed, the interior of the country has by no means been fully explored; vast tracts of territory, especially towards the western side, having never been trodden by the foot of a white man. The electric telegraph, however, which connects Australia with England by way of India, completely crosses the continent from north to south.

The aborigines, a singularly degraded race of blacks, are fast dying out, and are now seldom seen in the settled districts. They live in summer in the open air, and in winter shelter themselves behind strips of bark formed into a screen rather than a hut. They practise polygamy, and have some strange customs with regard to the burial of their dead.

The rivers of Australia are, for the most part, inconsiderable, and in the dry season are mere chains of pools. The Murray, however, which is the largest of all the Australian rivers, is open for barge traffic for a very considerable distance, and affords by its tributaries communication between South Australia, New South Wales, Victoria, and Queensland.

Australia possesses several considerable mountain

ranges, of which the Blue Mountains, the Australian Alps, the New England range, the Grampians, and the Darling range are some of the principal.

The government of the country is carried on by means of a Governor in each colony (who represents the British Crown), and Chambers of Legislature, two in each colony, which manage all colonial affairs subject to the sanction of the Crown.

The leading industry of Australia is *sheep-farming;* and it is to the wool thus produced in vast quantities for exportation that Australia owes its rapidly increasing prosperity rather than to its gold-fields, which although of service in the first instance by attracting labour to the colonies, are believed to have been of little permanent value to the country.

Large numbers of *cattle and horses* are bred in most of the colonies; the former chiefly for the hides and tallow; although of late years the carcases have been utilized in the preparation of preserved meat and "Liebig's" extract of beef. In 1879, the number of sheep in Victoria alone was computed at ten millions; while in New South Wales there were nearly twenty-four millions. Of cattle there were nearly three millions in New South Wales, and more than one million in Victoria; and the number of horses at the same date was, in New South Wales, 366,000, and in Victoria 210,000. At the end of 1879 the horses in the whole of the Australasian colonies numbered over 1,000,000, the cattle nearly 8,000,000, the sheep 66,000,000 and the pigs 800,000. All these figures are larger than those in the previous year.

Agriculture was much neglected by the earlier colonists, but now the area under cultivation is rapidly increasing year by year, and not only is enough grain of most excellent quality grown for home consumption, but large quantities are annually exported to other countries.

The production of *wine* is much on the increase. In 1879, the quantity manufactured was 684,000 gallons in New South Wales, and 574,000 gallons in Victoria. The wines of Australia, which are rapidly gaining public favour, are excellent in quality, and bid fair in the future to command a very extensive sale. In addition to European products, *sugar*, *cotton*, *maize*, *arrowroot*, and *silk* are cultivated in some districts.

Fruits of all kinds are largely grown in the colonies. The European kinds are produced in immense quantities in Tasmania and in the more southern districts of the mainland. In the warmer localities, semi-tropical fruits abound, such as the orange, banana, passion-fruit, olives, etc.

In all the Australian colonies the greatest drawbacks, both to pastoral and agricultural pursuits, are the prolonged droughts that occur periodically, and which often cause the death of tens of thousands of sheep and cattle from want of pasturage. These droughts are sometimes followed by floods, which are almost equally destructive, and many settlers have been ruined by both these causes; though, since the nature of the climate has been better understood, it has been found possible, by forethought and management, to provide in some measure against the disastrous effects both of droughts and floods.

The *mineral* productions of Australia are very important, and comprise, besides gold, copper, tin, silver, mercury, antimony, iron, lead, and zinc. The three latter metals are found chiefly in Western Australia. Coal fields of great extent exist in several parts of Australia, the most important mines being at Newcastle, near the mouth of the Hunter river, in New South

Wales. Kerosene is obtained in large quantities at Petrolia Vale, Hartley, and also at Wollongong. The shale from which it is distilled yields as much as seventy-five gallons to the ton.

Amongst the numerous articles exported from the various Australian colonies to Great Britain and other countries may be mentioned the following: wool, tallow, coals, coffee, gold, tin, lead, maize, wheat, flour, leather, hides, sugar, preserved meat, timber, bark, cheese, butter, wine, live-stock, cotton, tortoiseshell, whale oil, jams, etc.

The *railways* of Australia are becoming rapidly developed. In New South Wales there are three lines, two of which start from Sydney and one from Newcastle, the total number of miles open in 1878 being 688. In Victoria there were in January, 1879, no less than 1,100 miles of railway open for traffic, and many miles more in course of construction. South Australia had 450 miles open and 500 miles in course of construction at the same date. In Queensland there were, in 1879, nearly 500 miles of completed line. Tasmania had, in 1877, about 134 miles of railway open for traffic,—the main line running from Launceston to Hobart Town. The total number of miles of railway open or in course of construction in the colonies at the end of 1879 numbered 5,560, or an increase of 422 during the year. At the same period the miles of telegraph line numbered 28,363, and the miles of telegraph wire 43,950; the increase during the year of the former being 1,618, and of the latter, 3,316.

The colonies into which Australia is divided are the following:—*Western Australia*, which occupies the whole of the western portion of the continent, and is the largest of all the colonies; *South Australia*, which, since the

Northern Territory, or "Alexandra Land," was annexed to it, in 1863, is the second largest colony, and now occupies the whole central portion of the continent from north to south; *Victoria*, situated at the extreme south of Australia, and which, though the smallest of all the colonies of the mainland, is perhaps the most prosperous; *New South Wales*, the oldest of the colonies, occupying the south-east; and *Queensland*, occupying the north-east portions of the continent. *Tasmania* is an island lying to the south of Victoria, and separated from it by Bass' Strait.

The subjoined table (p. 208) will show a few leading facts with reference to each of the above-named colonies.

As the limits of a little work such as the present will not allow me to enter into anything like a general description of each individual colony, I will at once proceed to give a short account of the climate of Australia, and will then briefly describe such of the large cities and health resorts as are most likely to be visited by an invalid. Any of my readers who may desire further information as to the Australian colonies cannot do better than consult any of the excellent manuals that have been compiled for the use of emigrants and others, amongst which I may mention Messrs. Silver's "Australia and New Zealand," and the Government "Colonization Circular." Mr. Trollope's graphic description of his visit to the various colonies will also be found full of interest.

THE CLIMATE OF AUSTRALIA.—In a vast tract of country like that of Australia it may easily be understood that the varieties of climate and the differences of temperature are almost endless. The most northern point of Queensland extends far into the tropics, to within little more than $10°$ of the equator; while the southern coast of Tasmania reaches to nearly $44°$ south

Statistical Table of the Australian Colonies.

NAME OF COLONY.	DATE OF FIRST SETTLEMENT.	AREA IN SQUARE MILES.	POPULATION.	VALUE OF EXPORTS.	VALUE OF IMPORTS.	CAPITAL, WITH ITS POPULATION.	PRINCIPAL RIVERS.
New South Wales	1788	323,437	693,743 (1878)	£12,965,879 (1878)	£14,768,873 (1878)	Sydney (on Port Jackson): pop. 174,249	Darling, Murray, Murrumbidgee, Lachlan, Hunter, Hawkesbury, Clarence.
Victoria, erected into a separate colony in 1850	1803	88,198	879,442 (1879)	£14,925,707 (1878)	£16,161,880 (1878)	Melbourne (on Port Phillip): pop. 265,000	Murray, Glenelg, Goulburn, Yarra-Yarra, Snowy River.
South Australia, made a Crown colony in 1841	1836	914,730	260,000 (1879)	£5,355,020 (1878)	£5,719,611 (1878)	Adelaide (on Torrens river): pop. 90,000	Murray, Roper, Macarthin, Victoria.
Queensland, made a separate colony in 1859	1823	678,600	210,510 (1878)	£3,190,419 (1878)	£3,436,077 (1878)	Brisbane (on River Brisbane): pop. 33,000	Mary, Burnett, Fitzroy, Pioneer, Burdekin, Herbert, Mitchell, Flinders, Gilbert.
Western Australia	1825	978,300	28,166 (1878)	£428,491 (1878)	£379,050 (1878)	Perth: pop. 7,000	Swan, Murchison.
Tasmania, made a separate colony in 1825.	1803	24,600	110,000 (1879)	£1,315,695 (1878)	£1,324,812 (1878)	Hobart Town (on River Derwent): pop. 20,000	Tamar, Derwent, Huon.

latitude, or only about 6° less than the corresponding latitude of the south of England. While therefore the northern portions of the continent are exposed to the fierce heats of the tropics, the southern coasts enjoy a temperate climate.

But other causes besides latitude affect the climate of Australia. Thus the south-east trade-winds exercise an important influence in equalizing the temperature of the east coast of Queensland, and the climate of the more southern colonies is modified by the cool southerly winds that blow from the Polar seas on the one hand, and the hot northerly blasts, desiccated by their passage over the arid wastes of the interior, on the other hand. Then again, the climate of the coast districts is very different from that of the inland regions, the former being as a rule more humid and equable than the latter. Elevation also has much to do with the character of the climate, the high inland plains being distinguished by the dryness of the air and by the coolness of the nights as compared with the heat of the days. But besides all these general modifying influences there are local peculiarities of soil, moisture, vegetation, aspect, water supply, etc., which are special to each locality, and which will be of much importance with regard to its adaptability to each particular constitution.

From the above remarks it will be seen how impossible it would be to deal with such a vast subject as the climate of Australia with anything like completeness; but as even a few general hints may be of service to the invalid in search of a health resort, I will endeavour to give a brief sketch of the distinctive peculiarities of climate in each of the colonies, with the exception of Western Australia, which at present is not likely to prove attractive to a casual visitor.

1. *Victoria* possesses the most temperate climate of all the colonies of the mainland. It is also very dry, even

the coast regions being far less humid than those of New South Wales and Queensland. Its great drawbacks are the hot winds and the great and sudden changes of temperature to which it is subject. The south and south-west portions of the colony are at once the coolest and the least dry; while the country to the north of the dividing-range, being sheltered from the sea breezes, is hot and very dry. The high lands in the neighbourhood of the Australian Alps are cooler on account of their elevation, and are even visited in winter by severe snow-storms. Gipp's Land, a coast district to the east of Melbourne, backed up on the north by high mountains, is said to possess the finest climate in the colony, and to suffer less from hot winds than any other portion of Victoria. This is probably owing to the protection afforded by the mountains at the back. The warmest months in Victoria are January and February; the coolest, June and July. The mean annual temperature in Melbourne is 56·6, but the range between the highest and the lowest of the year is very considerable, being sometimes as much as $80°$, or even more. The highest recorded *shade* temperature appears to have been 115°, during a hot wind, and the lowest 27°, but the thermometer very rarely descends below 30° in Victoria, except in the high-lying inland districts. The average annual rainfall in Melbourne, deduced from observations extending over a period of fourteen years, is 25·65 inches. The greatest rainfall recorded in any one year was forty-eight inches, and the least, fourteen inches. In the coast districts more rain falls, as a rule, than in the inland districts, and the rainfall is less in the north-west portion of the colony than in any other. A few further particulars as to the hot winds and the climate of Melbourne will be given when speaking of that city.

2. The climate of the southern districts of *South Aus-*

tralia is characterized by its extreme dryness. Not only is the annual rainfall very small, but the great difference between the dry and wet-bulb thermometers—amounting in some cases to as much as 40°—indicates how small is the amount of humidity in the air. In summer, the hot winds are even more trying than in Victoria, and the heat is often intense; and although the dryness of the atmosphere renders it less unbearable than it would be in more humid districts, it is very trying to Europeans. But in winter—in fact, for eight months of the year—the climate is delightful and well suited for invalids; indeed, Adelaide is one of the best winter resorts for those suffering from pulmonary complaints that is to be found in the Australian colonies.

The following particulars as to the climate of Adelaide are taken from the "Colonization Circular" for 1877:—

Meteorological Observations at Adelaide.	Deg.
Mean annual temperature	63·94
Mean daily range	20·98
Highest recorded shade temperature	115·0
Lowest ,, ,, ,,	33·0
Mean annual humidity (9 a.m., 1 and 5 p.m.)	58·25
	Inches.
Mean annual rainfall	22·763

The high-lying districts of South Australia, some of which are situated within twenty-five miles of Adelaide, are much cooler than the low-lying land near the coast, and the inhabitants of the capital are glad during the hot months of the year to escape, in some measure, from the intense heat by visiting the more elevated portions of the colony.

3. The climate of *New South Wales* is very varied. Not only does the colony extend through eight degrees of latitude, giving on this account alone a considerable range of temperature, but the differences of elevation are

also very great in the various districts. In the coast-regions the climate is a somewhat humid one, the rainfall and the amount of moisture in the air being both considerable. The temperature is, however, more equable than that of Victoria, neither rising so high nor falling so low as in that colony. The hot winds are also much less trying than in Melbourne, both as regards their intensity and the length of time they continue; but they usually bring with them clouds of dust, from which fact they have received the name of "brick-fielders," and on this account it is not advisable for invalids to remain out of doors during their continuance. In the late autumn and winter the climate is mild, equable, and delightful, and consumptives from the more southern colonies frequently pass the winter at Sydney, or if they desire a still warmer locality, at Port Macquarie, towards the north of the colony. In the elevated plains of the interior, considerably less rain falls than on the coast, but the climate even here does not attain the dryness of that of Victoria or South Australia, while the daily range of temperature is very considerable. The following table gives a few particulars as to the climate of Sydney and of Bathurst, a town situated on high ground 125 miles to the west of the capital, and having an elevation of 2,200 feet above sea-level. These two places may be taken as fairly representative of the coast region on the one hand and the high inland districts on the other.

Meteorological Observations.	Sydney.	Bathurst.
	Deg.	Deg.
Mean annual temperature	62·9	55·8
Mean daily range	14·4	30·6
Highest recorded temperature	106·9	107·0
Lowest ,, ,,	36·0	17·0
Mean annual humidity	72·7	71·6
	Inches.	Inches.
Mean annual rainfall	50·051	24·992

Although the climate of New South Wales is spoken of as being a humid one, it should be remembered that the mean annual humidity is even here far less than that of England.

4. *Queensland* possesses a climate differing in many respects from that of the other colonies of Australia. A great portion of its territory lies within the tropics, and a considerable part of its eastern coast is exposed to the south-east trade-winds. The rainy season, too, occurs in the summer instead of in the winter, as is the case in the more southern colonies. The coast districts in the neighbourhood of Brisbane, the capital of the colony, are characterized by a warm moist climate of much greater equability than that of either New South Wales or Victoria. In summer the heat is very great, and is rendered still more oppressive by the saturation of the atmosphere with moisture from the rains that fall copiously at that season. In winter, however, the climate is comparatively dry and pleasant, and well suited to consumptive invalids. The coast regions further to the north possess all the characteristics of the tropics, and are, as a rule, unsuitable as a residence for Europeans, although even here the climate would appear to be far less trying than in many other countries in a similar latitude. The high-lying districts inland, and more particularly the Darling Downs, possess a much drier climate than the coasts; and although, as is usually the case in all mountain plains, the range of temperature is greater than in the low-lying territories—the nights being much cooler than the days, and the heat of the sun being often very intense—yet these elevated plains of Queensland have gained a greater reputation as a winter health resort than perhaps any other part of Australia, and many well-authenticated cases are to be met with in which a residence on the Darling Downs has been the means of curing

bronchitis, and even consumption in its earlier stages. The hot winds of Victoria and New South Wales are almost unknown in Queensland, and the heat of the climate is greatly tempered and equalized by the sea breezes derived from the trade-wind currents, which during many months of the year blow constantly upon its coasts. The mean annual temperature at Brisbane is 68·7, and the mean annual rainfall 43 inches, but a few miles inland the rainfall is considerably less. The climate of the southern coast districts of Queensland is considered closely to resemble that of Madeira.

5. *Tasmania*, which it will be remembered is an island lying to the south of Victoria, and separated from it by Bass' Strait, possesses a climate which has caused it to be regarded as the sanatorium of the hotter colonies of Australia. The inhabitants of Victoria, and even of New South Wales, go there with their wives and families towards the close of the fierce Australian summer, as we do to the watering-places on the British coasts, for the sake of its comparatively cool air and refreshing sea breezes, while at all times of the year invalids debilitated by the heat of the warm districts of the mainland are sent to the island by their medical advisers to regain their strength and energy.

There can be little doubt that, for the majority of Englishmen, Tasmania is better suited as a residence for all the year round than any other of the Australian colonies; and it is probable that even many consumptive invalids, if compelled to remain in *one* place during the whole year, would find this colony the best suited to their constitution.

It has been said of Tasmania, that it has "a winter not more severe than that of the south of France, a summer not hotter than that of London, a spring equalling that of Montpellier, and an autumn like that of the south of

England."* The mean annual temperature of Tasmania is considerably below that of the mainland, and the range of temperature is much less. The south coast, on which Hobart Town, the capital, is situated, is the coolest part of the island, and is exposed to constant sea breezes, by which the heat of summer is greatly tempered. The hot winds of Victoria cause but little inconvenience in Tasmania, being greatly modified by their passage across Bass' Strait. For an island surrounded by vast tracts of ocean, the climate is a dry one, and the rainfall is moderate. The centre of the island is occupied by a table-land, with an elevation of about three thousand feet above sea-level, and here the air is even drier than on the coast, although the diurnal range of temperature is, as in all high-lying districts, considerable.

The following table, giving the results of meteorological observations extending over nearly thirty years, is from the "Colonization Circular" for 1877:—

Meteorological Observations at Hobart Town.	Deg.
Mean annual shade temperature	54·72
,, diurnal range	17·91
,, annual humidity	75·0
,, annual rainfall	Inches. 22·71

As regards the relative prevalence of the various *classes of disease* in the Australian colonies, the following facts may be of interest:—Yellow fever, cholera, and hydrophobia, are unknown. Malarious diseases are rare. Continued fevers (typhus, typhoid, etc.) are prevalent to about the same extent as in Great Britain. Diseases of the liver and of the alimentary canal (such as diarrhœa and dysentery) are rather more frequent than in England

* "Forty Years in Tasmania."

and Wales, and so also are diseases of the heart, brain, and nervous system.

But it is in diseases affecting the respiratory organs that the difference between Great Britain and the Australian colonies is most marked. In Australia these diseases do not stand at the head of the list amongst the causes of death, as they do in this country. In Tasmania, for instance, consumption stands third in the list—old age and heart disease occupying the first two places; and the deaths from consumption in one year amounted to less than *one-third* of the English rate of mortality.

Amongst the cases of illness treated in the Sydney and Paramatta gaols, diseases of the respiratory organs occupy about the fourth place as to frequency; and it is highly probable that, were it possible to obtain trustworthy data as to disease in some of the high-lying districts most favourable to those suffering from pulmonary complaints, the results would be found still more satisfactory.

THE PRINCIPAL CITIES AND HEALTH RESORTS OF AUSTRALIA.—As Melbourne is the destination of most of the larger sailing vessels from England, it will be best to begin with that city, and to make it the starting-point for further travels.

Melbourne, the capital of Victoria, and the most thriving city of Australia, although not remarkable for its natural advantages, cannot fail to strike a new-comer with feelings of astonishment when he remembers that some forty years ago its site was occupied by only a few wooden huts. It now has a population of over 250,000, and is rapidly increasing in extent and importance. Its streets are very wide, quite straight, and perfectly regular, and they intersect each other in every case at right angles. The principal thoroughfares run east and west, and of these

Collins Street is the fashionable promenade—the Regent Street of Melbourne—and Bourke Street its great business thoroughfare.

Between the principal streets are narrower ones, which were originally intended to give access to the backs of the houses in the main thoroughfares from which they take their names. Thus there are Little Collins Street, Little Bourke Street, etc. But with the growing requirements of the city, these smaller streets have long since been alienated from their original uses, and are now lined on either side with important warehouses and offices. The shops in the main thoroughfares, although perhaps not equal to those of London or Paris, are sufficiently attractive, and the streets are busy and thronged with passengers, who look marvellously like those to be seen in any large English town, except that here there is a good sprinkling of coloured people, and occasionally one sees a Chinaman trudging stolidly with a long bamboo over his shoulder—at each end of which is suspended a huge basket usually containing vegetables, large quantities of which are cultivated by these industrious people. Their pigtails are seldom to be seen, but they are always somewhere under their hats, twisted neatly round their heads.

The banks of Melbourne are numerous and magnificent; they are built of solid stone or granite, and many of them possess considerable architectural merit. The public buildings are large, but, for the most part, not otherwise remarkable. A huge new Government House has been built of late years, but though vast and imposing, it would scarcely strike any one as being beautiful. There is a good Public Library, free to all and open up to ten o'clock at night every day in the week except Sunday. There is also a University, which does not, however, provide residence for the students; and near this is a well-arranged Museum. The Post Office and the Town Hall are large and imposing buildings. As for the churches, especially those belonging to the Church of England, but little can be said in praise of their external appearance. The Roman Catholic Cathedral is the largest, and some of the Dissenting places of worship have good spires; but, as a rule, the ecclesiastical architecture of Melbourne is certainly not of a high order.

The public gardens, or parks as we should probably call them in this country, are numerous, extensive, and conveniently situated; but none of them have any of the natural advantages of site enjoyed by those of Sydney and Hobart Town. The Botanical Gardens *as* botanical gardens are excellent, and contain many rare specimens, especially of shrubs and trees; but, like the parks, they lack beauty of situation and maturity of timber.

A feature of Melbourne which seldom fails to strike a stranger is the enormous width and size of the gutters. So wide and deep are they, in fact, that little wooden foot-bridges are placed at all the crossings, and at intervals along the streets. Even in dry weather some of them contain so much water, that if the pedestrian wishes to cross one of them without going round to a bridge, he will find it necessary to take a short run and to jump with some agility. But during heavy rains— and it *can* rain in Australia—the gutters become roaring torrents, and one can almost believe the legend that is told of a man who was once swept away and drowned in one! It is, I believe, a fact that children have more than once been drowned in the Melbourne gutters.

The vehicle of Melbourne is the "buggy," a kind of tilted cart on two wheels. The driver sits in front, the passengers behind, as one does in the back seat of a dog-cart. It is necessary to hold on tightly when jolting over a gutter. Melbourne is also well supplied with omnibuses.

Mosquitoes are not so plentiful in Melbourne as they used to be; but when they do occur, they usually show their preference for new arrivals, or, as the colonists would call them, "new chums." The bites are occasionally very troublesome, giving rise to much irritation, and in some cases causing sores. One of the best applications to the bites in their early stage is a lotion composed of a couple of table-spoonfuls of sal volatile to half a pint of water. Those who suffer much from the bites of these troublesome insects should always sleep within a mosquito net.

Considering its situation, close to the shores of a vast bay like that of Port Phillip, Melbourne possesses a remarkably dry climate; but it is subject, like the rest of Victoria, to great and sudden fluctuations of temperature, and in summer is liable to those terrible hot winds that are the scourge of the southern colonies of Australia. These winds are of course from the north, and traversing, in their passage from the equatorial regions, the great central deserts of the interior, they not only become heated by the burning sands, but are also desiccated to a remarkable extent. During the time the hot wind continues, the thermometer sometimes stands at from 100° to 110° in the shade, day and night. The wind, instead of bringing with it refreshing coolness, as it does in more temperate climates, is like the breath from a fiery furnace. The inhabitants seek relief by retiring into their houses and closing every aperture that could admit the hot blast; and sometimes whole families reside in their cellars until the wind shifts to a cooler quarter. The difference between the dry and wet-bulb thermometers is often as great as from 20° to 30°, the vegetation withers, the fruit is dried up on the trees, and those who have to be out of doors suffer from a dry and parched skin. Fortunately this wind seldom lasts longer than four days at a time, and it is then succeeded by a refreshing breeze from the south; but it may be imagined that neither the hot wind itself nor the great change of temperature that takes place when it ceases, is very favourable to the health of invalids, although they suffer less from it than might be expected. The average number of days in the year during which the hot winds blow in Melbourne is said to be fourteen; but this number is often exceeded in individual years. Further particulars as to the climate of Victoria have been already given.

Those who feel any interest in the Australian gold discoveries may take the opportunity, while they are in Victoria, of visiting the towns of Ballarat and Sandhurst, distant respectively 97 and 100 miles from Melbourne. There are lines of railway to both these places; and they are both interesting, not only on account of their association with the gold-rush of 1851, but also from the extensive mining operations carried on at the present time. At Ballarat the gold is "alluvial," and the machinery attached to the mines is directed to the raising and washing of the dirt amongst which the grains of precious metal are found scattered. At Sandhurst (which was formerly known as Bendigo) the gold, on the other hand, is found imbedded in quartz, which is crushed to powder by powerful machinery, and the gold afterwards separated by means of mercury, with which it forms an amalgam. Finally, the mercury is driven off by distillation, leaving the solid metal behind. Ballarat is a thriving town, with a population of 25,000, and Sandhurst at the last census had 22,000 inhabitants.

A visit may also be paid to Geelong, a port situated on the south-western shores of Port Phillip harbour, not very far from its entrance. A railway, forty-five miles in length, connects it with Melbourne. Its population is about 16,000.

A few days will be found sufficient for seeing all that is of interest in Melbourne itself, and a week or so may be devoted to visiting other places of interest in the colony; and then the invalid who is really travelling for his health, and who is content to make that his first object, must take his future plans carefully into consideration. In coming to a decision, several circumstances will have to be borne in mind—such as the time of year, the constitution of the patient, and the length of time he has decided to remain in Australia.

From the short account that has been given of the climate of each of the principal colonies, it will be seen which of the districts mentioned is most suitable as a summer, and which as a winter residence. The previous experience of the invalid himself, and the advice of his medical advisers, will also do much to lead him to a decision as to the nature of the locality he should choose,—whether it should be a coast or an inland district, a dry or a humid climate, etc. But in the case of an invalid, who, having left England, say, in October, has arrived in Australia in January or February (*i.e.* the hottest part of the year), and is sufficiently well to enjoy a moderate amount of travelling—particularly if he does not intend to remain in the colonies more than three or four months —I should by no means advise a lengthened stay in Melbourne, which possesses but an indifferent summer climate, and is in many respects not a very desirable residence for those in delicate health.

The best course will be at once to cross over to Tasmania, where the remainder of the summer can be spent healthfully and pleasantly; and in the autumn to go on to Sydney, Brisbane, Adelaide, or any of the other principal cities that it may be desired to visit, returning to Melbourne in time to embark for the homeward voyage. In this way each of these localities will have been visited at the season of the year in which its climate is most suitable for those in delicate health. I will therefore at once accompany the reader on a visit to Tasmania, the great health resort of the Victorians, and in some cases also of the inhabitants of the more distant colonies.

Tasmania is separated from Victoria by Bass' Strait, a channel about 102 miles across—the actual sea passage by steamer only occupying about twelve hours. Steamers run from Melbourne to the ports of Tasmania two or three times a week; and those who intend to visit the island cannot do better than take their passage to Launceston, the most northern and nearest of the ports, taking care to secure their berth two or three days in advance. The steamers—although, perhaps, rather too small for comfort, considering the rough weather that is sometimes met with in the Strait—are in other respects commodious and handsome little vessels, and are both well fitted and well found. They start from a wharf on the Yarra-Yarra—the river upon which Melbourne is situated—and follow its windings for a mile or two before emerging into the open bay of Port Phillip. The Yarra, as it is called for shortness, is but a narrow, insignificant little stream, muddy, low-banked, and tortuous, and presenting nothing of interest except some wool-scouring establishments and a few manure-works, which add but little to the pleasure of the passers by. Port Phillip harbour, which has now to be crossed, has been already described; its passage by steamer occupies only from three to four hours. In passing through the "Rip" in a small steamer, its peculiarities are much more evident than in a large sailing vessel. Here sea-sickness lays hold of unaccustomed voyagers; and even the passenger who has just landed from a three months' voyage must not be surprised if he also falls a victim to the malady—so different is the motion of a small steamer from that to which he has been accustomed, and so trying is the vibration of the screw.

As the steamers for Tasmania generally sail from Melbourne in the afternoon, it will be late in the evening before they have passed through Port Phillip Heads, and emerge upon the open sea in Bass' Strait; and by this time those who feel sea-sick cannot do better than turn in for the night. In the morning, if the run during the night has been a tolerably good one, the coast of Tasmania will be visible, and will be found far more interesting than that of the opposite mainland. Soon the mouth of the river Tamar will be entered, and a series of very beautiful views will present themselves in a constantly changing panorama, until the steamer, after following the windings of the river for about forty-five miles, arrives at Launceston. Trees and shrubs, strange to European eyes, line the water's edge in endless variety, and strange birds flap lazily overhead, or stand on long stilt-like legs upon the sand-banks that run out into the stream. Human habitations are few and far between, and when they occur, consist mostly of solitary log-built huts.

Launceston, although it boasts a population of some 12,000 inhabitants, is a very deserted-looking town. The houses are for the most part poor and the gardens ill kept; but there are a few good buildings, of which the post-office is one. There are several churches belonging to various denominations; public gardens, and two or three small hotels, of which the " Launceston Hotel " is probably the best, although even that is (or was) but a primitive establishment, with a *table d'hote* dinner at one o'clock and a tea at six. Launceston prides itself upon being well supplied with water and gas, and upon its English appearance generally; but its streets are dull and deserted, except on Saturday nights and on public holidays, when its inhabitants turn out in force.

The lion of Launceston, in the way of scenery, is the "Cataract," as it is called—a term likely to raise expectations that will scarcely be realized. A craggy valley, between two high hills of basaltic rock, with a slender stream, which, rushing over rocks and boulders, churns itself into foam, is what is really to be seen. The climate of Launceston is much superior to that of Melbourne —in the summer, at any rate—for it is cooler, and the hot winds, being tempered by their passage across the Strait, reach the island only in a mitigated form. A local handbook says: "Launceston may be called a city of calms. Lying in a bay of hills, high winds and thunderstorms are very rare; and facing northwards, so that the sun's rays have full effect all day, in spite of occasional winter fogs, it is a remarkably dry and healthy town."

But there is little to tempt any one to make a prolonged stay in Launceston, and it will be better after a day or two to push on to Hobart Town. The journey thither can, I believe, now be performed by railway; but at the time I was in the island the only communication between the two towns was by coach; and if the coaches still run, I should strongly advise the reader to choose that mode of conveyance. It affords infinitely better opportunities for seeing the scenery and wayside features of colonial life, and is altogether more enjoyable.

Driving out of the town between the high sweetbriar hedges, for which Tasmania is celebrated, the coach soon reaches high ground, and a panorama of fine mountain scenery opens out on the left side. Then comes a forest of "gum-tree scrub," lasting for many miles; and by this time the passenger will have discovered that the road along which he is driving is a very fine one—the finest in the colonies, in fact—and equal to any turnpike-road in England. The whole of the road between Launceston and Hobart Town was formed by convict labour, and not only is it admirably constructed, but it is planned with considerable engineering skill.

The journey between Launceston and Hobart Town by coach can, if desired, be managed in one day, but it will be better and less fatiguing to take two days about it. The usual halting-place is Campbell Town, distant forty miles from Launceston. Several villages are passed on the way; and although some of them appear to consist of no more than half a dozen tiny cottages and the inevitable public-house or "hotel," yet they are spoken of as towns, and dignified by pretentious names such as Cleveland, Breadalbane, etc.

The road ascends all the way to Campbell Town, a place which boasts a population of some 1,600, and which is considered by the Tasmanians to be quite an important town. It is situated on the table-land of the interior, at an elevation of about 1,500 feet above sea-level; and the air here, although cold at night and in the early morning, is beautifully clear and bracing; and those who have plenty of time, and who wish to explore the central and eastern parts of Tasmania, may with advantage stay here for two or three days. The "hotel," though small and primitive, according to English notions, is clean and tolerably comfortable. Although Campbell Town is only one-third of the total distance (121 miles) between Launceston and Hobart Town, yet it really divides the journey with tolerable fairness, on account of the long ascent before reaching the high ground on which it is situated.

After leaving Campbell Town, the scenery changes, and assumes a more sylvan character. The English traveller might now almost fancy that he is passing through some of the rich valleys of Cornwall and Devonshire, were it not that flocks of brilliantly coloured parrots and parroquets, or of screaming white cockatoos, constantly remind him that he is in a foreign land.

There are, however, immense numbers of veritable English rabbits, which, although they were introduced into Tasmania only a few years ago, have increased to such an enormous extent as to interfere seriously with the cultivation of the land. Lately, I believe, science has been brought to bear upon the subject in the shape of dynamite, with which the unfortunate rodents are blown to pieces in their burrows.

The names of the towns (!) that are passed in the latter part of the journey are somewhat " mixed." There are Bagdad, Lemon Springs, Green Ponds, Melton Mowbray, Brighton, Jerusalem, Jericho, while near the road are the River Jordan and the Lake of Tiberias!

Many miles before reaching Hobart Town the towering summit of Mount Wellington comes into view, and the road soon descends into the valley of the Derwent, where glimpses of beautiful river scenery are from time to time obtained. The country is here much more closely populated than during the first part of the journey, and pretty houses and farms dot the sides of the hills in increasing numbers as the capital of the island is approached.

Hobart Town will, I think, strike any new-comer as being a lovely city. It is situated upon the shores of a harbour, formed by the estuary of the Derwent, which, although not so large as that of Sydney, is scarcely inferior to it in beauty. On every side rise lofty mountains, with finely wooded valleys between them. The town itself is built upon the sides of hills which slope gently down to the quays and warehouses lining the water's edge. Mount Wellington, 4,166 feet in height, appears to rise just behind the town, but its summit is in reality some ten miles distant. On the opposite side of the estuary is Mount Nelson, of inferior height, but very picturesque, rising above a beautiful inlet of the harbour called Sandy Bay.

The town itself, which contains a population of upwards of 20,000 inhabitants, is very English in appearance, and has several streets of good width, in which are to be found the principal shops and public buildings. Except in the main thoroughfares the houses are for the most part but one storey high, with wooden verandahs and pretty gardens, in which our own choice plants, such as geraniums, fuchsias, roses, and calceolarias, flourish in great luxuriance. Interspersed among these, however, are more unfamiliar plants—such as large grotesque-looking cactuses and various indigenous flowering shrubs, while on every hand are the eternal stiff, scraggy gum-trees. The Government House at Hobart Town is certainly the handsomest and the most beautifully situated, if not the largest, of any in the colonies; and the other public buildings are commodious, if not imposing. There is a new cathedral in the Gothic style, and the services there are remarkably well conducted. As is usual in all colonial cities, there is a public park. At Hobart Town it is called the "Domain," and is large, undulating, well timbered, and splendidly located near the shores of the harbour.

The hotels in Hobart Town are good, and less expensive than in Melbourne; there are also several boarding establishments, where comfortable accommodation can be obtained.

The climate of Hobart Town, the favourite health resort of Tasmania, has been already described as not only remarkably dry, considering the position of the town and the small size of the island, but also as being much cooler than either Melbourne or Sydney. Particulars as to meteorological observations taken at the observatory have also been given. Although the middle of the day may be sometimes hot, yet the evenings and nights are usually cool and bracing. The hot winds of the continent are felt here even less than in the north of the island, and when they occur, seldom last more than twenty-four hours; but sometimes during that time the thermometer stands as high as 90° in the shade. This is, however, exceptional, the usual range in summer being from 55° to 75°. As a rule, I think those with delicate chests will feel more inclined to complain of the coolness than of the heat of Hobart Town; not that the temperature is actually low, but that there are often somewhat sudden changes from heat to cold that may be found trying. The Tasmanian winters, although, of course, colder than in the more northern colonies, are, on the whole, beautiful, and far more equable than the summers. The same remark applies to the autumn; and some of the inhabitants maintain that there is really no true summer in Tasmania, only a prolonged spring that merges into autumn.

On the whole the climate is a delightful one, and perhaps the best that is to be obtained within an easy distance of Melbourne; while its many natural beauties, and the comforts that are within the reach of an invalid, render Hobart Town as pleasant a place of sojourn as can be met with in the Australian colonies.

Those who feel inclined to do so may fill up their time very pleasantly by excursions to the many places of interest in the neighbourhood; and any one who wishes to see the heart of an Australian forest, with its gum-trees 250 feet in height, and its tree-ferns twenty or thirty feet high, should not miss the opportunity of making the journey by coach to the Huon river.

Letters of introduction will ensure the visitor a hearty welcome at Hobart Town, and the society there is remarkably pleasant and English-like.

In enumerating the advantages of Tasmania as a residence, I must not forget to mention its comparative freedom from mosquitoes, and also the great abundance of its fruits. Some districts of the colony resemble a vast orchard, in which are grown apples, pears, cherries, plums, and other European fruits, in such quantities that it is often impossible, owing to scarcity of labour, to gather them when they become ripe, and they are allowed to drop from the trees. Preserves are made in vast quantities, and exported to neighbouring colonies, and would be manufactured to even a larger extent, were it not that a heavy duty is imposed upon them.

Those who wish during their stay in the colonies to visit the capital of New South Wales can reach it easily by steamer either from Melbourne or from Hobart Town. The time occupied by the voyage is nearly the same in either case—viz., from two to two and a half days. The Melbourne boats are, however, larger and more punctual than those of the Tasmanian line; but both are equally well found as regards provisions and attention to the comfort of the passengers. The coast scenery both between Melbourne and Sydney and Hobart Town and Sydney is interesting to a stranger; but in the latter route less land is visible than in the former. The coast is for the most part mountainous and barren; and in the summer, when the season is a dry one, hundreds of bush-fires are to be seen raging amongst the gum-tree forests. As the neighbourhood of Port Jackson is approached, the scenery becomes more bold and striking; and after passing through the narrow entrance to Sydney harbour, with its rocky "Heads" only three-quarters of a mile apart, the view that opens up is one of the most beautiful that can be imagined. The calm, smooth expanse of water stretching away into numberless bays and coves; the rocky points, sometimes bare and rugged, sometimes clothed with foliage down to the water's edge; the lovely little islands, and the picturesque villas half hidden in semi-tropical vegetation; and, lastly, the imposing city in the distance, with its white houses and tall spires—all combine to form a picture of dream-like loveliness, scarcely to be equalled throughout the world.

Anthony Trollope appears to have been greatly struck with the beauty of Sydney harbour. He thus speaks of it: " I despair of being able to convey to any reader my own idea of the beauty of Sydney harbour. I have seen nothing equal to it in the way of land-locked sea scenery —nothing second to it. Dublin Bay, the Bay of Spezzia, New York, and the Cove of Cork are all picturesquely fine. Bantry Bay, with its nooks of sea running up to Glengarriff, is very lovely. But they are not equal to Sydney, either in shape, in colour, or in variety. I have never seen Naples, or Rio Janeiro, or Lisbon; but from description and pictures I am led to think that none of them can possess such a world of loveliness of water as lies within Sydney Heads. The proper thing to assert is that the fleets of all nations might rest securely within the protection of the harbour. How much acreage of sea the fleets of all nations might require I cannot even surmise; but if they could be anchored together anywhere, they could surely be so anchored at Sydney. . . . I doubt whether I ever read any description of scenery which gave me an idea of the place described, and I am not sure the effect can be obtained in words. . . . I know that the task would be hopeless, were I to attempt to make others understand the nature of the beauty of Sydney harbour. I can say that it is lovely, but I cannot paint its loveliness. The sea runs up in various bays and coves, indenting the land all around the city, so as to give a thousand different aspects of the water—and not of water broad, unbroken, and unrelieved, but of water always with jutting corners of land beyond it, and then again of water and then again of land. And you—the resident—even though you be a lady not over-strong; though you be a lady, if possible, not over-young, will find, unless you choose your residence most unfortunately, that you have walks within your reach as deliciously beautiful as though you had packed up all your things and travelled days and spent pounds to find them."

The City of Sydney, with its suburbs, is built upon the shores of numerous bays, coves, and creeks, and presents none of that unity of design which is seen in the arrangement of Melbourne. The streets are in many cases irregular and sometimes narrow, but there are nevertheless some fine business thoroughfares, and these, as well as the shops themselves, have a far more English appearance than those of the capital of Victoria. It is easy to see, too, that Sydney is by far the older city, for here are many traces of the first beginnings of the settlement, and indications of the manner in which it has been added to from time to time. The suburbs, particularly the more modern and fashionable ones, such as Darlinghurst, are exceedingly picturesque, and are built upon jutting points and upon the shores of bays, and most of them command lovely views of the harbour. Some of the more important of the suburban residences are beautifully situated, surrounded by grounds in which everything that can be done by art to enchance their natural advantages has been done.

Sydney boasts some fine public buildings. The Government House, although not so handsome as that of Hobart Town, not so pretentious as that of Melbourne, is much older than either, and is very beautifully situated, with a little bay of the harbour all to itself. The cathedral is quite new, and is a large building in the Perpendicular style, with a central as well as western towers, and makes a fine architectural addition to the *coup d'œil* of the city. The Town Hall, also new, is an imposing structure; and the new Post Office is a great improvement upon the old one, which was a wretched building. The Museum is perhaps the finest in the colonies, and contains most interesting zoological, ornithological, conchological, entomological, and mineralogical collections, besides many other objects of interest. The University is in one of the suburbs of Sydney. It is a large and imposing building, and has a very fine hall, with a handsome carved oak ceiling, and some very good stained glass. The students are non-resident. The botanical gardens are very beautiful both as to situation and arrangement. They are placed in a magnificent position, overlooking Sydney harbour, and contain, in addition to a fine botanical collection, many interesting specimens of live animals and birds.

Although Sydney is the parent-city of the colonies, it does not contain nearly so many inhabitants as its younger rival Melbourne. At the last published census its population was only 174,249, whereas that of Melbourne was 251,000.

There are many places of interest in the neighbourhood of Sydney. The Paramatta river, which empties itself into Sydney harbour at its western extremity, is navigable by small steamers for a considerable distance, and affords some fine river scenery. The small town of Paramatta, at which the steamers disembark their passengers, is celebrated for its extensive orange orchards, which when in blossom or covered with fruit present a lovely spectacle.

Near the North Head, at the entrance to the harbour, is Manley Beach, a small watering-place and favourite health resort during the hot months of summer. The main street of the village passes across the neck of land which here divides the harbour from the ocean. At one end it opens upon a calm land-locked bay; at the other upon the surf-beaten shore of the open sea.

Some little idea of the vast extent of Sydney harbour may be obtained from the following statement put forward by some of the colonists with a view to astonishing newcomers. They say that if a man were to start from the South Head, and were to walk round the shores of every bay, creek, cove, inlet, river, and estuary, he would have traversed upwards of a thousand miles before arriving at the North Head! This estimate must probably be taken *cum grano salis;* but any one can see for himself that the coast-line is enormous.

The hotels of Sydney are less pretentious than those of Melbourne, and much less expensive. One of the oldest established, and perhaps the best, is Petty's Hotel, a very comfortable, homely house, where you are aroused in the morning and called to meals by a great bell which, vigorously rung through the corridors, carries you back to your youthful school-days. Boarding-houses are numerous both in Sydney itself and in the suburbs; at these the charge for board and lodging, exclusive of wine, etc., is about 30s. per week.

Fruits are exceedingly plentiful and very cheap at Sydney. Besides those grown in its own neighbourhood, it is plentifully supplied from Tasmania with the English fruits, and from Queensland with the semi-tropical kinds. At some of the hotels I have seen great bowls of fruit placed on the table, in which were to be found grapes, bananas, passion-fruit, oranges, guavas, pine-apples, peaches, apricots, nectarines, pears, and apples, besides other varieties.

The climate of Sydney, though more equable than that of Tasmania or Melbourne, and not liable to hot winds to so great an extent as the latter, is, as has been already seen, more humid than either. Although the temperature seldom rises above 90°, the *sensation* of heat is sometimes very great, and the comparative dampness of the atmosphere, not allowing of the free evaporation of moisture from the skin, sometimes produces the unpleasant sensation of being in "a bath of perspiration." But often, when the heat is at its greatest, the wind will suddenly veer to the south, and there comes up, with little warning, a great storm often accompanied by hail, rain, and lightning, familiarly known to the colonists as a "southerly buster." The temperature at once falls some 20° or 30°, with most refreshing effects, but with some little danger as regards those who are susceptible to sudden changes.

But notwithstanding these drawbacks, the climate of Sydney is, for many months of the year, a very enjoyable one for those in health, and suits even some invalids admirably. Sometimes in the autumn, for weeks together, there is scarcely a cloud to be seen, and days of brilliant sunshine, tempered by a refreshing breeze from the sea, succeed each other with unbroken regularity. The winters in Sydney are also very beautiful, and far more healthful than the summers.

For most consumptive and bronchitic invalids, however, Sydney possesses a climate too humid and relaxing to render it a suitable residence except for a short time, and it will be desirable to proceed without unnecessary delay to one or other of the elevated inland districts of the interior. A visit may be paid to the Blue Mountains, or the high-lying plains beyond. A railway, which is quite a triumph of engineering skill over natural difficulties, has been constructed, at a great expense, over the Blue Mountains to Bathurst, a town built at an elevation of 2,200 feet above sea-level, particulars as to the climate of which have already been given. The railway ascent is by a series of zigzags, and the views of mountain scenery obtained from them are very fine.

Another line of railway goes to Goulburn, which also lies high upon a spur of the mountain range, and has a good climate.

Another high-lying district and health resort is that of Liverpool Plains, easily reached from Newcastle, the seaport which supplies Sydney with coal. A voyage by steamer of some seven hours takes the passenger to Newcastle, and from thence there is a railway direct to Liverpool Plains.*

Brisbane, the present capital of Queensland, is situated about 500 miles north of Sydney, from which it is reached by the usual means of inter-colonial communication—viz., by steamer. The town is prettily situated upon a river of the same name, and has a population of about 20,000 inhabitants. It has well-laid-out public gardens, and the usual public buildings found in all the capitals of the colonies—viz., a government house, houses of parliament, courts of justice, a museum, churches belonging to various denominations, etc., etc. The heat and humidity of its climate at most seasons of the year render it an unsuitable residence for invalids, who should at once proceed to one or other of the high-lying towns or stations situated upon the Darling Downs, a district which, amongst all the highlands of Australia, has perhaps gained the greatest reputation as a health resort for cases of chest disease. There is a railway as far as Warwick, which has the name of being one of the prettiest towns in Queensland.

Adelaide, the capital of South Australia, is situated in the Great Australian Bight, about 550 miles west of Melbourne, and is within easy reach of the latter place

* In each of these districts there are numerous towns, in most of which fair accommodation can be obtained, as well as medical attendance.

by means of steamers which run two or three times a week. The capital is eight miles from the seaport, which is called Port Adelaide, and is itself a place of some importance. The city of Adelaide is pleasantly placed in a plain, with a background of hills rising towards the north. The Torrens river, upon which the town is situated, is during eight or nine months of the year little more than a dry watercourse, but in the rainy season it becomes quite a torrent. The city is built with the greatest regularity, the general arrangement being even more rectangular than that of Melbourne. All the streets run either north and south or east and west, and there is no deviation from this general plan. It has a government house, houses of parliament, a town-hall, and a particularly fine post-office, of which the inhabitants are justly proud; besides which there are banks, hospitals, orphanages, and other public buildings. It is also very abundantly supplied with churches belonging to all denominations. The water supply of Adelaide is particularly good, and the streets are well lighted with gas.

The climate of Adelaide is, as has been already shown, remarkable for its dryness, and is said much to resemble that of Sicily or Naples. During eight or nine months of the year it is delightful as a residence; but in the three summer months—December, January, and February—the heat is often very intense, the thermometer not unfrequently rising as high as 110° or 115° in the shade, while the hot winds which then prevail do not tend to improve matters. But even in the hottest weather relief may easily be obtained by visiting some of the high districts which are within very easy reach of the city—such as Mount Lofty, which is only eight miles, or Mount Barker, twelve miles from Adelaide; and at either of which the thermometer will stand many degrees lower than in the plains.

The rainy season at Adelaide is in the winter, but an Englishman would probably regard the weather that then prevails as resembling a rainy summer in England rather than winter; and as the total annual rainfall is but small, and in some years little or no rain falls even in the rainy season, no one is at any time likely to find the amount of moisture excessive.

Such is a sketch—necessarily slight and imperfect—of the principal cities of Australia; and it is hoped that enough has been said of the climate of each to enable an invalid, making only a short stay, to choose his places of sojourn judiciously and at the same time to see as much as possible of the colonies. To those who intend to *remain* in Australia I will not here attempt to offer any advice beyond mentioning the general fact that, as a permanent residence for consumptive or bronchitic invalids, the high-lying plains of the interior have been found far more favourable than the coast districts of the various colonies.

CHAPTER XII.

NEW ZEALAND.

Position—Area—Discovery—History—Divisions—Government—Geographical features—Harbours—Productions, industries, and exports—Railways—Cities and principal towns—The Maories—Scenery and points of interest—Lake Wakatipu—The Southern Alps—The island of Kawau—The volcanic district—Hot lakes and geysers—The pink and white terraces of Rotomahana—Forests—Flowers and fruits—Animals and birds—Reptiles—Fishes—The climate of New Zealand—Hints to invalids.

NEW ZEALAND, situated more than a thousand miles to the east of the Australian continent, is, as everybody knows, nearly the antipodes of England. Noon with us is midnight with the New Zealander.

Under the general name of New Zealand we find three principal islands—of which one is much smaller than the others—and several outlying groups of less importance. The three principal islands, which are arranged in a chain having a general direction from north-east to south-west, were formerly called respectively North, Middle, and South Islands, but are now known as North, South, and Stewart's Islands.

The length of the principal group is roughly estimated at 1,100 miles—the extreme breadth at 200 miles. The united area is about 104,272 square miles, or rather less than that of Great Britain and Ireland together. North Island is divided from South Island by Cook's Strait, while South Island is separated from Stewart's Island by Foveaux Strait.

The *discovery* of New Zealand is attributed to Tasman, who first sighted the west coast after leaving Tasmania in 1642. He landed for water in the South Island, where several of the sailors were killed by the always warlike natives. Captain Cook visited New Zealand in 1769 and on subsequent voyages; and about this time other English and French navigators called there, but not without severe loss to their crews from the hostile spirit of the New Zealanders, who were much addicted to killing and eating their visitors.

The first white *settlers* were, as has been so often the case in the history of our colonies, runaway convicts from the penal settlements of Australia and Van Diemen's Land. Missionary effort and public and private enterprise soon led to more general immigration—the tone of society improved, and the wild excesses of the white settlers, as well as the terrible scenes of massacre and cannibalism on the part of the natives, which had marked the early days of colonization, gradually ceased under the influence of advancing order and civilization. In 1832, a British Resident was appointed; and in 1839, Captain Hobson was made Lieutenant-Governor—New Zealand at that time being considered in the light of a dependency of New South Wales. Finally, in 1841, New Zealand was erected into a separate colony. Since that time, notwithstanding many serious troubles and sanguinary conflicts with the native inhabitants, the country has steadily and rapidly increased in wealth and prosperity, and is now one of the most flourishing of our colonial possessions.

New Zealand was formerly divided into ten *provinces*, viz., Auckland, New Plymouth (or Taranaki), Wellington, Nelson, Canterbury, Otago, Napier (or Hawke Bay district), Marlborough, Westland, and Southland. Each of these provinces had a government of its own. But in

1875 these provincial districts were abolished by act of Parliament, and a system of counties established instead. The provincial boundaries are however still retained as a matter of convenience.

The *government* of New Zealand is now carried on at Wellington, which takes rank as the capital of the colony, and at which place the General Assembly, or Parliament, is held. The machinery of government includes a Governor appointed by the Queen; a Legislative Council of forty-nine members appointed for life by the Governor; a House of Representatives, with eighty-eight elected members, of whom four are Maories; and an Executive Council, composed of the Governor and nine members, of whom two are Maories.

The *geographical features* of New Zealand are of much importance, and largely affect the character of the climate. Both the principal islands of the group are mountainous. The South Island contains the loftiest ranges, while the North Island possesses numerous volcanic peaks and extinct craters. The ranges of the North Island are of no great elevation—the principal ones are the Rua Hine and the Coromandel; some of the detached volcanic peaks, however, attain a height of more than 8,000 feet. The most important of these are Ruapehu, Edgecombe, Tongariro, and Egmont.

The South Island possesses a well-marked range of mountains—the Southern Alps—which, running from north-east to south-west, form a central ridge or backbone. Some of the principal peaks are of considerable elevation. Mount Cook is more than 13,200 feet in height, only 2,500 feet short of the height of Mont Blanc; many other summits nearly approach, and some exceed, 10,000 feet. The higher peaks rise above the snow-line which is found on Mount Cook, at 7,880 feet above the sea. Glaciers of vast magnitude descend from

GEOGRAPHICAL FEATURES. 241

the eastern slopes of the mountains. The Tasman Glacier, near Mount Cook, is twelve miles long and a mile and three-quarters wide. The lower mountain-spurs and the surrounding valleys are clothed with magnificent semi-tropical forests. To the east of the Alps there is a second mountain range of less importance, viz., the Wakefield range. Between the latter and the Alps are situated the high-lying Canterbury Plains, with a mean elevation of from 3,000 to 4,000 feet above sea-level.

Both the North and South Islands possess many inland *lakes*, some of them of large size. In the North Island they are mostly formed of the craters of extinct volcanoes, which have become filled with water. Lake Taupo, which is the most extensive body of inland water in the North Island, lies at an altitude of 1,887 feet above the sea, and covers an area of about 300 square miles. Rotorua, one of the largest of the circular volcanic lakes, lies to the north-east of the Taupo basin, and has an island in its centre. The principal lakes of the Southern Island are Tekapo, Pukaki, Hawea, Wanaka, and Wakatipu. The latter, which is commonly called by the settlers "Wakatip," is famed for its scenery. The lakes of the South Island are mostly long narrow bodies of water, and somewhat resemble the Swiss lakes. Hot springs, geysers, and sulphurous pools abound in the volcanic regions of the North Island.

The rivers of New Zealand are numerous, but with the exception of some of those on the east side of the South Island, they are of no great length. Some of the principal streams are the Waikato, the Wanganui, the Wairoa, and the Thames in the North Island; and the Molyneux (or Clutha), the Waitaki, the Rangitata, the Rakia, the Hurunui, the Clarence, the Wairau, and the Gray in the South Island.

New Zealand possesses some magnificent harbours.

Those on the west coast of both islands are, with a few notable exceptions, small, and are nearly all obstructed by shifting sand-bars, owing to the prevalence of the westerly winds. The other coasts are particularly rich in fine natural harbours, formed by estuaries, inlets, and land-locked bays. In some of these, to use a common figure of speech, the united navies of the world might safely ride at anchor. On the north-east coast of Auckland is the great land-locked anchorage of the Hauraki Gulf, with the safe and commodious inner harbour of Waitemata. Only seven miles distant on the west coast is the large Manukau harbour. The town of Auckland lies on the neck of land between these two great sheets of water. Other harbours of the North Island are Kaipara, Hokianga, and Port Nicholson. In the South Island, opening upon Cook's Strait, there are Queen Charlotte's Sound, Pelorus Sound, Blind Bay, and Massacre Bay. On other parts of the coast we find Milford Haven, the Bluff Harbour, Port Chalmers, Akaroa, and Port Cooper.

PRODUCTIONS, INDUSTRIES, EXPORTS, ETC.—The indigenous productions of New Zealand are not numerous. They consist of (1) timber of a very fine quality, especially the kauri pine, found only in certain localities, and much valued for ship-building purposes, on account of its lightness and elasticity. (2) The resin of the same tree, known as kauri gum, which forms a most valuable article of export, its price in some years being as high as £70 per ton.* (3) Native flax (*Phormium tenax*). This also constitutes an important article of export.

The mineral productions of the colony are of considerable importance. Gold is found in paying quantities in

---

* The gum, which is found beneath the surface of the ground, is the product of the decay of former generations of kauri pines.

many districts, and is largely exported.* Silver, copper, iron, tin, platinum, nickel, antimony, and graphite are also found in several parts of the colonies. Coal exists at Greymouth, Port Chalmers, Auckland, Westport, Raglan, the Bay of Islands, and other localities, and is worked to advantage.

Farming.—Under this head may be included both agricultural and pastoral pursuits. The South Island, taken as a whole, is far superior to the North Island for agriculture. Some parts of the North Island are, however, exceedingly productive. The following table will show the number of acres under cultivation in each island up to 1878:—

1878.	Wheat.	Oats.	Barley.	Potatoes.	Artificial Grasses.	Totals.
N. Island	13,711	12,506	990	7,048	328,640	362,895
S. Island	229,695	177,838	21,723	10,516	748,814	1,188,586

There are not so many great squatters in New Zealand as in Australia. The country for the most part is not well suited for large runs. On the other hand, as the soil of New Zealand admits of being laid down in artificial grasses, a comparatively smaller area of land may be rendered equal, in its stock-raising capabilities, to much larger tracts of the arid pastures of the Australian continent. This is particularly the case with regard to sheep. The farmers of New Zealand frequently combine agricultural and pastoral pursuits: dairy farms are of frequent occurrence. The stock returns exhibit from year to year an enormous increase in the pastoral wealth

* The province of Otago is the most rich in gold. The whole lake-district of that region may in fact be regarded as one vast gold-field. "The glittering metal is everywhere found in the beds of the numberless watercourses that belong to the tributary valleys of the Clutha basin and its lakes."

of the colony. In 1878 there were in New Zealand 137,768 horses; 578,430 cattle; 13,069,338 sheep; 222,061 pigs.

Wool is being produced in large and increasing quantities, and now forms the principal export. In 1853 the yield was only a little over a million pounds; whereas in 1878 it had reached a total of nearly sixty millions of pounds. In consequence of the abundance of timber found in some parts of New Zealand, and its value for exportation, a large number of saw mills have been erected in various localities. In 1878 there were over 200 in the two islands.

The low price of cattle and sheep has led to the establishment of a considerable number of tanneries. Several meat-preserving companies have come into existence of late years, and tallow and soap works are also met with in several places, in connection with the same group of industries. Other trades and manufactures are much the same as in other colonies.

Exports.—The principal exports, arranged in order of value, are as follows:—Wool, gold, wheat, tallow, kauri gum, preserved meats, timber, oats, barley, flax, leather, butter, farm produce, potatoes, etc., hides, sperm oil, etc.

The total value of the exports for 1879 amounted to £5,743,126.

Railways.—The total number of miles of railway open for traffic up to October, 1880, was 1,194. Several fresh lines were also in course of construction.

The following table, contributed to the *English Mechanic* in January, 1881, by Mr. Charles Rous-Martin, F.R.G.S., F.M.S., will show the number of miles open in the various districts, together with the receipts and paying qualities of the various lines during *twenty weeks* of the financial year.

Districts.	Miles of railway open.	Total receipts to date.	Percentage of expenditure to receipts.	Average receipts per mile per annum.
		£ s. d.		£ s. d.
Kaipara	16	1,963 11 2	107·05	319 1 7
Auckland	107	22,157 0 3	72·91	538 7 9
Napier	65	8,976 9 9	85·46	359 1 2
Wellington	53	11,045 2 2	95·53	558 14 0
Wanganui	108	13,208 10 6	71·54	342 14 9
New Plymouth	33	3,459 7 7	86·58	272 11 2
Amberley—Kingston *	755	245,328 16 5	63·37	844 16 9
Greymouth †	8	3,709 13 8	53·97	1,205 13 0
Westport	10	959 0 7	148·56	248 16 7
Nelson	20	3,170 14 6	79·03	412 3 9
Picton	19	2,130 8 7	89·20	291 10 7
Total	1,194	316,108 15 2	67·14	—

In 1879 there were 8,000 miles of telegraph wire for the conveyance of messages in the colony. The number of miles is now probably considerably greater. A submarine telegraph cable unites New Zealand with the Australian continent.

CITIES AND PRINCIPAL TOWNS.—The progress of New Zealand, as shown by the growth of its cities and towns, is something marvellous, remembering that little more than forty years have elapsed since it became a British colony, and remembering also the many troubles it has passed through in the course of its brief history. The Rev. James Buller, in his useful and interesting work entitled "New Zealand, Past and Present," after contrasting the means of travelling some thirty-nine years ago —when the only roads were the native war paths—with those of the present day, when nearly all the districts which are not yet supplied with railways have good

* South Island Main Trunk Line.   † Mineral Line.

roads and an excellent coach-service, goes on to point out the alteration which has taken place in the aspect of the towns within his recollection. He says, "In the early stage of our colonial history, our towns were little more than misshapen collections of tents, huts, and shanties. The streets, so called, were quagmires in wet weather. Delicate ladies did not despise a bullock-cart as a means of locomotion. But what do we now see? Beautiful cities, containing from 20,000 to 35,000 people in each; well-paved streets, lighted with gas, crowded with vehicles of all kinds, and adorned with stately buildings, which compare favourably with those in the best English towns. There are many smaller towns, with a population ranging from 2,000 to 7,000. There are fifteen towns with from 1,000 to 2,000 inhabitants in each; and besides these are forty more with from 100 to 500. In some of the larger towns, steam trams are used. Museums, libraries, mechanics' institutes, etc., are found in all of them. Public parks, gardens, and show grounds are also provided. The annual agricultural, horticultural, and art exhibitions, are all on a very considerable scale."

Not only in the altered aspect of the towns, but also in the rapid increase of the population of the country generally, the progress of the colony is most strikingly shown. The population of the whole of New Zealand at the last census, taken in December, 1879, was estimated at 463,729. This did not include the native population, which in 1878 was computed at about 42,800.

The following is a brief description of some of the principal cities and towns of the colony:—

Wellington, the present capital and seat of government of New Zealand, is situated on the harbour of Port Nicholson, near the eastern entrance of Cook's Strait. It was formerly the capital of the province of Wellington, one of the districts of the South Island. Port Nicholson is one of the finest harbours in the colony. It is completely land-locked; and the position of the city on its shores, surrounded as it is by hills, the sides of which are dotted with villas, is exceedingly picturesque. Nearly all the buildings—even the Government House—are of wood, on account of earthquakes; but recently the colonists have begun to erect their houses and public buildings of more substantial material. It is a busy thriving town, with a steam-tram running from end to end, and has good churches, excellent public buildings, and extensive wharves. There are also handsome public and botanical gardens. Anthony Trollope, in his "New Zealand," thus describes the city: "The town of Wellington, now the capital of the colony, stands high up in a bay which was originally called Port Nicholson, and is still so named on the map. The site as seen from the sea is very lovely, as the town is surrounded by hills, and is open only to the water. It reminded me much of St. Thomas—among the Virgin Islands; but in appearance only. St. Thomas is one of the most unhealthy places frequented by man, whereas there is perhaps no spot more healthy than Wellington. It is, however, noted for being windy, and the character seems to be deserved." The population of Wellington in December, 1879, was 21,582.

Christchurch, the former capital of the provincial district of Canterbury, is situated near the east coast of the South Island. It is distant about eight miles from its seaport, Port Lyttleton, with which it is connected by a railway which passes through a tunnel piercing the range of hills which separates the town from the harbour. The town was founded in 1850, by a Church of England

Association which bore the name of the "Canterbury Pilgrims." The older buildings are in the Mediæval style, and the streets have ecclesiastical names. The streets, which have asphalt pavements, are arranged on the rectangular plan. Canterbury possesses a park, a college, a training school, and a museum.

Situated on the banks of the Avon, a pure and limpid stream, and commanding lovely views of the distant snow-clad Alps, the city may be regarded as possessing great natural advantages, while its comfortable and English appearance renders it an attractive residence for emigrants from the old country. Many of the houses and some of the churches are, like those of Wellington, built of wood, on account of the earthquakes by which the district from time to time is visited. A road across the mountains, constructed at great expense, affords communication with the towns of the west coast, viz., Hokitika, Greymouth, and Westport, to which places coaches run twice a week. The mountain scenery on the way is described as most magnificent. The population of Christchurch in 1878 was nearly 25,000.

Dunedin, the capital of Otago, is situated on the southeast coast of the South Island, eight miles from Port Chalmers, its seaport. The town was founded in 1848, by colonists connected with the Free Church of Scotland. At the back of the town rise hills, the sides of which are dotted with villas and terraces of houses. It comprises upwards of ninety streets, many of which are between sixty and seventy feet wide. The main street is two miles and a half long. There is a large public park, and the public buildings are handsome and commodious. Mr. Anthony Trollope says, "Dunedin is a remarkably handsome town—and, when its age is considered, a town which may be said to be remarkable in every way. The main street has no look of newness about it. The houses are well built, and the public buildings, banks, and churches are large, commodious, and ornamental." Population in 1878, 22,490; in 1880, nearly 35,000.

Invercargill, the most southerly of all the important settlements of New Zealand, is situated on Foveaux Straits, twenty miles from its seaport, Bluff Harbour, with which it is connected by a railway. It is a rising town, and was formerly the capital of the Southland district. In 1878 it contained a population of 3,753. From Invercargill, Lake Wakatipu, considered one of the finest bits of scenery in the colony, can be easily reached.

Hokitika, on the west coast of the South Island, is, like Greymouth, a mining town. It was the former capital of Westland, and at the time of the gold discoveries was of considerable importance. It is a well-built town, with broad streets, but suffers from the drawback which is common to all the towns on the west coast, of having a harbour which is only available for small vessels, on account of the sand-bar which obstructs its entrance. The scenery around Hokitika is, however, magnificent, comprising some of the grandest portions of the Alpine range culminating in the glaciers of Mount Cook.

Nelson, situated at the extremity of Blind Bay, is the most northern port of the South Island. It was the former capital of the provincial district of Nelson. The climate is considered one of the best in the colonies, and the situation is very beautiful. As a quiet place of residence, it is delightful, but it is not of great commercial importance. Anthony Trollope, speaking of this town, says, "Though sleepy, it seemed to be happy. I was there about the beginning of September—a winter month

—and nothing could be sweeter or more pleasant than the air. The summer heats are not great, and all English fruits and grass and shrubs grow at Nelson with more than English profusion. Every house was neat and pretty. The site is, I think, as lovely as that of any town I ever saw. Merely to breathe there, and to dream, and to look around, was a delight."

Wanganui. Passing to the North Island, we find the rising town of Wanganui situated on Cook's Strait, 120 miles to the north of Wellington. A railway connecting the two places is almost completed, and in the meantime the transit can be made either by coach or by steamer. In either case the journey is made through some very fine scenery. Wanganui is situated on a river of the same name,—navigable for ships of moderate size, and spanned by a handsome iron bridge, 700 feet long. Wanganui is the centre of an extensive trade, and bids fair to be a place of considerable importance. Its population in 1879 was about 3,000.

New Plymouth, the former capital of the provincial district of Taranaki, is situated on the south-west coast of the North Island. It has only an open roadstead, passengers being compelled to land in surf-boats. Iron, in the form of iron-sand, is found in large quantities in the neighbourhood, and works have been established for the extraction of the metal. The Rev. James Buller says of this town, " It looks well from the sea, the ground gradually sloping upwards from the beach, and a dark-green belt of bush still rising in the middle distance, until the landscape culminates in a glorious background of the majestic snow-clad cone of Mount Egmont. The central point of the foreground is Marsland Hill, crowned with the Immigration Barracks—most commodious, but certainly not prepossessing in appearance. In front and to the right and left of this point churches and other buildings are seen peeping from amidst the trees, which have been plentifully planted by the settlers. Taranaki, of which fine district New Plymouth is the chief town, has been aptly compared with Devonshire in England. It is well watered, beautifully wooded, and has a most fertile soil. It was laid waste in the unhappy war which began in 1860. It has now far more than recovered its former condition, and is in a very prosperous state." The population of New Plymouth in 1878 was 2,678.

Auckland is situated in the northern peninsula of the North Island, on a neck of land only four miles in width. To the east is the Hauraki Gulf and Waitemata harbour, and to the west is Manukau, or Symonds' harbour. It is built on the banks of the Waitemata river—an important stream. From its position, Auckland has been somewhat extravagantly compared to "Corinth for commerce, and Naples for beauty." It was founded in 1840, and soon became recognised as the capital of the province of Auckland. It is a rapidly increasing town; for the population, which in 1878 was only 13,731, had reached nearly 26,000 in 1880. The surrounding district is covered with orchards and vineyards, and dotted with pleasant villas. It has good streets, fine public buildings, and a handsome "domain" and public park. The suburb of Remuera, which contains the residences of the wealthier inhabitants, is very picturesque. There are many native settlements in the neighbourhood of Auckland.

Napier, the former capital of the Hawke Bay district, is situated on the east side of the North Island, towards the southern extremity of Hawke Bay. It is a "pretty and prosperous town," and has the advantage of a good and dry climate—one of the best, in fact, in the whole of the islands. Its harbour, Port Napier, is small, and will not at present accommodate vessels of any great size: larger vessels have to anchor in the open roadstead. A railway, connecting Napier with Wellington, will soon be completed. The population of Napier in 1878 was 8,368.

There are many other towns of less importance, amongst which may be mentioned *Lyttelton*, the seaport of Christchurch, with a population of about 3,000; *Grahamstown*, a mining settlement on the Thames gold diggings, thirty miles from Auckland, with a population of over 2,000; *Shortland*, also on the Thames diggings; *Collingwood*, on Massacre Bay; *Greymouth*, a mining town on the west coast of the South Island; *Blenheim* and *Picton*, in Marlborough; *Gisborne*, on Poverty Bay; *Campbelltown*, on the Bluff of Southland; *Akaroa*, the French port on Banks Peninsula; and *Kaiapoi*, on the Courtenay.

THE MAORIES.*—The native inhabitants of New Zealand are so interesting as a race, and their history is so bound up with that of the colony, that they deserve more than a passing notice. Although geographically so near to each other, nothing can be more striking than the contrast between the Maories and the degraded aborigines of the Australian continent. Instead of the stunted forms, prominent abdomens, retreating foreheads, and low type of intellect which constitute the main characteristics of the Australian Bushmen, we find amongst the natives of New Zealand tall, robust, well-knit frames, handsome and intelligent countenances, and an aptitude for mental and social improvement which is truly surprising. The Maories have straight dark hair, an olive complexion, and well-proportioned hands and feet. Formerly the practice of tattooing the body was almost universal amongst them: now it is passing away, with other old customs.

* Pronounced *mowries*, the *ow* being sounded as in *how* and *now*.

In their original state, before the advent of the white man, the Maories, although shocking cannibals, were in many respects far in advance of most other savage tribes. Those who first visited their shores found them numerous and prosperous, with their own system of religion and laws. They lived in well-built houses, and their weapons, canoes, and household utensils were well made and highly ornamented. They possessed a calendar, and understood the points of the compass. Their religion was particularly interesting. Though they believed in a future state, and were not idolaters, they had little idea of one supreme God, but had an elaborate system of mythology, which bore many traces of having been derived from that of the ancient world. At the same time, some of their rites, such as sacrificial offerings and circumcision, pointed to a Jewish origin. They were constantly at war amongst themselves; and although, before guns were introduced by the white settlers, their weapons were not very formidable—consisting principally of javelins, spears, and stones flung from slings—yet their inter-tribal conflicts were often very fatal, and were rendered the more horrible from the prisoners being almost invariably cooked and eaten. This slaughter of prisoners was even in more recent times sometimes carried on to a frightful extent. According to Dr. Thompson, "in 1822, Hongi's army ate 300 persons after the capture of Totara on the river Thames; and in 1836, during the Rotura war, sixty beings were killed and eaten in two days." It is believed that even within the last few years the practice has been secretly indulged in by the native tribes in some of the remote inland districts.

Like most of the inhabitants of the Pacific Islands, the New Zealanders were an almost amphibious race. I was assured by a gentleman who had for many years lived amongst them in the earlier days of the colony, that some of their exploits in the sea were truly marvellous. In the part of the country in which he resided, the young men—and in some cases even the young women—would swim out into the surf to fight the sharks which abounded on the coast, and whose flesh was used by them as an article of food. Their only weapon was a knife carried between the teeth. They were nearly always victorious. Swimming round and diving under the shark with surprising agility, they would seize an opportunity to plunge their knife into the belly of their adversary, until after repeated wounds he was despatched. It was, as may be imagined, a hazardous encounter, and every now and then one of these adventurous swimmers paid the penalty of his rashness with his life.

Although the word Maori is said to mean indigenous, yet the current traditions amongst the natives point to the fact that they originally came either from the Navigator or Sandwich group of the Pacific Islands, somewhere about the beginning of the fifteenth century. The chiefs and others who owned land traced their pedigree direct from the first settlers, and they still adduce this descent as their title to territory. Always a brave and warlike race, the Maories naturally resented what appeared to them as an unjust appropriation of their native soil by the white man, but even in their wars they sometimes proved themselves generous and even chivalrous foes. In spite of the disasters which attended some of the earlier missions, the Maories were not slow to embrace the tenets of Christianity, and were gradually induced to forsake the revolting cannibalism which had so long prevailed amongst them.

The Maories did not escape the disastrous effects which the first contact with white settlers seems almost invariably to produce upon coloured races. They at first acquired the vices, without copying the virtues, of civilization. Drunkenness, disease, and war carried off their thousands of victims, rapidly thinning the ranks of the once numerous tribes, until it is computed that at the present time there exist only about 40,000 native inhabitants out of the 100,000 that were found in New Zealand in Captain Cook's time. Those who now remain are for the most part prosperous, and in some cases even wealthy, as some of the tribes have made large sums of money by the sale of their lands. As has been seen, they send representatives to Parliament, and take a considerable interest in politics. They do not, however, amalgamate at all freely with the white settlers, whom they regard with suspicion, especially in the matter of the sale of land. They have formed a land league amongst themselves, and can now seldom be induced to part with any portion of the territories that remain to them. By far the greater number have retired to the central portion of the North Island. Here they live in their own way, and obey their own laws. Two of their old customs, that of "tapu" (perhaps the same word as the "taboo" of the Sandwich Islands) and "muru," were still in full force when Mr. Trollope visited New Zealand not many years since, and are amusingly described by him.

The same author with a few graphic touches describes a New Zealand chief as he saw him in 1874. The picture is too good to be omitted : " At Horokiwi we dined and slept; and the governor, whose guests we were, asked an old chieftain who was coming along the coast to dine with us. He was tattooed all over, up to his hair, and round almost to the nape of his neck, and he wore a great chimney-pot hat, about fifteen inches high, as some men used to wear in London a quarter of a century ago. He was very careful with his hat, and ate his dinner solemnly, with excellent appetite. When asked his opinion about this and that other Maori chief, he shook his head in disgust. They were all bad men, and had had too much land awarded to them. He rode a wretched old horse, and said that he was going about for pleasure, to spend a month among his friends."

The Maories are regarded by many as a doomed people, and it is feared that before many years have passed away they will, as a race, have ceased to exist. Mr. Buller, however, takes a more hopeful view, and his opinion should have great weight from the length of time he has resided in the colonies. He thus speaks of the present condition and prospects of the Maories: "The Maories are a people of great capacity, and open to civilizing influences. There are few of them who cannot now read and write their own language. They can learn anything to which they choose to apply themselves. They know something of the principles of mechanics, such as the use of the inclined plane, the lever, the drill, the screw, and the pulley. They have names for everything that grows in the soil, that flies in the air, or that swims in the water. They are very independent, and live apart from the settlers, in their own villages. For the purpose of trade, politics, or pleasure, they come into the towns, but few of them live there. They are still the owners of millions of acres of land, and are very jealous of their rights. . . . . Though very few of them have yet acquired the knowledge of English, all of them command enough of it to make bargains; they are, however, now fully alive to the importance of the English tongue, for they are politicians, merchants, and landowners. For the adult it is a hard task to pronounce English, but as many as two thousand of their children are now learning it in schools, subsidized by the Government, and supplemented by fees from the parents. In this way, it is to be hoped, they will in time become anglicised, and that will be a great factor in effecting an amalgamation. . . . . By many it is a foregone conclusion that they are a doomed race; and if the present rate of diminution continue, they cannot long exist as a people. But it may not. I am not without hope that they will learn to be more faithful to sanitary laws, and so turn the corner. An analgamation of the two races of Maories and Anglo-Saxons is much to be desired."

Perhaps no more striking instance can be given of the way in which the Maories have adapted themselves to the spirit of the times than the readiness they have shown to take advantage of the fame of the lakes and terraces of Rotomahana—situated in the heart of their own territory—to levy upon sight-seers most exorbitant charges for their services as guides, boatmen, etc. So high were these demands, that the ubiquitous Messrs. Cook considered it necessary to send an agent to negotiate with the chiefs. After a solemn palaver with the "committee of Ngati Hinemeti, acting on behalf of the several Maori chiefs interested," a fixed and satisfactory tariff was arranged. Messrs. Cook's tourist tickets are now accepted by the same race who, little more than half a century ago, would not have hesitated to kill and eat any white stranger who might have ventured amongst them!

SCENERY AND POINTS OF INTEREST.—Apart from the interest attaching to the progress of the colony, as shown in the size and prosperity of its towns and the increasing importance of its industries and commerce, New Zealand possesses much in the way of scenery and natural history that is well worth a long journey to see. Notwithstanding the fact that Messrs. Cook's tickets have found their way even to some of the remoter districts of the islands, yet much of the country is still untrodden by the general run of tourists, and possesses even now some of the charms of freshness. In the matter of scenery there is probably no country in the world that comprises so much variety in so small a compass. There is lake scenery equal to that of Scotland, mountain scenery similar to that of Switzerland, volcanic scenery even more wonderful than that of Iceland, semi-tropical forest scenery not unlike that of South America; besides some unique features such as the pink and white terraces of Rotomahana, which are peculiar to New Zealand itself.

The scenery of the two islands is, as we should expect from their geological formation, widely different. In the North Island is to be found the peculiar beauty derived from the wild rugged desolation of volcanic upheavals, mingled with the luxuriant growths of semi-tropical vegetation; while the South Island presents the quieter features and more solemn grandeur of a primary formation, with its lofty mountain ranges and inland lakes.

In the limits of the present chapter it will be possible only to indicate very briefly a few of the best districts for scenery.

We will first take the South Island, with Invercargill as a starting-point. From this town the tourist can, without any great fatigue, make the journey to Lake Wakatipu, shortened by the colonists into "Wakatip," situated towards the centre of the southern portion of the island. The distance from Invercargill is about seventy miles, and the greater part, if not the whole, of the journey can now, I believe, be performed by rail. Near the southern extremity of the lake is Kingstown, and from this place a steamer crosses to Queenstown on the opposite shore, and also makes trips from the latter place round the northern portion of the lake. The scenery is very grand: the mountains, with their glaciers and snow-covered summits, surround the lake on every side. To the south-west of Wakatip are Lake Teanua and Lake Manipori, the scenery of which is said to be very fine; and on the south-west are a series of sounds somewhat resembling the fiords of Norway. This district is very sparsely inhabited, and is somewhat difficult of access, but the wild beauty of its scenery will well repay any one who is sufficiently enterprising to explore it. From Lake Wakatip the tourist can, if he prefers to do so, go on to Dunedin by coach, instead of returning to Invercargill.

The journey from Dunedin to Christchurch can be made either by rail or by steamer. When at Christchurch, a tourist who is in tolerably robust health should not miss the opportunity of visiting the district of Westland on the western coast of the island. The mountain road along which the journey is performed has been made at great expense (some £150,000), and passes through some of the most magnificent scenery in the island, comprising the glaciers of Mount Cook and all the grandeur of the Southern Alps. A coach runs twice a week from Christchurch to the principal towns of the west coast—Hokitika, Greymouth, Westport, etc. The journey each way occupies two days. Hokitika and most of the other towns of the west coast owe their origin to the gold discoveries; and now that the gold rush has ceased, and steady mining operations are alone carried on in the district, these towns, although they have perhaps lost some of their importance, are much more pleasant as places of sojourn than they were formerly. The climate of this part of the colony is, however, too rough, damp, and rainy for invalids, and those who are suffering from any pulmonary complaint should make only a very short stay in the district.

In the North Island, the tourist in search of the picturesque should make his head-quarters at Auckland. The town itself is pleasant, and the surrounding district is full of interest. Maories and half-castes, who in Dunedin and Invercargill are rarely, if ever, to be seen, are constantly met with in the streets of Auckland; and their pahs or settlements abound in the neighbourhood. Excursions can be made northwards to the lovely island of Kawau, the residence of Sir George Grey; to the Wai-Wera hot springs, where the hotel accommodation is said now to be amongst the best in the colony; and to the beautiful Bay of Islands, with its delicious climate and picturesque scenery. The interest of the North Island, however, culminates in the volcanic district which lies between the mountain of Tongariro—itself an active volcano 6,000 feet high—and the shores of the Bay of Plenty. The whole of this region is like a huge cauldron. Craters, geysers, boiling springs, hot lakes, sulphur lakes, mud pools; jets which discharge gas, jets which puff out steam, and jets which throw up mud, abound in every direction. In some places the crust of earth is so thin that the thrust of a walking-stick is sufficient to break it. Near the centre of the district is the largest lake of New Zealand, Lake Taupo. This is itself an immense ancient crater which has become filled with water. Most of the other lakes of the North Island bear traces of the same volcanic origin.

But the lions of the whole district are the remarkable pink and white terraces of Rotomahana. These may be briefly described as a series of lofty terraces formed of fantastic incrustations—coloured deep pink in the one case, pinkish white in the other—deposited by the constantly overflowing water from a hot lake situated on their summit. Mr. Anthony Trollope's description of these terraces is so forcible and graphic, that I must be excused if I give it *in extenso:* "The glory of Roto Mahana is in the terraces. There are the white terraces on the side on which we had slept, and the pink terraces across the lake. I will endeavour, in describing these, to avoid any word that may seem to savour of science—

being altogether ignorant in such matters—and will endeavour simply to say what I saw and felt. These terraces are formed of a soft friable stone, which is deposited by the waters streaming down from the hot pools above. The white terraces are in form the finer of the two. They are about three hundred feet in width, and rise nearly two hundred in height from the lake. As you ascend from the bottom, you step along a raised fretwork of stone, as fine as chased silver. Among this the water is flowing, so that dry feet are out of the question; but the fretwork, if the feet be kept on it, assists the walker, as the water, though it runs over it, of course runs deeper through it. As you rise higher and higher, the water, which at the bottom is hardly more than tepid, becomes warmer and warmer. And then, on one terrace after another, there are large shell-like alabaster baths, holding water from three to four feet deep, of different temperatures as the bather may desire them. Of course the basins are not alabaster, but are made of the deposit of the waters, which is, I believe, silica; but they are as smooth as alabaster, only softer. And on the outside rims, where the water has run, dripping over, century after century, Nature has carved for herself wonderful hanging ornaments and exquisite cornices, with that prolific hand which never stints itself in space because of expense, and devotes its endless labour to front and rear with equal persistency. On the top terrace is the boiling lake from whence the others are filled.

"We had swum in Roto Mahana early in the morning, and did not bathe at the white terraces, having been specially recommended to reserve ourselves for those on the other side. So we crossed the lake to the pink terraces. In form, as I said before, the white terraces are the finer. They are larger and higher, and the spaces between the pools are more exquisitely worked,—and to my eye the colour was preferable. Both are, in truth, pink. Those which have the name of being so are brighter, and are salmon-coloured. They are formed after the same fashion, and the baths are constructed— of course by nature—in the same way. But those which we last visited were, I was told, more delicious to the bather. I can, indeed, imagine nothing more so. The bather undresses upon a piece of dry rock a few yards distant, and is in his bath in half a minute, without the chance of hurting his feet; for it is one of the properties of the stone flooring which has here been formed, that it does not hurt. In the bath, when you strike your chest against it, it is soft to the touch; you press yourself against it, and it is smooth; you lie about upon it, and, though it is firm, it gives to you. You plunge against the sides, driving the water over with your body, but you do not bruise yourself; you go from one bath to another, trying the warmth of each. The water trickles from the one above to the one below, coming from the vast boiling pool at the top, and the lower therefore are less hot than the higher. The baths are shell-like in shape, like vast open shells, the walls of which are concave, and the lips ornamented in a thousand forms. Four or five may sport in one of them, each without feeling the presence of the other. I have never heard of other bathing like this in the world.

"And from the pink terraces, as you lie in the water, you look down upon the lake which is close beneath you, and over upon the green broken hills which come down upon the lake. The scene here, from the pink terraces, is by far the lovelier, though the white terraces themselves are grander in their forms. It is a spot for intense sensual enjoyment, and there comes perhaps some addition to the feeling, from the roughness you have encountered in reaching it; a delight in dallying with it, from the roughness which you must encounter in leaving it."

This remarkable tract of country was formerly somewhat difficult of access, but now there are at least two routes by which the tourist can reach it with comparative ease; in fact, I believe that the whole journey, which formerly occupied some two or three weeks, can now, if necessary, be performed from Auckland and back in five or six days. The journey can be made either entirely by land or partly by sea; in the latter case the passenger is taken in a coasting steamer to the small town of Tauranga, in the Bay of Plenty. From thence the journey is made by coach, or on horseback, canoes belonging to the Maories being used for crossing the lakes, etc. Fairly good accommodation can now, I believe, be obtained at all points of the journey, and the charges, though high, are much less exorbitant than they were formerly. If the excursion is made overland, advantage is taken of the railway which now runs southward from Auckland for a considerable distance towards the centre of the island. The latter part of the journey is performed by coach, canoe, etc., as in the former case.

The forests of New Zealand are particularly lovely, and entirely different in character from the "gum-tree scrub" of Australia. The greater humidity of the climate is shown in the more vivid colouring of the tree-foliage, in the luxuriant undergrowth, and the abundance and vigour of the parasitical forms of vegetation. In their general aspect the forests somewhat resemble those of South America, but most of the species of plants are peculiar to New Zealand. Ferns are particularly abundant, and there are three species of tree-ferns, some of which attain the height of forty feet. These and the palm trees give a semi-tropical character to the scenery. "The floral landscape of New Zealand may be divided into three distinct kinds. First, there is the primeval forest, composed of lofty pines and other evergreen trees of vast size, beneath the shelter of which flourish the tree-ferns and the graceful *nikau* palm (*Areca sapida*), which itself grows thirty feet high. All this forest is bound together and rendered well-nigh impassable by the rope-like stems of the *smilax*, or supple-jack. The whole is shaded externally from the sun by the lofty canopy of foliage overhead, and nourished by the ceaseless moisture that drops from every spray, rendering these antipodean forests rank with vegetation. Parasites sprout from the loftiest trees, while mosses and smaller ferns clothe their trunks with green, carrying a profusion of vegetable life up into their topmost branches. All is of the deepest green, and amidst the gloom an almost unbroken silence reigns; whilst the warm, damp, windless air is laden with the delicious fragrance of the blossom of the wax-like pink *hoya;* and the tangled undergrowth of fuchsias is rendered gay by the large star-like blossoms of a species of white clematis. Coming suddenly out of the forest, the traveller enters upon vast tracts of undulating land, without a tree, except here and there a solitary *dracena* or *cordyline*, the whole being densely covered with the social fern, breast-high, through which wind the narrow footpaths of the natives. The third phase of vegetation is represented by the swampy flats near the lakes and rivers, which are covered with clumps of the *Phormium tenax*, or New Zealand flax, and clusters of a sort of large Tussack grass, (the *Typha angustifolia*,) or *raupo* of the natives, who employ it for building and thatching their houses." *

The lower forms of vegetable life exhibit in New Zealand some remarkable curiosities. Some of the fungi

* Silver's Handbook of Australia and New Zealand.

are bright crimson, and some are luminous at night by their own phosphoric light; others attain a gigantic size. The mosses and lichens grow with great luxuriance, some of the cup-mosses being particularly elegant. One of the lichens resembles white coral. Amongst the most singular things found in the forest is the so-called "vegetable caterpillar" which the natives have named *Aweto*. It is a large caterpillar, from the head of which grows a long fungus bearing seed-spurs at the end. The Maories eat this caterpillar, as well as a large beetle which lives in rotten wood, and which they call *Wetu*.

The flowers natural to New Zealand are not numerous, but some of the forest trees and shrubs bear very beautiful blossoms. Most of the European species, however, grow with great luxuriance. The gardens in Auckland are filled with a profusion of flowers such as geraniums, fuschias, etc., as well as several semi-tropical plants, all of which grow in the open air all the year round, and often attain a great size.

New Zealand has no indigenous fruits of any consequence, but all the European varieties grow in the greatest profusion. Figs, peaches, grapes, plums, and melons abound; but, as in Australia, they have scarcely the same delicate flavour they have in England.

There are not many countries in the world with so few indigenous animals as New Zealand. The sole representatives of the zoology of the country are believed to be a couple of species of bat and a small rat. The latter is fast disappearing, if it has not already disappeared, before its more voracious European relative, which has been introduced into the colony. The Maories have always had a small domestic dog, but it is probable that they originally brought it with them. The so-called wild pigs that have been plentiful in the islands are the descendants of the pigs which were introduced by Captain Cook.

The ornithology of New Zealand is full of interest. Up to probably 200 or 300 years ago there existed a gigantic race of wingless birds allied to the cassowaries, and called by the natives *Moa*. From the skeletons that have been found, Professor Owen divides the family into ten species, of which the largest attained the enormous height of ten to thirteen feet. It is believed that the natives destroyed these birds in considerable numbers when they first came to the islands, so that they gradually became extinct. In some places heaps of the bones of moas have been found, all of them broken, leading to the inference that the marrow had been extracted and eaten by the Maories. In one case a perfect and unbroken egg was discovered. A species of Apteryx, called by the natives Kiwi, and closely allied to the moas, still exists in some of the more remote districts. It is a wingless bird, the size of a fowl; its body is covered with hair-like feathers, and it lays a solitary egg of enormous dimensions in comparison with its own size.

Some of the more curious birds, which in the first days of colonization were tolerably numerous, are now almost extinct. Amongst these may be mentioned the "laughing owl," a night-bird of extraordinary appearance. It is spotted with chestnut and black, has a small head and beak, long legs, and green feet. There was also a remarkable nocturnal parrot, which fed on the ground at night, nibbling the grass like a rabbit. The "parson-bird," so called from two tufts of white feathers on the throat—the rest of the plumage being black—is still tolerably plentiful. It is about the size of a rook. Several species of wild ducks and pigeons are found in considerable numbers, and are not only much esteemed for the table, but afford excellent sport.

Of reptiles there are very few. There are no snakes of any kind—New Zealand in this respect presenting a marked and very pleasing contrast to Australia. There are a few species of harmless lizards. Insects are not particularly numerous, but mosquitoes are found plentifully in the marshy districts.

Fish abound on the coasts, and there are a few kinds in the rivers of New Zealand. More than 150 species have been described, many of which are very valuable as food, and afford good sport to those who are fond of fishing. Sharks, as we have already seen, are very numerous, and one kind—the "tiger shark"—is particularly ferocious.

The marine mammalia are represented by several species of seals, including the sea-lion, sea-leopard, and the fur-seal. There is also a species of porpoise met with on the coast, called the New Zealand dolphin (*Delphinus Zelandiæ*), and one or two species of whales occasionally visit the shores of the colony.

THE CLIMATE OF NEW ZEALAND.—It will greatly help us in forming an estimate of the climate of a colony such as New Zealand, if we first of all attentively consider the position, surroundings, and physical characteristics of the country taken as a whole. It will then be easier to appreciate the advantages or disadvantages, in point of climate, of any particular district.

The following facts should be borne in mind :—

(*a*) New Zealand may be practically regarded as a long narrow tract of land stretching for a distance of more than a thousand miles almost due north and south. Its northern extremity, reaching to a latitude of 34° south, is nearly in the same parallel as Sydney, New South Wales, or Buenos Ayres in South America; whereas its most southern point is in the latitude of 47° south, considerably nearer the Pole than the most southern point of Tasmania. It will be observed that no portion of the colony corresponds in latitude with England, which lies between 50° N. and 56° N.

(b) A glance at a map of the world will show us that New Zealand is placed in a vast ocean-belt which stretches around the globe almost without a break. The "brave west winds" of the southern hemisphere, which, as we have seen, partaking of the nature of a gigantic cyclone, blow with but little interruption from some point between north-west and south-west, expend their full force upon the western shores of New Zealand.

(c) These winds come loaded with the watery vapour of thousands of miles of ocean, without undergoing, as in Australia, any desiccating process by passing over vast sandy deserts.

(d) Both the principal islands of the New Zealand group are mountainous, and the ranges for the most part have a general direction parallel to the western coast-line. In the South Island this is especially the case—the lofty Alpine range running close to the west coast throughout nearly its whole length. The vapour-laden winds from the west, in passing over these mountain ranges, deposit much of their moisture in the form of rain and snow.

(e) The various districts of the colony present great differences as regards elevation. Canterbury Plains have an elevation of some 3,000 to 4,000 ft. Otago also has extensive elevated plateaux.

(f) New Zealand, although so narrow in extent, possesses numerous rivers and inland lakes. In some localities there are also marshy districts. In these respects it presents a marked contrast to the broad Australian continent, with its great sandy deserts.

From the foregoing facts we may draw the following conclusions as to the general characteristics of the climate :—

1. That different parts of New Zealand will vary considerably in temperature, according to latitude and elevation.

2. That the winds blow with great force especially upon the western shores of the islands.

3. That the climate is a humid one, partly on account of the vast ocean tracts by which the colony is surrounded, and partly owing to the streams, lakes, and forests of the country itself.

4. That, on account of the protection from the prevalent westerly winds afforded by the mountain ranges, the eastern portions of the islands are both less rainy and less humid than the western side.

As we proceed, it will be seen how far these conclusions are borne out by facts.

The meteorological conditions of New Zealand may be studied under the heads of Temperature, Rainfall, Humidity, Winds, and Atmospheric pressure.

Temperature.—The mean temperature for the whole of New Zealand, as deduced from several years' observations, is 55°·2. The mean for the North Island is 57°·9, for the South Island 52°·7. In its mean annual temperature therefore the climate of the North Island resembles that of Rome or Milan; while the South Island in this respect resembles Jersey. As compared with the mean temperature of our own climate, the North Island is found to be about 8° warmer, and the South Island about 3° warmer, than the neighbourhood of London.

The yearly range of temperature would appear to be for the North Island 56°, and for the South Island 65°.

But although these averages may enable us to form a

rough estimate of the general climate of a country, they give us but little idea of the characteristics of the various distrcts of which it is made up. The information obtained by comparing the mean temperatures of the various stations will be more practically useful. The following table gives in the first column the mean shade temperatures in several of the towns of both islands, as deduced from observations extending over a period of thirteen years, 1867-79. In the second and third columns the highest and lowest recorded shade temperatures are given.

Stations.	Average for 13 years, 1867-9.	Highest recorded.	Lowest recorded.
N. Island.	Deg.	Deg.	Deg.
Auckland	59·2	90·4	31·9
Napier	58·8*	94·0	30·0
Wellington	55·4	83·0	30·0
S. Island.			
Nelson	55·4	92·0	25·0
Christchurch	52·7	95·7	21·3
Hokitika	52·8	82·4	26·9
Dunedin	50·5	88·0	27·0

* 1870-79.

This table shows very clearly the gradual decrease in mean temperature as we pass from the north to the south of the colony. It also brings out the fact that while the yearly range is very considerable at all the stations, the climate of the North Island is on the whole more equable than that of the South Island. This is no doubt due partly to the fact that the North Island is more densely wooded than the South. All the published observations are taken on the coast, where the climate is to a certain extent equalized by the sea—in the interior the extremes of temperature are probably much greater.

The elevated plains of Canterbury and Otago, in common with all high table-lands, possess a most variable climate. In summer the heat is often intense, while in winter severe frosts occur, and snow sometimes lies upon the ground for many weeks at a time.

The hottest months in New Zealand are January and February—the coldest, July and August.

Rainfall.—The quantity of rain varies greatly in different parts of the colony; the amount that falls is much greater in some years than it is in others.

The following table gives the average rainfall for the thirteen years from 1867 to 1879 inclusive. The average number of rainy days is also given for a series of years.

Stations.	Inches.	No. of rainy days.
N. Island.		
Auckland	44·98	183
Napier	35·69	74
Wellington	53·78	143
S. Island.		
Nelson	61·70	84
Christchurch	25·33	107
Hokitika	119·11	206
Dunedin	35·79	182

From this table we gather that, of the stations mentioned, Hokitika on the west coast is, as we should expect, the most rainy; whereas Napier and Christchurch—which occupy sheltered positions on the east coast—have the least quantity of rain. It will be observed that at all of the stations the rainfall is greater than in England, where the yearly average, as deduced from thirty-nine years' observations, is 24·76 inches.

Droughts such as those which occur in Australia are unknown in New Zealand.

Snow.—All the loftier mountains throughout the colony are, as we have seen, covered with snow. The snow-line on the Southern Alps is at about 7,800 feet. In the North Island snow occasionally falls, but except in the most elevated districts it does not lie upon the ground. In many districts of the South Island snow falls plentifully at times. This is particularly the case in the elevated plateaux of Canterbury and Otago. In Southland, in 1873, fifteen inches of snow lay on the ground for five days.

Humidity.—As might be expected from its position and physical configuration, New Zealand possesses a moist climate. Except on the west coast, however, the humidity would not appear to be so great as in England. At Greenwich the mean yearly relative humidity (for thirty-nine years) is 81.

From Government returns, published in the "Colonization Circular," the mean relative humidity, as deduced from several years' observations at the various stations, would appear to be as follows:—

North Island.

Auckland	72
Napier	79
Wellington	68

South Island.

Nelson	74
Christchurch	76
Hokitika	90
Dunedin	71

The extreme humidity of the climate of Hokitika, on the west coast of the South Island, is brought out very prominently in this table. In fact, the western slopes of the Southern Alps are in many places too humid, both as regards climate and rainfall, for successful agriculture. In some districts the dampness of the air is shown by the fact that all articles made of leather quickly become covered with mildew. The luxuriant parasitical growths in the forest also testify to the humidity of the climate.

Throughout both islands a considerable amount of dew is deposited; but in the North Island the fall is said to be heavier than in the South. Fogs are but seldom experienced in the North Island, but in the South Island, and especially on the west coast, and in winter, they are not unfrequent.

Wind.—The prevailing winds in the North Island are westerly, varying from N.W. to S.W. The warm, moist equatorial current is of course from the north, the cold, dry, polar current from the south. Owing, however, to the irregular shape of the islands, and the numerous mountain chains and peaks, the local winds are, for the most part, but eddies from the great main currents. The storms in this colony, as in Australia, are usually from the south—frequently from the south-east. They are often accompanied by hail. In the southern hemisphere the wind veers with the sun, but in a contrary direction to the hands of a watch; whereas in the northern hemisphere the wind, while veering with the sun, coincides with the movements of the watch.

Strong winds, as we have seen, prevail throughout the colony, and on the west coast especially, they often attain great force, and lash the sea into fury. The greatest velocity that has been registered is said to be 84·5 miles per hour. This represents a hurricane of terrific violence. Cook's Strait and Foveaux Strait, lying open as they do to the prevailing winds, are often visited by gales and sudden squalls.

The hot winds of Australia are but little felt in New Zealand generally. The Canterbury Plains, however, and other districts to the east of the Alps, are sometimes visited in summer by hot currents of air from the north-west, which descend the sides of the mountains, melting the snow on the upper slopes. Some difficulty has been experienced in accounting for this phenomenon. The most likely hypothesis is that the hot winds of Australia rise after leaving that continent, and again descend upon passing over the mountains of New Zealand.

Atmospheric Pressure.—The observations taken at the various stations show a greater average barometric pressure in the North Island than in the South. The mean for the former is given as 30·010, for the latter as 28·831. In its general indications the barometer follows the same laws as in the rest of the southern hemisphere; it falls for the warm equatorial currents from the north, with their accompaniments of rain and moisture, and rises for the cold, dry polar currents from the south.

Earthquakes are felt at times over the whole area of New Zealand, but are most frequent in the neighbourhood of Cook's Strait, especially in Wellington. The most serious shocks were experienced in 1848, when some of the houses in Wellington were thrown down. As a rule, however, the shocks are slight, and though somewhat alarming, are not dangerous, and it is believed that the subterranean disturbances of which they are the outcome are gradually subsiding. At any rate, the colonists have of late years taken heart of grace, and are now substituting houses of brick and stone for the more temporary structures which it was at first thought best to erect in Wellington and elsewhere.

Thunderstorms are neither particularly violent nor very frequent in New Zealand. They vary greatly in different localities, but are on the whole most felt on the west coast and in the neighbourhood of the mountain ranges.

The Aurora australis is a phenomenon that is frequently seen, especially in the more southern parts of the colony.

General observations.—It will be seen from the foregoing particulars that the climate of New Zealand is not marked by great extremes in any direction. It is in fact not altogether unlike that of England, although on the whole somewhat warmer. Hence there is no colony which, as regards climate, is more suitable as a residence for an average healthy Englishman, especially one who has to gain his livelihood by outdoor pursuits. All the habits of the old country can be maintained; the constitution has not to undergo any of the troubles of acclimatisation, as in hotter countries; neither is there any alteration of the physical type in the course of a few generations, as in some other colonies. Dr. Dieffenbach says with regard to the climate of New Zealand, "The purity of the atmosphere, resulting from the continual wind, imparts to the climate a vigour which gives elasticity to the physical powers and to the mind. Heat never debilitates, not even so much as a hot summer's day in England; and near the coasts especially there is always a cooling and refreshing breeze. The colonist who occupies himself with agriculture can work all day, and the mechanic will not feel any lassitude, whether he works in or out of doors."

The seasons in New Zealand are of course just the reverse of our own, but they scarcely present the same abrupt changes they do with us. Dr. Thompson, writing on this subject, says: "An idea of the seasons in New Zealand may be drawn from English strawberries being ripe in November, December, and January; apples, pears, plums, and peaches in February; and melons, figs, and grapes in March and April. Spring, in short, commences in September, summer in December, autumn in April, and winter in June. The summer mornings, even in the warmest parts of the colony, are sufficiently fresh to exhilarate without chilling, and the seasons glide imperceptibly into each other. The beauty of the day is in the early morning; and at this hour, away from the settlements of men, a solemn stillness pervades the air, which is only broken by the shrill and tinkling voices of birds. Summer nights are often singularly beautiful and mild, and on such occasions the settlers are frequently enticed from their houses to wander about in the open air."

We have now to consider the question of the suitability of the climate for invalids, especially for those who are suffering from chest delicacy. It will be seen at once that for the latter the west coast of the colony, with its heavy rainfall, its damp atmosphere, and boisterous winds, would be quite unsuitable as a residence. The high-lying plains of Canterbury and Otago, although in some respects more favourable than the west coast, do not possess the same advantages as the high table-lands of Australia. The climate is subject to great and sudden changes, owing to the vicinity of the snow-covered mountains of the district, and has little of the distinctive dryness which in Australia is caused by the great sandy deserts of the interior. The driest and most equable climates are to be found in the sheltered bays and harbours situated on the east side of protecting mountain ranges. Thus, while Auckland, although warm and tolerably equable, is damp and rainy, the Bay of Islands, further to the north, being well protected by mountains, has a far drier climate and smaller rainfall. Passing down the east coast, we find that the Hawke Bay district has an excellent climate—Napier, its principal town, being strongly recommended as a residence for invalids. Nelson, occupying a sheltered position in a deep bay at the northern extremity of the South Island, and being also well protected by mountain ranges, is another locality which has gained a great reputation as a sanatorium, as well as a pleasant place of residence. It has been called the Madeira of New Zealand. Christchurch, although considerably cooler, and subject to greater extremes of temperature than Napier and Nelson, has a very moderate rainfall, and is in some respects fairly suitable as a place of sojourn for invalids suffering from chest complaints.

Concluding Hints to Invalids.—Those of my readers who intend to visit New Zealand in the course of a voyage undertaken for the express purpose of benefiting the health, will do well to bear in mind the following points :—

1. Although the climate of this colony is one of the best in the world for those in good health, it is not generally so well suited as that of Australia for invalids who are suffering from chest delicacy.

2. The New Zealand winters, especially in the South Island, are, as a rule, too cold and damp for chest invalids. Those therefore who visit the colony for health, should, if possible, so time their arrival as to avoid spending any portion of the winter there.

3. Invalids should avoid making a prolonged stay on the west coast of the islands.

4. After visiting such places of interest as are within the compass of their strength, health-seekers should, if possible, spend the rest of their time at one or other of the following towns : Napier, Nelson, Wellington, Christchurch, or Auckland. Of these, the first two (especially Napier) have the best, driest, and most equable climates. Wellington and Auckland have a tolerably equable climate, but both are humid, from their position. Christ-

church is dry, but subject to great variations of temperature. Auckland is the warmest of all the towns mentioned.

Suggestions as to the length of stay it is advisable for invalids to make on shore before starting on the return voyage have been given in Chapter IX. It is only necessary to add that chest invalids who propose remaining in the colonies during a winter should, if possible, cross over to the Australian continent, and pass the colder months in one or other of the winter health resorts that have been already recommended.

CHAPTER XIII.

SOUTH AFRICA.

Districts comprised in South Africa—Cape Colony—Population—Rivers—Mountains—Industries and productions—Exports—Ports—Cape Town—Suburbs of Cape Town—Railways—Cape wines—Port Elizabeth — East London — Natal — Durban — Pietermaritzburg—Orange Free State—Elevated plains of the interior—Bloemfontein—The Transvaal—Climate of Cape Town and its neighbourhood—The "Cape doctor"—Health resorts of the interior—Graham's Town—Cradock—Colesburg—Bloemfontein—Conveyances—Cobb and Co.'s coaches—Passenger carts—Mail carts—Private conveyances—Ox waggons—Climate of the inland plains; its dryness—Thunderstorms—Droughts—Meteorological observations—Influence of the climate on disease.

FOR the information of those who have chosen the voyage to the Cape of Good Hope in preference to the longer Australian passage, it is proposed to give in the present chapter some little account of South Africa and its climate, with special reference to those localities that have been found most suitable for invalids. It will, of course, be impossible to do more than give a brief outline of the subject, but even a few hints may prove of service to those who intend making some little stay at the Cape before returning home.

The term *South Africa*, in its widest sense, includes several colonies and districts situated in that portion of the African continent which lies to the south of 22° S. lat. It comprises the following territories, viz. :—

1. The colonies that belong to Great Britain—viz.,

Cape Colony (including the incorporated provinces of British Kaffraria, Griqualand West, and British Basutoland), *Natal*, and the *Transvaal* (annexed in 1877).* In addition to these there are certain irregular districts, virtually British, situated in Kaffirland (or Kaffraria), and known collectively as the "*Transkeian Territory.*"

2. An independent Dutch republic, the *Orange Free State.*

3. Countries inhabited by, and still under the dominion of, native tribes—viz., *Kaffirland, Zululand,* etc.

4. Certain *Portuguese possessions* in the neighbourhood of Delagoa Bay, to the north of Natal.

It will only be necessary for the purposes of the present work to glance briefly at three or four of the colonies that have been enumerated above—viz., Cape Colony, Natal, the Orange Free State, and the Transvaal. The rest are of comparatively little importance to any one visiting South Africa only for a short time, or as an invalid.

CAPE COLONY comprises that somewhat triangular portion of the African continent which is bounded by the South Atlantic and South Indian Oceans on the south-west and south-east respectively, and by the Orange River on the north. The extreme length of the colony is 770 miles, and its breadth 470.

The entire population is about 720,000,—of whom about 236,000 are Europeans; 11,000 Malays; 98,000 Hottentots; 73,000 Fingoes; 214,000 Kaffirs or Bechuanas; and 87,000 mixed and various races. The European inhabitants of the colony are of several nationalities, and comprise a large number of Dutch boers or farmers, many of them the descendants of the original Dutch settlers, by

* At the present time (1881) this colony occupies a somewhat anomalous position. It has an independent government, but acknowledges the queen as "suzerain."

whom the country was held with but little interruption until the beginning of the present century. In addition to these, the colony contains English, German, French, and Portuguese inhabitants, besides others of various races.

The *rivers* of Cape Colony are, for the most part, unimportant, the want of navigable and perennial streams being one of the great drawbacks to South Africa. Although in the rainy season they are often raging torrents, at other times many of them are little more than detached pools of water; and the estuaries, even of the largest, are mostly filled up with sand, rendering them useless for purposes of navigation. The most important of the rivers of Cape Colony are Orange river, Oliphant's river, the Breede, Camtoos, Gauritz, Sunday's river, Great Fish river, the Keiskamma, Buffalo, Kei, and Bashee rivers. The last four are perennial streams.

The *mountain systems* of the colony are of considerable importance to those seeking a health resort, because upon them depend the differences in the elevation and climate of the various districts. In the southern portions of the colony, the land, as it recedes from the coast, rises in a series of natural terraces, until, at an average distance of about 130 to 150 miles from the sea, a system of lofty mountain ranges is reached, which crosses the southern portion of the continent from east to west, and has been called the "Backbone of Africa." On the north of these mountains are situated the highest districts in the colony. But before reaching the "backbone of Africa," one or more secondary parallel ranges of mountains will have been crossed, and all of these, including the highest, act, as it were, as retaining-walls or buttresses to the elevated plains beyond them; for they slope steeply and precipitously towards the south, but very slightly, if at all, towards the north. It is to this peculiar configuration of the country that the great dryness of the more elevated plateaux is partly due; for the damp winds blowing from the sea deposit their moisture on the southern face of the mountains in the form of rain, which goes to feed the rivers of the district below. The communication between the tracts of country of different elevations is by means of roads constructed with much skill through the narrow passes or "kloofs" which pierce the mountain ranges at intervals. The high-lying districts to the north-east of the colony are those that have been found most suitable for chest complaints requiring a dry climate. The Nieuwoeld, the provinces of Cradock and Colesberg, and the districts extending northwards towards the diamond fields, are the localities that have been most recommended.

The natural resources of the colony are considerable. Besides agricultural pursuits, the farmers of the Cape are engaged in rearing large numbers of *sheep, cattle,* and *horses,* for the pasturage of which the grass lands of the interior are admirably suited. *Ostrich farming* is also becoming a favourite pursuit, and appears to be profitable. In 1875 there were some 22,000 birds in the colony. A pair of breeding birds is worth as much as £150, and the artificial incubation of the eggs is now practised to a considerable extent. *Wine making* is carried on principally in the neighbourhoods of Constantia, Stellenbosch, Worcester, Robertson, and Oudtshoorn. *Tobacco, cotton,* and *coffee* are grown in some districts, but, with the exception of tobacco, not to any great extent. The *fruits* of the Cape are various, and include oranges, citrons, guavas, bananas, peaches, apricots, plums, quinces, grapes, etc. *Grain* is raised in large quantities, and the wheat of South Africa is amongst the best in the world. *Game* of all kinds is still plentiful in many of the inland districts, and the botanist will find an immense field for research in the varied and beautiful *flowers* and *trees* of the colony.

THE DIAMOND FIELDS—CAPE TOWN.

The *diamond fields* are situated in Griqualand West, which was formerly a separate colony, but in 1873 was incorporated as one of the provinces of Cape Colony. The diamond diggings are of two kinds, known as "river diggings" and "dry diggings." The former extend along the banks of the Vaal river between Hebron and Sifonel; the latter are included within a radius of little more than two miles in the neighbourhood of Kimberley, which is the principal town and the seat of magistracy of the district. The largest diamond yet found weighed 288 carats. By a glance at the map it will be seen that the diamond fields are situated at the extreme north of Cape Colony; and although the climate is a good one, the length and difficulties of the journey render it unsuitable for an invalid.

The most important *exports* of Cape Colony are copper, corn, aloes, ostrich feathers, cured fish, dried fruits, hides, skins, ivory, wine and brandy, wool, diamonds, etc.

The principal *ports* of Cape Colony are Cape Town and Port Elizabeth, in Algoa Bay; other ports, at present less important, are East London and Port Alfred. It will only be necessary to describe the first three.

Cape Town, the capital of Cape Colony, is built on the sloping shores of Table Bay, which, although an open roadstead, is so enclosed and protected by surrounding hills and mountains, and by an island—Robben Island—as to afford secure anchorage for vessels even of the largest size in all ordinary states of the wind.

A large breakwater, which has been constructed at great expense, affords additional security.

Immediately behind the town rises in bold relief the singular flat-topped mountain so universally known as Table Mountain,[*] and on its right and left are the Lion

---

[*] 3,582 feet in height.

Mountain and Devil's Peak, while other mountains stretch away in rugged succession as far as the eye can reach.

The streets of Cape Town are, for the most part, tolerably regular and of good width. Many—perhaps I should say most—of the houses have been built by the Dutch settlers, and some are of venerable age and picturesque appearance. With the exception of these, Cape Town possesses very few buildings, either public or private, of much interest to the stranger. Besides the English, Dutch, and Roman Catholic Cathedrals, there are many churches and chapels, none of which, however, possess any architectural pretensions. The Market Place is a large open space, surrounded by a few handsome buildings—principally banks, warehouses, and shops. The public Botanical Gardens are pretty, home-like, and well-timbered. Facing these is the Government House—a homely old-fashioned brick building, beautifully covered with luxuriant creepers, and surrounded by lofty trees. Near the Government House is a large building containing the Museum, Public Library, and Reading Rooms. The Museum does not contain anything of very great interest, but the Reading Rooms are particularly comfortable and well-arranged, and being perfectly free to all, are a great boon both to inhabitants and strangers.

There are at present two lines of railway from Cape Town. One extends to Wynberg, the nearest station to Constantia; the other, which is still in course of construction, will eventually run some three hundred miles into the interior, to Beaufort, and is at present open for a distance of about a hundred and fifty miles. Branches from the main line run to Stellenbosch and Malmesbury respectively.

Cape Town is surrounded by suburban villages, most of which are very pleasantly situated, and form a much more desirable residence for invalids than the city itself.

Some of the most important are Constantia, Wynberg, Rondebosch, Sea Point, Kalk Bay, etc.

Nothing can be more lovely than the scenery in the neighbourhood of Constantia. The roads between Cape Town and those places are, at first sight, very English in appearance, owing to their being fringed on either side with trees of various familiar kinds, amongst which the oak of our native shores is conspicuous. These oak trees are, however, not indigenous to the country, but were introduced by early Dutch settlers, and are, in some places, planted so closely together as to form by their over-arching boughs an almost impenetrable screen from the heat of the sun during the summer. We are, however, soon reminded that we are far away from home by the hedgerows of lofty aloes, and of the cactus, known as the prickly pear; while the coloured population of every shade that clusters round the wayside cottages speaks yet more unmistakably of a foreign land. The best wine in the colony is made at Constantia, and the vineyards are for the most part owned by wealthy descendants of the original Dutch settlers. Both the vineyards themselves and the fine old houses of the proprietors are well worth a visit. The Cape wines, especially the lighter kinds, grown at Constantia, are genuine, wholesome, and palatable; and the visitor should not allow any prejudice he may have previously entertained to stand in the way of his making use of them during his stay, especially as English beers and foreign wines are excessively dear and inferior in quality.*

The street conveyances of Cape Town consist mostly of roomy well-built Hansom cabs, which are very wisely painted white at the top, for the sake of coolness. The

* The genuine Cape wines are very different to the brandied compounds that have found their way into England under that name.

drivers are, with scarcely an exception, men of colour. Longer journeys are made in the Cape cart—a two-wheeled conveyance capable of accommodating four or even six people, and furnished with two or four horses. For very long journeys into the interior, ox waggons are often employed.

There are several hotels in Cape Town, the best of which are perhaps the "St. George" and the "Royal," but the "Masonic" and the "Commercial" are also very respectable houses. The accommodation at all these is fairly good, and the charges are much the same as in England. There are also boarding-houses, at which good accommodation may be obtained for about £2 per week. Lodgings are almost unknown in the colony.

Cape Town contains a population of about 32,000 souls, of whom nearly half are Europeans; the rest are Malays (descendants for the most part of the servants and slaves of the Dutch East India Company), Kaffirs, natives of Mozambique, Bonny, etc. The true Hottentots are almost, if not quite, extinct, but they have left their impress on the mixed population. The Malays, who nearly all profess the Mussulman religion, are many of them in affluent circumstances. Some of the younger men and women are very handsome, and most of the race possess features of great intelligence. The European population contains, of course, a large proportion of Dutch; there are also many English residents, and a fair sprinkling of French, Germans, and other nationalities.

Taken altogether, Cape Town is an interesting city, and a visitor is little likely to forget his first impressions of its general aspect. The picturesque town, with its magnificent background formed by Table Mountain, and the perhaps still more striking Lion Mountain—the variety of the population, presenting every shade of colour, from the ebony black of the negro to the scarcely noticeable bronze of the half-caste Malay—the gorgeous colours in which the women love to dress themselves—the curious head-dresses of the men—the semi-tropical fruits, flowers, and vegetation,—all combine to form a picture upon which the memory will dwell with pleasure for many a long year.

Port Elizabeth, the second port of Cape Colony, is situated in Algoa Bay, about 500 miles east of Cape Town. The bay, which is bounded by Cape Padrone on the east, and Cape Recife on the west, while protected from the north-west gales, is exposed to those from the south-east; and although somewhat sheltered by a few rocky islets, it is at present far from a desirable harbour. Much expense has been incurred in the attempt to improve it, but hitherto with only partial success, owing in a great measure to shifting bars of sand in the bay. Port Elizabeth is a busy thriving town, with a population of over 13,000 inhabitants; and, considering how recently it was founded, it has grown more rapidly than almost any other town in the colony. It possesses several churches, banks, and insurance offices; a hospital, barracks, gas-works, etc.; and if only provided with a good harbour, would no doubt become a place of very considerable importance, especially as it is the terminus of two railways towards the interior—viz., the North-eastern and the Midland lines. Seventy-six miles of the former and sixty-five miles of the latter are already open for traffic.

As Port Elizabeth is at present the best port for Grahamstown, Cradock, Bloemfontein, and other favourite health resorts of South Africa, it is of considerable importance to the invalid visitor to the Cape; but it must be borne in mind that the climate of Port Elizabeth itself is perhaps one of the worst in South Africa for chest complaints, and that the stay there should be as short as possible.

There are two lighthouses in Algoa Bay—one on Cape Recife, and the other on Bird Island.

East London, the next port in importance to Port Elizabeth, is the seaport of British Kaffraria, and is situated at the mouth of the Buffalo River, about 700 miles east of Cape Town. Although the anchorage is at present open and exposed, extensive harbour-works are in course of construction; and as East London is the terminus of the partially completed railway to Queenstown (distant 120 miles), it is likely to become a place of considerable importance, especially as it is the natural port for King Williamstown (the railway to which is already completed) and other large towns. At present, the landing of passengers is often difficult, and in some states of the wind almost impossible.

NATAL, which is situated on the south-east coast of Africa, to the north of Kaffraria and Basutoland, has a coast-line of some 150 miles, and extends inland for a distance of about 130 miles at its broadest part. It has only one port available for shipping—viz., *Durban*, situated in the harbour of Port Natal. This harbour is sheltered and land-locked, and has a length of about three miles and a half, and a width of two miles and a quarter, while it is only 600 yards wide at its entrance, which is still partially obstructed by a sand-bar, notwithstanding all that has been expended in attempts for its removal. A lighthouse has been built on a bluff near the entrance.

Durban is the oldest town in the colony, and is regularly built. It has a population of about 6,500. A short line of rail connects the landing-place with the town. There are also iron-foundries, steam-mills, etc.

Pietermaritzburg, the capital of the colony, is about fifty-four miles inland from Durban. It is built on high land, and at some seasons of the year is liable to very severe thunderstorms. The population of Pietermaritzburg is about 6,800.

Since the commencement of the Zulu war the railway between Pietermaritzburg and Durban, which has so long been a desideratum for the colony, has, I believe, been completed and opened for traffic.

The total population of Natal is about 307,000,—of whom 18,600 are whites, 6,700 imported coolies, and 281,700 natives.

The fertility of its soil, and the great variety of the products that can be grown on the successive plateaux into which it is naturally divided, render Natal probably the most flourishing of the South African colonies. On the low-lying district next the coast, cotton, tobacco, coffee, and sugar are successfully cultivated, together with many other tropical and semi-tropical productions. On the plains of medium elevation crops of barley, oats, etc., are raised in great perfection, as well as the fruits and vegetables of Europe; while the highest and most inland plateaux are suitable for pasturage, and supply meat and butter to the more densely populated districts below.

The principal exports of Natal are sugar, wool, cotton, ostrich feathers, hides, ivory, coffee, arrowroot, butter, etc.

THE ORANGE FREE STATE is a republic which owes its existence to Dutch boers, who, dissatisfied with British rule, migrated northwards from Cape Colony, and formed themselves into an independent state. It comprises the territory which lies between the two streams that unite to form the Orange river, and is far removed from the coast; Port Elizabeth, the seaport from which it is most easily reached, being situated more than two hundred miles from its frontier.

The population of the state is believed to be nearly

50,000, of whom about half are Europeans and the remainder natives. Of the Europeans the greater proportion are descendants of the original Dutch settlers.

Some of the highest land in South Africa is to be found in the Orange Free State. The vast undulating plains of which it mainly consists are covered with long grass, and in many districts stretch in unvarying monotony as far as the eye can reach, while in others they are broken by rocky hills, locally called "kopjes." These plains are admirably adapted for grazing purposes, though, in common with all the high-lying districts of South Africa, they are liable to violent thunderstorms. Diamonds, garnets, and other precious stones are to be found in considerable numbers, though not to the same extent as in the neighbouring district of Griqualand West. Game of every kind abounds, and affords unlimited scope for the energies of those addicted to field sports.

Bloemfontein, the capital and seat of government, is situated on very high ground towards the centre of the state, having an elevation of some 4,000 feet above sea-level. An English missionary bishop resides there, and it possesses two or three churches, banks, etc.; but it is far from imposing as to appearance and size, boasting only a population of about 1,000. There are hotels, but they are expensive, and the accommodation is far from good. A home for consumptive invalids was founded a few years since, under the auspices of the Bishop of Bloemfontein.

Bloemfontein can be reached either from Cape Town or Port Elizabeth. The latter is the best route for invalids, and will be more fully described further on.

THE TRANSVAAL, or, as it was formerly called, the South African Republic, lies north of the Vaal river, and from this fact it takes its name. Like the Orange Free

State, it owes its origin to a migration of dissatisfied Dutch boers. In 1877 it was formally annexed by Great Britain, since which event public attention has been a good deal directed to its resources, and at one time some little emigration to the colony took place; but the present anomalous position of the Transvaal with respect to England, no less than the recent war, will, it is to be feared tend to check for the present any further enterprise in that direction.

The population is believed to amount to about 300,000, of whom only some 25,000 or 30,000 are whites. The greater number of the Europeans are, as may be supposed, of Dutch origin. The natural characteristics of the country are much the same as those of the Free State, presenting a series of elevated plateaux, which in some districts attain an elevation of as much as 7,000 feet above sea-level. The Transvaal is, however, better timbered, and possesses a greater variety of climate and scenery.

The capabilities of the colony are great and varied. It already supplies large quantities of grain to neighbouring territories, and breeds cattle, horses, and sheep in considerable numbers. Gold has been discovered in paying quantities in several districts, both in quartz-reefs and alluvial deposits; and the country also produces silver, copper, lead, tin, iron, cobalt, coal, sulphur, and saltpetre. Coffee and sugar are grown in the warmer and more sheltered districts.

The principal towns are *Potchefstroom*, situated only a few miles north of the Vaal river, and *Pretoria*, which is considerably farther north. The latter is the seat of the local government. Neither of the towns is at present of any importance as to size, but Potchefstroom is said to be pleasantly situated and of picturesque appearance.

The Transvaal is most easily reached by way of Natal; but the difficulty of transit, to say nothing of recent troubles, renders it scarcely a suitable place of resort for those in delicate health.

CLIMATE AND HEALTH RESORTS.—It must not be imagined that any one visiting South Africa for the sake of its climate has only to land at one of the ports in order to enjoy its full benefits. This is very far from being the case; and indeed the invalid in search of a health resort should be as careful in his selection of a locality, even for a temporary residence, as he would be under similar circumstances in England. He must, in fact, bear in mind that there is a greater difference in the climate of the various parts of Cape Colony alone, than there is between the health resorts of the south of England and the Hebrides or the Orkney Islands.

In the first instance the invalid cannot do better than land at Cape Town, and take up his quarters there until he has decided upon his future plans—especially if he should arrive in the colony at the commencement of the summer, as will be the case if he has left England in the autumn. Here he will be able to obtain good accommodation and most of the luxuries and conveniences of civilization, as well as the best medical advice in the colony. The climate, although not perfection, is still a good one, and will seldom fail to be of benefit to those suffering from pulmonary complaints.

The future movements of the invalid must be guided by several considerations, viz.:—

1. As to the kind of climate that from his own experience and in the opinion of his medical advisers is most likely to suit his particular case.

2. Whether his state of health is such as to enable him to bear the fatigue and discomforts of a long inland journey, with perhaps very indifferent accommodation when he arrives at his destination.

3. As to the season of the year that is before him.

4. The length of time he intends to remain in the colony.

If his case is one that is most likely to be benefited by a warm, equable, marine climate of moderate humidity—if his state of health is such as to render a long journey and the discomforts of travelling unadvisable—if his stay in the colony is to be short—and especially if he has the summer season before him, he cannot do better than remain in the neighbourhood of Cape Town during the whole of his stay, as there is probably no other climate along the coast, or in the more accessible portions of the country adjacent to it, that is preferable, and certainly no other place where so many comforts are to be obtained.

If, on the other hand, his case is one for which the dry, keen air of the elevated inland districts is most suited—if his constitution is still sufficiently sound to bear the fatigues of travel, and to put up with a good deal of rough accommodation—and if there is plenty of time at his disposal, he may with much advantage visit some of those localities beyond the inland mountain ranges which have been specially recommended for invalids.

Leaving for the present the description of these high plains of the interior, I will now endeavour to give a slight sketch of the climate of the coast regions, with special reference to Cape Town and its neighbourhood.

The district surrounding the base of Table Mountain, and occupying the peninsula lying between Table Bay and Simon's Bay, possesses a climate which is essentially of a marine character. Like most other coast climates, though tolerably equable, it is somewhat humid, the winds from the sea being more or less loaded with moisture. The seasons are of course the reverse of our own—the hottest weather occurring towards the end of January, the coldest about the middle of July. The *winter* is the rainy season in all the coast districts of the colony; whereas in the inland districts, as will be seen farther on, it is the *summer* that is the rainy season. In winter Cape Town and its neighbourhood is damp; it is therefore not so desirable a residence for invalids in winter as in summer. Owing to the reflexion of the heat from the enclosing sides of Table Mountain, Cape Town itself is sometimes unpleasantly hot in summer; but this objection does not apply to some of its suburbs, such as Constantia and Wynberg, which, being situated on the other side of the spur of the mountain, and being moreover well wooded, are pleasant summer resorts.

Cape Town is visited from time to time by violent winds from the south-east, which have received the name of the "Cape Town doctor," because by them the streets are cleansed from any noxious effluvia that might be the cause of disease. It is to these winds that the immunity of the town from most epidemics is believed to be largely due, especially as the arrangements as to drainage and water supply are by no means perfect. But however advantageous these winds may be in a sanitary point of view, they are by no means well suited to invalids who are suffering from pulmonary complaints. Not only do they blow with extreme violence, but they carry with them clouds of dust, which may prove very irritating to the bronchial mucous membrane. Delicate persons should therefore as much as possible avoid going out in these winds; and it may even be necessary for them to remain in the house for days together during their continuance. The suburbs of Cape Town are in a great measure sheltered from these winds; and in this respect, as well as from their greater coolness, they will prove a much more desirable summer residence for invalids than the town itself. In the winter season, however, these places, owing to the number of trees by which they are surrounded, are even more damp than Cape Town itself. In all the coast districts the time of sunset is said, on account of its dampness, to be trying to invalids, who should therefore avoid being out of doors at that hour.

In South Africa the spring months—viz., September, October, and November—are the pleasantest for Europeans; the heat is not then oppressive, vegetation is at its freshest, and the profusion of wild flowers will be a constant source of pleasure to those who take an interest in such things.

Those who find the climate of Cape Town and its neighbourhood unsuited to their constitution, or who, having spent the summer there, wish to avoid the winter rains, cannot do better than turn their attention to the high-lying districts in the north-eastern portions of Cape Colony, or the high plains of the Orange River Free State. All these districts are best reached by way of Port Elizabeth, to which port steamers belonging to the Union Company and to Messrs. Donald, Currie, and Co. run several times each month. The passage usually occupies two or three days, and is sometimes rather rough and unpleasant; the landing, too, in Algoa Bay is occasionally somewhat difficult, but not sufficiently so to prevent even invalids, unless very ill indeed, from undertaking the voyage.

Port Elizabeth, as has been previously mentioned, is one of the worst places for invalids to be found along the coast. It will be advisable, therefore, to push on at the earliest opportunity to *Grahamstown*, a distance of about eighty-five miles. The journey thither can be made by coach in one day, and good accommodation is to be had there.* The climate of Grahamstown, although

* The greater part, if not the whole, of the journey can now, I believe, be accomplished by railway.

somewhat humid, and partaking to a certain extent of the characteristics of the coast regions, is, on the whole, a pleasant one. The town is situated on a plain about 1,700 feet above sea-level. The distance from the coast in a direct line is only about twenty-five miles; the new harbour in course of construction at Port Alfred being only about twenty-eight miles distant. The town contains some 8,000 inhabitants; and besides churches possesses banks, military barracks, and other public buildings. It is the seat of an English bishopric, and there are forty-eight clergymen in the district. Good waggon-roads connect Grahamstown with various other places, and render it a good point of departure for the interior. The principal hotels are "Wood's," the "Masonic," and Belman's "Commercial." There are also private boarding-houses.

After a good rest at Grahamstown, the invalid cannot do better than proceed to *Cradock*, 115 miles farther towards the interior. During the latter part of the journey the Great Winterberg range of mountains will have been crossed, and the traveller will now find himself upon an inland plateau possessing an elevation of some 3,000 feet above sea-level. The town of Cradock is situated upon the Great Fish River, and has a population of about 2,000. Very fair accommodation is to be obtained there, and the climate of the district is probably one of the best for pulmonary complaints to be found in the whole of South Africa. The invalid may therefore safely take up his quarters there for as long as he feels inclined to do so; and should he not care to encounter the fatigues of further travel, he may with advantage remain there during the whole winter.

If, however, he should wish to go farther into the interior, he may push on to *Colesbery* (a town of 1,400 inhabitants), situated some 230 miles north of Cradock.

From thence he can travel by easy stages to *Bloemfontein*, the capital of the Orange Free State (see p. 290), and one of the most celebrated of the South African health resorts.

It must, however, be borne in mind that, as a general rule, the farther the invalid recedes from the coast the more difficult he will find it to obtain good accommodation and those comforts and luxuries that are required in illness.

The conveyances that are available for passenger traffic between the coast and the interior are of several kinds.

The railway, which is eventually to connect Port Elizabeth with Cradock, and by a branch with Grahamstown, is still unfinished, but about seventy-six miles are already open for traffic. Portions of the line to Graaff Reynet are also completed.

Passenger carts run daily between Grahamstown and Alicedale, the nearest station on the main line.

Cobb and Co.'s coaches leave Port Elizabeth twice a week for the diamond fields, passing through Grahamstown and Cradock, and are comfortable conveyances.

Passenger carts occasionally run between Port Elizabeth, Grahamstown, and Cradock.

The mail carts also take passengers under certain circumstances. This is the quickest mode of conveyance, but should only be adopted by those in robust health, as the wear and tear of travelling continuously for long distances, without proper time being allowed for rest and refreshment, is very great.

Those who, contemplating a long journey into the interior, prefer to travel by their own private conveyance, will have two courses open to them. They can either follow the example of Mr. Anthony Trollope during his journey through the South African colonies, and purchase a Cape cart and a team of horses, selling them for as much as they will fetch at the end of the journey; or they can adopt the patriarchal Dutch plan of travelling by bullock waggon. The latter method, though very tedious, is said to be exceedingly pleasant, and is well adapted for large parties with much baggage. The huge covered waggon serves for travelling by day, and provides sleeping accommodation, if necessary, at night, while preserved provisions and any other comforts that may be required during the journey can be carried in any quantity. It need scarcely be mentioned that the two latter modes of travelling are expensive, and are only suited to those with ample means.

The Orange Free State can be reached not only from Port Elizabeth, but also from Cape Town, by the coaches that run to the diamond fields, from whence the rest of the journey can be made by mail cart; but this route is so fatiguing as to be quite unsuited for an invalid.

As regards the *climate* of the elevated plains of the interior, unfortunately few trustworthy and systematic records are to be obtained relating to the principal health resorts. A few facts, however, seem to be well established. One of these is the extreme *dryness* of the air in these districts. At Graaff Reynet, for instance, the mean annual percentage of humidity is only 55·98, whereas at Cape Town it is 72·00. During the winter, little, if any, rain falls, and the air is light, keen, bracing, and invigorating. The nights are cold, but in the middle of the day the sun is often extremely powerful. The daily range of temperature is very considerable; but, owing to the great dryness of the air, this does not seem to act prejudicially upon consumptive patients; on the contrary, in all parts of the colonies testimony is forthcoming as to the wonderfully restorative effects of the climate of these districts in cases of pulmonary disease that had previously been considered hopeless. In summer, these regions are visited by thunderstorms of great violence, often accompanied by deluges of rain. These storms refresh the air, and render it cool and pleasant for a time, but in the intervals the heat is sometimes intense. All these districts are subject to long-continued droughts, which are very destructive to vegetation. On the whole, the high-lying plains of the interior are not so desirable for a summer as for a winter residence for invalids, although, all the year round, they appear fairly suitable to most constitutions.

The following table will show at a glance the great differences which exist between the climate of Cape Town and that of Graaff Reynet, the only high-lying station at which anything like regular meteorological observations appear to have been taken.

Abstract of Mean Annual Results from the Meteorological Stations at the Royal Observatory, near Cape Town, and at Graaff Reynet, in the Sneeuwbergen Mountains.*

Meteorological Observations.	Royal Observatory.	Graaff Reynet.
Mean height of barometer (corrected)	Deg. 30·031	Deg. 27·508
Mean annual temperature	62·38	64·41
Mean daily range	14·11	24·52
Highest recorded temperature	99·5	105·0
Lowest „ „	39·8	28·0
Mean annual humidity (9 a.m., 1 and 5 p.m.)	Per cent. 72·00	Per cent. 55·98
Mean annual rainfall	Inches. 22·476	Inches. 13·196
Mean annual number of thunderstorms	15	23
Height of the stations above sea-level	Feet. 37	Feet. 2,517

* From the Appendix to the "Colonization Circular" for 1877.

By the above table the following facts are brought into prominence: viz., that while the mean annual temperature of Graaff Reynet is only about two degrees higher than that of Cape Town, the mean daily range is nearly ten degrees greater; that the mean annual humidity of Graaff Reynet is rather more than 16 per cent. less than at Cape Town; and that the rainfall at the latter place is some 9¼ inches more than at the former.

It now only remains to add a few general remarks as to the influence of the climate of South Africa on disease. Unfortunately the statistics bearing on this subject are very imperfect, but the following are a few of the facts that appear to have been established. Asiatic cholera, yellow fever, and hydrophobia are unknown in the colony; the liver diseases of tropical climates are rare; small-pox, measles, and scarlatina occur occasionally in an epidemic form, but not so frequently as in England; typhoid fever occurs from time to time, but is probably not so prevalent as in Europe; while dysentery and diarrhœa are rather more frequent, as are also some nervous disorders, such as neuralgia. But it is as regards lung diseases that the climate of South Africa compares most favourably with that of Europe. In the tables, compiled by Major Tulloch, from observations extending over twelve years, it is shown that only 82 per 1,000 of white troops stationed on the Cape frontier were attacked by lung disease, as compared with 148 per 1,000 of the troops stationed in the United Kingdom. The deaths from the same class of diseases were at the Cape only 2·4 per 1,000, whereas in the United Kingdom they were 7·7 per 1,000.

There can, in fact, be little doubt that upon lung diseases of every kind, including phthisis in all its stages, the various climates of the Cape, when selected with judgment, are capable of exerting a most beneficial and in many cases a curative effect, and it is to be regretted that the advantages of the colony in this respect have not been more freely tested by invalids from this country.

The climates of Natal and the Transvaal have not been specially alluded to in the foregoing short account of the health resorts of South Africa, because that of Natal would not seem to possess any special characteristics that would render it a particularly desirable residence for invalids (the coast districts being less favourable to the health of Europeans than those in the neighbourhood of Cape Town, and the elevated inland plateaux being considerably more humid than those of Cape Colony), while the climate of the Transvaal is very similar to that of the more accessible Orange Free State; and most of the particulars given as to the climate of the latter will apply equally well to that of the former.

Although the disturbing influences of the unhappy wars which have so thoroughly unsettled the South African colonies during the past few years, may perhaps have caused some interruption in the arrangements as to conveyances, etc., that have been mentioned above, and have rendered the resources of the country, for the time, less available for invalids, yet there can be little doubt that any such derangement is only temporary. Now that we may venture to look forward to more peaceful times, not only will any interrupted lines of communication be speedily re-opened, but, owing to the public attention drawn to this part of our colonial possessions, a fresh impetus will in all probability be given to the construction of railways and the provision of other means of inland conveyance, while there is also every reason to expect that the tide of emigration will set more strongly towards our South African colonies than it has done for some time past.

The following books give much valuable information

with regard to the Cape, and may be consulted with advantage by any of my readers who wish for a more detailed description of any of the colonies: Silver's "Handbook for South Africa," the Government "Colonization Circular," Trollope's "South Africa," and "A Year's Housekeeping in South Africa," by Lady Barker.

CHAPTER XIV.

THE METEOROLOGY OF THE OCEAN.

Instruments required for taking observations—Barometer—Thermometer—Thermometer screen—Hygrometer—Method of determining the humidity of the air—Observations of shade temperature—Surface temperature of the sea—The meteorological journal—Estimation of the amount of cloud—Direction and force of the wind—Observations of rainfall not reliable—Special meteorological conditions at sea—Distribution of storms—Log and meteorological tables of a voyage to Australia—Log, meteorological tables, and weather report of homeward voyage by Cape of Good Hope.

THOSE who feel inclined to study the meteorology of the ocean on their own account will find the subject one of great interest.

The instruments required will be a barometer and a good thermometer, or preferably a pair of dry and wet-bulb thermometers, with a small louvre-boarded screen in which to mount them, also a second thermometer for taking the surface temperature of the sea. A rain-gauge mounted on gymbals may be added if desired; and a meteorological journal should be provided, in which to enter the observations taken.

The barometer may be an aneroid, as this is not only the least expensive and most portable form of instrument, but also the easiest to read. It will give the *relative* changes of atmospheric pressure with the same precision as a more expensive and less handy instrument; but it must be borne in mind that for accurate scientific observations it is necessary that an aneroid should be frequently compared with a standard mercurial barometer, and corrected by it. The aneroid should be secured to one of the bulkheads (*i.e.* partitions) of the cabin, in such a way that it will not swing independently of the movements of the vessel. It should also be placed in a good light, and at a convenient height for reading. The best aneroids, compensated for temperature, cost five guineas each; but a sufficiently good one for ordinary purposes may be obtained for from two to three pounds.

The thermometer should be a mercurial one, as it is more sensitive and less likely to get out of order than a spirit thermometer. A standard mercurial thermometer, with a Kew certificate, costs about £1; but a sufficiently good one may be obtained for about ten shillings.

The thermometer should be suspended in a small wooden screen, to which the external air is freely admitted by means of a louvre-boarded front and sides. The screen may be obtained to order through a meteorological instrument maker, or can be made by any intelligent carpenter at the cost of a few shillings. The front, which should be made to open on hinges, in order to allow the readings to be taken, may be secured by a brass lock and key. The back of the screen should be provided with cross slips of wood, for the purpose of keeping it separated from the surface against which it is fixed. The dimensions of the screen should be such as to freely accommodate the thermometer or thermometers it is intended to employ.

The selection of the position in which the thermometer screen is to be placed is of considerable importance, and on board a ship is often a matter of some difficulty; but the courtesy of the captain and officers will generally afford facilities to those who wish to make scientific observations. The screen should be in the open air, and secured to some part of the vessel where it will be, if possible, always in shade. It should be at a height of from four to five feet above the deck. In the case of a steamer, care must be taken that the thermometers are not influenced by the heat from the engine-room or funnel. The fore part of the vessel in a steamer will generally be found to be the most suitable position.

In order to determine the humidity of the air, it is necessary, instead of a single thermometer, to employ the arrangement known as a Mason's hygrometer, the cost of which will be from about £1 to £2. This instrument consists merely of a pair of ordinary thermometers, reading exactly alike, and fixed vertically on a wooden back, a few inches apart. The left-hand thermometer gives the temperature of the air in the shade, and is known as the "dry-bulb" thermometer. The right-hand thermometer is called the "wet-bulb" thermometer, because its bulb is intended to be kept in a constantly moist state. This is effected by means of a covering of muslin and a wick conveying water to it from a little bottle that is supplied with the instrument. The wet-bulb thermometer gives the temperature of an evaporating surface. In order to place the covering on the thermometer bulb, take a small piece of perfectly clean muslin about an inch square, and after dipping it in distilled water (or clean rain-water), wrap it closely round the bulb in such a way as to completely cover it; then secure it with a piece of cotton tied round the stem of the thermometer, just above the bulb. The covering is now complete. Next take four threads of coarse crochet or darning-cotton, each about ten or twelve inches in length, dip them in distilled water, place them side by side, and then double them. There will now be a loop at one extremity and eight ends at the other. Pass the eight ends through the loop, and place the noose thus formed round the stem of the thermometer, just above the bulb, where the single thread confining the muslin had previously been tied. It now only remains to fill the little bottle with distilled water—rain-water, if perfectly clean, will answer—and to place all the eight ends of the wick in it in such a way as to absorb the water and distribute it over the muslin covering of the bulb. Although this is a long description, the process itself will be found very simple.

In order to obtain satisfactory results, the following hints should be borne in mind:—1. The bottle should be kept constantly supplied with water; 2. In putting on a new covering, the hands should be perfectly clean; 3. The covering should be renewed as often as it becomes discoloured; 4. The noose of the wick must not be drawn too tightly round the stem of the thermometer, or the passage of the water through it will be checked.

The humidity of the air is determined by the difference between the readings of the dry and wet-bulb thermometers. When the air is dry, evaporation goes on briskly from the wet surface of the muslin covering the wet-bulb thermometer; and this, by a well-known physical law, reduces the temperature of the mercury contained in the bulb. When, on the other hand, the air is saturated with moisture, evaporation is altogether checked, and the two thermometers will indicate the same temperature.

A table will be found in the appendix, showing the relative humidity of the air for each 2° of temperature from 40° to 86°, and for every half-degree of difference between the readings of the dry and wet bulb thermometers up to 10°. To use this table, first find the nearest degree in the extreme right or left-hand columns corresponding to the dry-bulb temperature, then run the eye along that line until it reaches the column of the nearest half-degree of difference between the readings of the dry and wet-bulb thermometers, and the value there found will be the relative humidity. Example: suppose the readings to be, dry bulb 52°, wet bulb 47½°, the difference between these is 4½°. On the line of 52°, and under the difference of 4½°, we find 72, which is the relative humidity required. In the scale of relative humidity, complete saturation of the air is represented by 100.

As a rough guide for determining the amount of moisture in the air *at sea*, it may be stated that a difference of less than two degrees between the dry and wet-bulb readings at noon indicates unusual humidity; when the two thermometers read alike, the atmosphere is completely saturated with vapour; when the difference amounts to three or four degrees, it may be considered about the average; when the difference is five degrees, it shows that the air is dry; and when it reaches six degrees or more, it may be regarded as unusually dry.

In taking an observation of the shade temperature by the dry-bulb thermometer, it should be carefully noticed that the bulb is bright and undimmed by any deposition of spray or mist. Should there be any appearance of moisture, the bulb should be carefully wiped with a soft handkerchief, and the reading taken in a quarter of an hour or twenty minutes from that time. If in very hot weather the sun should be found to be shining on the screen, and the thermometer be thought to be unduly influenced by it, or if for any other reason a doubt should exist as to the correctness of the reading indicated, it would be better in such cases to rely upon the surface temperature of the sea, and take this as representing the approximate air temperature. Or a still closer approximation to the true air temperature may be obtained by applying a correction to the surface temperature reading for the difference found to exist between the sea and air temperatures, when reliable observations of the latter were last made.

The temperature of the surface of the sea may be taken by simply baling up a little water by means of a small bucket, which may be easily extemporised from any tin capable of holding a pint or two of fluid. A good mercurial thermometer should be plunged in the water immediately after it is drawn up, and held in it for fully one minute, when the temperature should be carefully noted. A bucket made of canvas is very convenient, as it possesses the advantage of portability when travelling.

The meteorological journal should be ruled in columns for the reception of the observations taken each day. The first column should contain the date, the second and third the latitude and longitude, the fourth the barometer; the fifth the surface temperature of the sea, the sixth and seventh the dry and wet-bulb temperatures, the eighth the relative humidity (which may be ascertained from the table of relative humidity which will be found in the appendix, and entered at any time afterwards), the ninth for the amount of cloud, the tenth and eleventh for the direction and force of the wind, and the remaining space for a short description of the weather prevailing at the time of observation. On an adjoining page may be entered a description of the weather of the previous twenty-four hours, with notes of any special phenomena that may have been noticed during the day.

All the observations should be taken each day at the same hour or hours, and at once entered in the journal. In ordinary weather one observation taken at noon will be quite sufficient, but during the prevalence of unusual weather more frequent observations will be of advantage; and an entry each evening, giving a brief description of the weather that has prevailed during the day, will greatly increase the value and interest of the journal.

In estimating at any time the amount of cloud, the whole of the visible heavens is to be taken into consideration. If the sky be cloudless, the amount of cloud should be entered as 0; if two-tenths be covered, it should be entered as 2; if half be covered, as 5; and so on, total obscuration of the sky by cloud being represented by 10.

For the direction and force of the wind a passenger cannot do better than consult one of the officers on duty at the time, as considerable experience is required accurately to determine either of these points. The direction of the wind should be according to the true, not the apparent, or magnetic, meridian. The force is estimated according to the "Beaufort scale," which ranges from 0, representing a dead calm, to 12, which is the most violent hurricane that can blow. In the appendix is a table giving this scale, with its equivalents in miles per hour.

It will be noticed that in the form recommended for the meteorological journal no column has been set apart for the record of the daily rainfall. It has been omitted because it is so difficult to obtain a good position in which to place the rain-gauge; added to which the movements of the ship, the draughts from the sails and various other causes are so likely to prove sources of error, that the observations cannot be regarded as reliable, and are therefore scarcely worth the trouble they involve. At the same time an interesting field of inquiry is open to those who by their ingenuity could overcome these difficulties.

In the course of a long voyage, however, there will be sure to occur occasions when a rain-gauge mounted on gymbals might be used with advantage; for instance, when the ship is becalmed in the equatorial regions. It may be added that a novel form of marine rain-gauge, the invention of Mr. W. J. Black, which has been found to work well at sea, will be found described in "Nature," vol. vii., p. 202. Notes on the character and duration of the rainfall should always be entered in the journal, in the space devoted to a description of the weather of each day.

On a page at the commencement of the journal should be inserted a short description of the instruments used; their known errors; the names of the makers; their position with respect to surrounding objects; their height above deck, with any other particulars that may be considered to affect their readings.

To any one who has not previously taken meteorological observations, the foregoing directions may appear somewhat complicated and troublesome, but in practice this is not the case, and ten or fifteen minutes each day will be amply sufficient for taking all the observations, and entering them in the journal, while the amusement and interest that will be derived from the study of the weather at sea will go a long way towards relieving the monotony of a long voyage.

The few instruments named may be obtained of any good meteorological instrument maker. Of those in London, Messrs. Negretti and Zambra, of Holborn Viaduct, and Mr. L. Casella, of Holborn Bars, may be named as thoroughly trustworthy.

The following are a few hints which may be found of interest in connection with the various instruments as illustrating some of the special meteorological conditions that prevail at sea.

Barometer.—Several interesting facts as to the variations of barometric pressure will be noticed during a voyage to Australia.

1. In the tropics, and particularly near the equator, the range of the barometer is very slight, extending only to a few tenths, except on very rare occasions, such as the occurrence of a hurricane; whereas in both temperate zones (as in England) the mercury ranges through a space of two inches or more.

2. The "diurnal range" of the barometer, which in the

temperate zones is masked by rapid and constant changes of pressure, is perfectly well marked in the tropics. So regular is the rise and fall of the mercury, that with a little practice it is said to be possible to tell the time by it. The total variation for diurnal range amounts to about one-tenth of an inch, and the fluctuation occurs twice in the twenty-four hours. The first period of maximum pressure is at about 10 a.m., the corresponding minimum being about 4 p.m. The second maximum is at about 10 p.m., and the second minimum about 4 a.m.

3. In the southern hemisphere the behaviour of the barometer with regard to the direction of the wind is exactly the reverse of what it is in the northern hemisphere: *i.e.*, it *rises* for southerly winds, and *falls* for northerly winds.

Admiral Fitzroy's remarks, which are so often printed upon barometers in England, can be rendered applicable to the southern hemisphere simply by substituting north for south throughout. Thus :—

NORTHERN HEMISPHERE.		SOUTHERN HEMISPHERE.	
RISE FOR NORTH N.W., N., N.E., DRY OR LESS WIND.	FALL FOR SOUTH S.E., S., S.W., WET OR MORE WIND.	RISE FOR SOUTH S.E., S., S.W., DRY OR LESS WIND.	FALL FOR NORTH N.W., N., N.E., WET OR MORE WIND.
EXCEPT WET FROM NORTH.	EXCEPT WET FROM NORTH.	EXCEPT WET FROM SOUTH.	EXCEPT WET FROM SOUTH.

4. Another feature worth yof notice is that in the northern hemisphere, when standing with the back to the wind, the barometer will be lower on the left-hand, and higher on the right-hand, and the stronger the force of the wind, the greater will be the difference in atmos-

pheric pressure. The converse of this obtains in the southern hemisphere.

Temperature.—The most noticeable fact with reference to the temperature of the air at sea is its equability.

After passing the Bay of Biscay, and getting well away from land influences, the temperature (which then stands, say, at somewhere about 60° to 65°) steadily and gradually rises as the ship sails southwards, until, near the equator, it attains its maximum of about 84°. It then gradually falls until it reaches its minimum of 40° to 45° in the cold latitudes to the south of the Cape of Good Hope.

By referring to the detailed meteorological observations appended to this chapter, it will be seen how the temperature of the air at sea thus rises by almost insensible gradations day by day as the ship sails southwards from England, and how, after the equator is passed, it again as steadily and gradually falls; presenting none of those sudden and trying variations which we so often experience on land*—variations sometimes amounting to 30° or 35°, or even more, in the twenty-four hours.

Nor is it only from day to day that the changes are so slight; the *daily range* of temperature is also very small. The air at night is but little cooler than it is in the shade during the day, and the thermometer often indicates but a few degrees of difference between the greatest heat during the day and the lowest temperature at night.

Humidity.—The amount of moisture in the air at sea is, as a rule, during the daytime, in excess of that on land in England. But it must be remembered that the humidity of the ocean is altogether different in its character and in its effects upon the constitution to that of inland districts. This is, no doubt, greatly owing to the presence in the atmosphere of saline particles and other constituents only met with at sea, but it is probably also

---

* Of course, in a steamer the alteration of temperature is more rapid.

partly due to the fact that the amount of moisture is very much less variable: the difference between the humidity of the night and day, and also from day to day, being generally inconsiderable. On damp evenings it will be noticed that those parts of the deck that have been wetted with salt water are the first to become moist.

Dew is said to be rarely deposited upon the surface of the ocean itself, but the decks of a ship, and the upper surfaces of other floating objects, are found to be freely covered with it when the conditions are favourable for its deposition. It is deposited most copiously on clear, calm, cloudless nights, when the air is humid, and especially when the temperature of the surface of that portion of the sea over which the ship is passing is considerably lower than the temperature of the air above it.

Rainfall.—As already mentioned, observations of the rainfall at sea are difficult to obtain, and not altogether reliable. It may, however, be stated in general terms, that, except within the limits of the calm-belts, much less rain falls at sea than in most countries situated in the temperate zones, and that less rain falls in the southern than in the northern hemisphere. The number of fine days to be enjoyed at sea will contrast most favourably with the previous experiences of those who have resided in the British Islands.

Storms.—Recent researches have tended to establish the fact that all storms are cyclonic; or, in other words, that they are circular eddies of wind of greater or less diameter.

Most storms possess in common the following characteristics. They rotate much more rapidly near their centre than at their circumference, and have a central space or core, in which a comparative calm prevails. In the northern hemisphere their rotation is N.W.S.E., or in an opposite direction to the hands of a watch; in the southern hemisphere, on the other hand, their rotation is

N.E.S.W., and therefore with watch hands. Besides their rotatory motion, they have also a progressive motion, which may cause them to travel a distance of many hundreds of miles.

The following may be given as a few general indications of the distribution and character of the atmospheric disturbances met with in the regions through which a ship passes on its way to and from Australia:—

1. Strong winds and occasional gales are met with in the northern region of prevailing westerly winds, especially during the winter months.

2. In the calm-belts and in the trade-wind regions gales are seldom experienced; but short squalls of greater or less violence are frequent in the calm-belts, and occur more rarely in the trade-wind regions.

3. In the southern region of prevailing westerly winds boisterous weather, with occasional heavy gales, may again be expected, especially during the winter. Maury, in his "Physical Geography of the Sea," considers that "we may contemplate the whole system of these 'brave west winds' in the light of an everlasting cyclone on a gigantic scale." But he also states that actual storms are less frequent in the southern than in the northern hemisphere.

4. In returning from Australia by the Cape of Good Hope, the ship's course through the South Indian Ocean is some ten or fifteen degrees to the north of the outward track, and lies either within the calm-belt of Capricorn or on the southern border of the south-east trades. This course will bring the vessel, when nearing the Cape, within the district of the Maurtitius hurricanes; and during the first four months of the year it is possible that one or more of these hurricanes may be encountered at this stage of the voyage; but as they are here at some distance from the focus of the district, they are seldom of extreme violence.

As regards the behaviour of the barometer with reference to storms, it may be stated in general terms that the nearer the storm approaches the lower the mercury will fall, and that it will continue to descend until the centre of the storm is reached. As soon, however, as the centre of the storm has passed, the glass will begin to rise; but this first rise is often followed by the most violent part of the gale, making true the proverb—

> "*First* rise after very low
> Indicates a stronger blow."

The weather immediately preceding a storm is usually warm, cloudy, and wet; that following it, cold, bright, and fine.

Appended are two tables of meteorological observations taken on board ship during voyages to and from Australia. The first is extracted from the meteorological log of the ship *Newcastle* (Capt. Chas. Le Poer Trench), and shows the observations taken each day during a voyage from England to Melbourne in the autumn of 1876. It serves admirably to exhibit the gradual and steady increase in temperature that occurs between the English Channel and the equator; and the subsequent equally steady decrease until the southern limits of the passage have been gained. It also illustrates some of the points with reference to the behaviour of the barometer at sea that have been referred to above.

The second series of observations were taken by Edward Mawley, Esq., F.M.S., during a voyage from Melbourne to London by way of the Cape of Good Hope. The short description of the weather that is appended to each day's observations, and the careful summary at the end of the table, as well as the figures themselves, give a very graphic picture of the weather that is to be expected in a voyage of this kind.

TABLE I.

Extract from Meteorological Log of Ship "Newcastle," Capt. CHAS. LE POER TRENCH.

Date (civil time). 1876.	Position. Latitude. N.	Position. Longitude. W.	Wind. Direction. True.	Wind. Force 0—12.	Barometer (corrected and reduced to 32° Fah.) In.	Temperature. Dry bulb Ther. Deg.	Temperature. Wet bulb Ther. Deg.	Remarks.
Oct. 15	49° 5'	5° 20'	S.S.W.	4	29·935	59	55	Off the Lizard Point.
,, 16	49° 10'	7° 25'	S.	7	29·350	58	57½	
,, 17	49° 10'	7° 20'	S.W.	2	29·490	57	54½	
,, 18	49° 10'	7° 20'	W.N.W.	2	29·665	57	53½	
,, 19	46° 55'	10° 40'	N.W.	5	30·005	58	53½	
,, 20	44° 5'	12° 35'	N.W.	4	30·065	58	52½	
,, 21	42° 0'	14° 10'	N.W. by N.	2	30·130	59	54	
,, 22	40° 25'	15° 0'	Calm	0	30·175	64	59	
,, 23	40° 5'	15° 15'	S.S.W.	1	30·060	65	62	
,, 24	38° 30'	17° 10'	S.S.E.	6	29·735	68	64	
,, 25	37° 15'	18° 25'	N.W. by N.	3	29·820	66	60	
,, 26	35° 30'	19° 15'	N.N.E.	2	30·105	68	61	
,, 27	33° 50'	20° 10'	S.E.	4	30·100	71	69	
,, 28	32° 30'	20° 40'	S. by W.	4	29·905	72	71	
,, 29	31° 0'	19° 45'	W.S.W.	4	29·835	72	71	
,, 30	28° 45'	18° 10'	S.S.W.	4	29·905	74	72	Sighted Island of Ferro.
,, 31	27° 55'	18° 35'	W.	5	29·835	74	72	
Nov. 1	25° 5'	17° 55'	W.	4	29·935	74	72	
,, 2	23° 50'	18° 25'	N.N.E.	2	30·005	75	71	

THE METEOROLOGY OF THE OCEAN.

Date	Lat.	Long.	Wind		Bar.			Remarks
Nov. 3	22° 35′	19° 5′	N.E.	3	30·030	78	71	Saw a land-bird.
,, 4	21° 15′	19° 50′	E.N.E.	1	30·020	81	73	
,, 5	20° 15′	20° 5′	N.	2	30·025	75	68	Caught a bat, saw a hawk and a
,, 6	18° 25′	20° 35′	N.N.E.	4	29·990	78	74	dragon-fly.
,, 7	16° 10′	21° 20′	N.E. by N.	1	29·950	82	79	Brilliant meteors.
,, 8	15° 10′	21° 35′	E.N.E.	3	29·980	81	77	Dragon-fly seen.
,, 9	13° 40′	21° 50′	E.	1	29·905	82	74	
,, 10	13° 30′	22° 0′	S.S.E.	1	29·920	84	79	
,, 11	13° 15′	22° 15′	S.E.	1	29·925	83	78	Two waterspouts seen.
,, 12	12° 25′	22° 40′	E.	3	29·920	83	78	
,, 13	11° 0′	22° 55′	E.S.E.	3	29·900	82	79	
,, 14	10° 15′	23° 0′	S.S.W.	1	29·980	78	76	Saw a wild duck much exhausted.
,, 15	8° 15′	23° 10′	E. by N.	3	29·965	85	80	
,, 16	6° 35′	23° 15′	E.S.E.	2	29·875	80	77	Many falling stars.
,, 17	5° 45′	23° 55′	S.E.	2	29·880	81	77	
,, 18	4° 10′	24° 40′	E. by S.	4	29·960	80	77	
,, 19	1° 25′	25° 40′	E.S.E.	5	29·980	79	77	
,, 20	S. 1° 55′	26° 25′	E.S.E.	5	29·955	79	75	Steady trade-winds.
,, 21	5° 30′	26° 40′	E.S.E.	4	29·945	79	75	Very brilliant meteors.
,, 22	8° 10′	27° 15′	S.E. by E.	4	30·025	80	75	Saw a land-bird like a cuckoo.
,, 23	11° 5′	27° 35′	E. by S.	4	30·055	79	75	
,, 24	14° 10′	28° 5′	S. by W.	4	30·050	78	74	Losing the trades.
,, 25	16° 30′	28° 35′	E. by S.	4	30·055	78	71	
,, 26	18° 35′	28° 50′	S.E. by E.	2	30·125	77	75	
,, 27	20° 0′	28° 55′	E.	1	30·125	78	76	Sighted the Island of Trinidad.
,, 28	22° 10′	29° 25′	E.N.E.	3	30·135	77	73	Large numbers of flying-fish.
,, 29	21° 15′	28° 55′	N. by W.	4	30·015	76	73	

* Kindly furnished by the Meteorological Office.

318   THE METEOROLOGY OF THE OCEAN.

TABLE I. (continued).

Date (civil time). 1876.	Position. Latitude. S.	Longitude. W.	Wind. Direction. True.	Force 0—12.	Barometer (corrected and reduced to 32° Fah.)	Temperature. Dry bulb Ther.	Wet bulb Ther.	Remarks.
Nov. 30	26° 40′	27° 5′	N.N.E.	5	In. 29·930	Deg. 73	Deg. 72	
Dec. 1	28° 15′	25° 25′	S.W. by W.	2	30·015	68	61½	Very brilliant meteor.
,, 2	29° 45′	24° 25′	S.W.	3	30·060	65	60½	Several whales.
,, 3	32° 5′	23° 10′	W. by S.	3	30·005	64	60½	
,, 4	34° 5′	22° 20′	N.	6	29·843	64	61	
,, 5	37° 5′	18° 35′	W.S.W.	1	29·950	57	53½	Brilliant meteors.
,, 6	38° 10′	16° 30′	N.E. by N.	1	30·190	59	53½	
,, 7	39° 10′	13° 50′	N.E.	1	30·040	59	56½	
,, 8	40° 40′	9° 50′	N.E. by N.	6	29·865	56	55½	Saw tern and divers.
,, 9	41° 5′	5° 40′	N.N.W.	3	30·070	55	54½	
,, 10	41° 20′	1° 40′	N.	4	30·115	56	55½	
		E.						
,, 11	41° 30′	2° 10′	N.N.W.	4	30·095	55	54½	
,, 12	41° 20′	5° 20′	S.W.	4	30·105	—	—	
,, 13	41° 40′	10° 45′	N.W. by N.	5	29·735	54	54	
,, 14	41° 35′	15° 55′	W.S.W.	5	29·378	52	48½	
,, 15	41° 35′	19° 50′	S. by W.	3	29·655	46	46	
,, 16	41° 45′	23° 30′	N.N.W.	4	30·010	—	—	
,, 17	42° 5′	28° 20′	N.	5	29·785	64	59	
,, 18	42° 15′	32° 30′	W.S.W.	2	29·785	64	51	
,, 19	42° 25′	35° 20′	N.W.	1	29·795	54	53	
,, 20	42° 30′	40° 30′	N.W. by N.	5	29·580	53	53	

THE METEOROLOGY OF THE OCEAN.

Date	Lat	Long	Wind		Barometer			Remarks
Dec. 21	42° 40'	46° 50'	N.	6	29·470	55	54	Quantity of seaweed.
,, 22	42° 40'	50° 50'	N. by E.	2	29·315	48	47	
,, 23	42° 50'	55° 0'	W.	4	29·220	50	48	
,, 24	42° 40'	59° 55'	W.	6	29·530	49	45	
,, 25	42° 40'	64° 55'	N. by E.	6	29·575	52	51	Brilliant meteors.
,, 26	42° 35'	68° 55'	S.W. by W.	4	29·965	56	56	
,, 27	42° 30'	73° 15'	N.W. by N.	5	30·120	58	56	
,, 28	42° 30'	78° 30'	N.W. by W.	5	29·935	56	55	
,, 29	42° 25'	83° 35'	S.W. by W.	5	29·990	51	48	
,, 30	42° 35'	88° 20'	N.W. by N.	6	29·855	55	54	
,, 31	42° 45'	93° 35'	N.W. by N.	6	29·755	54	53	
1877. Jan. 1	42° 50'	98° 45'	W.S.W.	6	29·735	50	48	Much seaweed.
,, 2	42° 30'	104° 0'	W.	7	29·790	53	51	
,, 3	42° 35'	108° 40'	W.S.W.	4	29·685	51	50	
,, 4	42° 30'	113° 0'	W.N.W.	4	29·580	54	52	
,, 5	42° 35'	118° 25'	W. by S.	8	29·215	54	51	
,, 6	42° 55'	124° 10'	W. by N.	4	29·580	52	48	
,, 7	42° 45'	129° 5'	N. by W.	7	29·520	57	55	
,, 8	42° 25'	133° 50'	S.W.	4	30·050	54	50	Water green, land-birds and fish.
,, 9	41° 0'	135° 45'	N.E. by N.	2	29·965	57	52	Brilliant meteor.
,, 10	40° 45'	137° 30'	W.	3	29·635	58	56	
,, 11	39° 25'	141° 20'	W. by S.	5	29·785	62	56	Sighted Cape Otway.

TABLE II.

Meteorological Observations taken on board the "Sobraon" (Capt. J. A. Elmslie, R.N.R.) by E. MAWLEY, Esq., F.M.S., during a voyage from Melbourne to London viâ the Cape of Good Hope.

DATE.	LOG.			METEOROLOGICAL OBSERVATIONS. (Taken each day at noon.)					REMARKS.
	Latitude. S.	Longitude. E.	Distance since previous noon	Barometer (corrected)	Tempera-ture of air in shade.	Relative humidity of air.	Wind. Direction.	Wind. Force 0–12.	
1875.			Miles.	In.	Deg.	%			
Feb. 14	......	......	......	......	......	......	......	......	Land last seen.
,, 15	39° 10'	142° 8'	(a)	29·93	......	......	......	......	
,, 16	39° 6'	139° 53'	126	30·00	......	......	S.	5	Bright, but cool.
,, 17	39° 3'	136° 47'	106	30·06	59·4	......	S. by W.	3	Bright, but cool ; sighted King's Island 10 p.m.
,, 18	39° 14'	135° 50'	145	30·00	60·4	......	E.	2	Bright, but cool.
,, 19	39° 15'	133° 11'	58	29·83	60·6	73	S.E.	2	Moderately bright, but cool.
,, 20	40° 22'	129° 56'	116	29·88	63·4	......	W.	5	Bright, and rather warmer.
,, 21	39° 26'	128° 41'	165	29·61	59·4	76	W.N.W.	7	Moderate gale, max. force of wind 8 p.m.
,, 22	39° 12'	127° 0'	78	29·94	59·7	77	W.	6	Dull, slight showers.
,, 23	39° 13'	126° 9'	79	30·15	57·5	81	S.	1	Dull and cold.
,, 24	38° 22'	123° 38'	40	30·18	59·3	77	E. by N.	2	Dull and cold.
,, 25	37° 33'	119° 18'	129	30·10	59·9	92	E.N.E.	3	Dull, cold, and wet.
,, 26			211	29·87	65·3	86	N.E. by N.	6	Bright and warm, strong breeze, heavy rain, early morning.

THE METEOROLOGY OF THE OCEAN.   321

Date	Lat.	Long.		Bar.			Wind		Remarks
Feb. 27	38° 1′	115° 36′	177	29·93	59·6	94	S.	5	Dull and damp—sea fog—off Cape Leewin.
„ 28	37° 30′	112° 40′	142	29·92	61·7	67	Z.	0	Bright, but cool.
Mar. 1	36° 22′	110° 5′	142	30·01	63·7	78	S.	4	Moderately bright and warm.
„ 2	36° 18′	107° 28′	127	30·16	65·4	61	E.	2	Bright, warm, and calm.
„ 3	36° 30′	105° 44′	84	30·18	62·1	60	S.	2	Dull, warm, and calm.
„ 4	36° 48′	104° 35′	58	30·07	62·0	65	S.W.	1	Dull, warm, and calm.
„ 5	36° 51′	102° 52′	84	30·08	63·2	67	E.	1 to 2	Bright, warm, and calm.
„ 6	37° 0′	101° 4′	86	30·12	63·9	64	S.	2	Bright, warm, and calm.
„ 7	36° 58′	100° 14′	40	30·08	66·4	71	W.N.W.	2	Bright but cool; squally evening.
„ 8	36° 21′	96° 30′	184	30·18	61·1	67	S.S.W.	3	Moderately bright and cool.
„ 9	36° 19′	94° 13′	111	30·18	62·6	68	E.S.E.	4	Moderately bright and cool.
„ 10	36° 16′	91° 44′	121	30·14	66·0	78	N.N.E.	1	Bright and warm, showery about 5 p.m., rain at night.
„ 11	36° 20′	89° 35′	105	30·11	66·5	92	N.E.	3	Dull, showers during evening and at night.
„ 12	36° 32′	84° 5′	227	29·38	66·3	93	N.W. by N.	7	Very heavy rain with gale, early morning—a whole gale between 2 and 4 p.m.
„ 13	35° 31′	84° 2′	75	29·82	64·1	84	W.	5 to 6	Squally.
„ 14	33° 49′	83° 06′	114	30·10	67·2	62	W.S.W.	2	Bright, with slight showers.
„ 15	33° 45′	81° 56′	63	30·20	68·9	60			Bright, calm, and warm.
„ 16	33° 47′	80° 46′	58	30·20	68·5	69	S.E.	1	Bright, calm, and hot.
„ 17	33° 57′	79° 54′	44	30·13	70·2	76	Z.	0	Bright, calm, and hot.
„ 18	34° 6′	79° 5′	42	30·05	70·3	73	W.N.W.	2	Bright and warm.
„ 19	34° 0′	77° 45′	67	30·01	68·5	83	N.	2	Bright and warm.
„ 20	32° 11′	76° 3′	140	30·06	70·1	75	S.W. by S.	3	Bright and warm; small waterspout observed at 7 a.m.
„ 21	31° 30′	74° 58′	68	30·05	72·6	72	N.W.	1	Bright and hot.
„ 22	31° 44′	73° 46′	63	29·96	69·6	85	Light and variable.	0	Squall at 6.30 a.m., then showery, moist, and dull.

TABLE II. (continued).

METEOROLOGICAL OBSERVATIONS.
(Taken each day at noon.)

DATE. 1875.	LOG. Latitude. S.	LOG. Longitude. E.	Distance since previous noon.	Barometer (corrected).	Temperature of air in shade.	Relative humidity of air.	Wind. Direction.	Wind. Force 0–12.	REMARKS.
Mar. 23	31° 0'	71° 12'	Miles. 139	In. 30·06	% 69·5	66	S.S.E.	4	Bright and warm.
„ 24	31° 16'	67° 51'	173	30·18	70·4	60	S.E.	4	Bright and warm.
„ 25	32° 0'	64° 3'	200	30·21	72·1	79	E. by N.	4 to 5	Bright, warm, and sultry.
„ 26	31° 48'	59° 56'	211	30·08	74·2	75	N.N.E.	5	Bright, hot, and sultry.
„ 27	31° 31'	55° 16'	241	29·75	72·6	100	N.E.	2 to 6	Heavy rain 4 a.m. till 2.30 p.m. Blowing a gale after 0.30 p.m., which reached its height about 3 p.m.
„ 28	30° 38'	53° 58'	86	29·82	69·4	73	W.	4	Bright and warm, passing showers.
„ 29	31° 26'	53° 13'	62	29·90	71·2	79	W.	3	Bright and hot, with light wind.
„ 30	32° 25'	52° 55'	62	29·95	73·9	74	N.W.	1	Bright, hot, and calm.
„ 31	32° 36'	50° 37'	118	30·10	65·9	68	S.	6	Bright, with cool wind.
April 1	32° 56'	45° 30'	261	30·18	67·4	64	E.	5	Rather dull, cool dry wind.
„ 2	32° 55'	40° 5'	274	29·78	72·2	86	N.N.E.	6	Bright, with fresh wind, occasional light squalls.
„ 3	33° 5'	36° 42'	171	29·65	72·3	79	N.W.	6	Bright, with fresh wind, squally, thunderstorm, and heavy squall at 1 a.m.; blowing hard all night.
„ 4	32° 37'	35° 32'	65	30·00	68·2	62	S. by W.	5	Bright, with pleasant breeze.

THE METEOROLOGY OF THE OCEAN. 323

Date	Lat.	Long.	Dist.	Bar.	Temp.	Hum.	Wind	Force	Remarks
April 5	32° 40'	33° 46'	90	29·97	67·6	63	N.E.	3	Rather dull, with dry air.
„ 6	32° 56'	29° 56'	194	30·18	67·9	60	S. by W.	5 to 6	Bright, but cool, with fresh, dry wind.
„ 7	33° 47'	27° 16'	143	30·16	67·6	66	E.	......	Bright; Cape Recife 70 miles distant at noon.
„ 8	31° 39'	24° 22'	155	30·03	70·4	74	E.	4	Bright, damp towards evening.
„ 9	35° 9'	20° 56'	172	29·85	64·2	94	N.E.	2	Bright, with damp air; particularly damp during the whole morning.
„ 10	......	......	......	29·88	65·5	94	variable	......	Dull, very damp and calm, frequent showers during afternoon
„ 11	35° 2'	18° 29'	121	29·90	63·5	87	S.W. by W.	3 to 5	Bright, and not quite so damp.
„ 12	......	......	......	......	......	......	......	......	Bright and hot, with dry air. Anchored in Table Bay about 3.30 p.m.
„ 13	......	......	......	......	......	......	......	......	Bright and warm.
„ 14	......	......	......	......	......	......	......	......	Bright and hot.
„ 15	......	......	......	......	60·6	......	......	......	Cloudy and cool.
„ 16	33° 17'	17° 1'	80	30·00	63·2	87	S.W.	......	Bright, cool, light air.
„ 17	32° 20'	14° 56'	121	29·90	63·7	72	S.W.	variable	Moderately bright, with cool, dry wind.
„ 18	30° 57'	13° 13'	121	29·97	67·0	85	N.W.	1	Tolerably bright, warm, and sultry.
„ 19	29° 40'	10° 33'	159	30·08	65·4	68	S. to S.W.	variable	Dull, with dry light wind.
„ 20	27° 59'	7° 3'	210	30·17	67·5	76	S.E.	5	Dull and warm.
„ 21	25° 34'	4° 14'	211	30·06	70·1	78	S.E.	5	Moderately bright, with soft dry air.
„ 22	23° 37'	1° 26'	193	29·98	72·2	71	S.E.	4	Bright and warm; St. Helena at noon N.W.¼N, 600 miles distant. During the morning entered the tropics.

TABLE II. (continued).

METEOROLOGICAL OBSERVATIONS.
(Taken each day at noon.)

DATE. 1875.	LOG. Latitude. S.	LOG. Longitude. W.	Distance since previous noon.	Barometer (corrected)	Temperature of air in shade.	Relative humidity of air.	Wind. Direction.	Wind. Force 0–12.	REMARKS.
April 23	21° 40′	1° 5′	Miles. 183	In. 29·95	Deg. 72·9	% 67	E.S.E.	4	Dull and rather sultry; passing showers.
„ 24	20° 21′	3° 0′	140	29·97	76·6	62	Z.	0	Bright and hot; St. Helena at noon N. 31° W., 294 miles distant.
„ 25	19° 7′	3° 39′	75	29·98	75·1	69	E.	0 to 1	Bright and hot.
„ 26	17° 30′	4° 39′	103	29·98	75·4	74	S.E. by E.	3	Bright and hot.
„ 27	......	......	108	......	......	......	......	......	Bright and hot; all day off St. Helena.
„ 28	14° 54′	7° 2′	100	29·94	77·3	75	S.E.	3 to 4	Bright and hot.
„ 29	13° 12′	8° 35′	136	29·93	78·2	71	S.E.	3	Bright and hot.
„ 30	11° 55′	10° 53′	150	29·94	78·0	63	S.E.	......	Bright and hot; very dry air; rain at night.
May 1	10° 14′	12° 44′	149	29·94	76·8	79	S.E.	3 to 4	Hot, rather dull and showery; Ascension Island N. 63° W., 170 miles.
„ 2	8° 31′	14° 42′	157	29·90	80·7	67	E.S.E.	3 to 4	Bright and hot, with dry air; Ascension Island in sight at sunrise, at noon N. 26° E., 38 miles.
„ 3	6° 29′	16° 8′	155	29·87	81·5	64	S.E. by E.	3	Bright and hot.

THE METEOROLOGY OF THE OCEAN.

Date	Lat.	Long.			Temp.	Wind	Force	Remarks
May 4	4° 31′	17° 18′	132	29·88	83·5 / 72	S.E. by S.	3 to 4	Bright and very hot.
" 5	2° 33′	18° 46′	148	29·86	82·6 / 76	E.S.E.	4	Bright and very hot; heavy tropical rain between 3 and 4 a.m.
" 6	1° 0′	20° 2′	120	29·82	81·5 / 81	S.E. by E.	2	Moderately bright and hot; heavy tropical shower about 3 a.m. and again at 11 p.m.
" 7	N. 0° 7′	20° 59′	94	29·82	85·0 / 72	N.E.	1 to 2	Bright and very hot indeed; heavy tropical shower 10 p.m.; lightning; crossed the line this morning.
" 8	0° 56′	20° 54′	55	29·87	78·5 / 89	S.	2	Moderately bright and hot; a heavy thunderstorm at 4 a.m.; vivid lightning.
" 9	2° 52′	21° 24′	116	29·86	80·7 / 88	N.E.	light airs	Dull, very close and rainy; about 1.30 p.m. a heavy storm came up astern; lost the S.E. trades.
" 10	3° 14′	22° 11′	53	29·83	82·5 / 76	N.E.	1	Bright and very calm and hot.
" 11	3° 47′	22° 15′	33	29·87	81·5 / 82	W.S.W.	light airs	Dull, hot, and sultry.
" 12	5° 2′	22° 15′	83	29·76	74·6 / 95	W.	5	Dull, sultry, very heavy rain from 11.30 p.m. yesterday; rain fell in torrents all last night and throughout the day.
" 13	6° 17′	23° 46′	94	29·84	79·5 / 78	N.E. by N.	4	Bright and hot; caught the N.E. trades.
" 14	7° 51′	26° 6′	168	29·87	78·3 / 78	N.E. by N.	5	Bright and warm.
" 15	10° 13′	28° 26′	199	29·90	77·3 / 73	N.E. by N.	4	Bright and warm.
" 16	12° 42′	30° 26′	189	29·83	75·1 / 74	N.E. by N.	4	Bright, with cool wind.
" 17	15° 40′	32° 33′	217	29·88	73·5 / 77	N.E.	4	Bright, with cool wind.
" 18	18° 30′	33° 57′	190	29·97	74·9 / 77	N.E.	3 to 4	Bright, with cool wind.

TABLE II. (continued).

METEOROLOGICAL OBSERVATIONS.
(Taken each day at noon.)

DATE.	LOG.				Barometer (corrected)	Temperature of air in shade.	Relative humidity of air.	Wind.		REMARKS.
1875.	Latitude. N.	Longitude. W.	Distance since previous noon.					Direction.	Force 0—12.	
					In.	Deg.	%			
May 19	21° 49'	34° 52'	Miles. 201		30·09	73·5	83	E.	3	Dull, warm, and sultry.
,, 20	23° 45'	35° 9'	117		30·10	75·4	79	E.	3	Bright, warm, rather sultry; lost the N.E. trades.
,, 21	24° 34'	35° 4'	50		30·12	4·5	79	E.	light airs	Dull, warm, and sultry.
,, 22	25° 39'	34° 42'	68		30·11	75·2	79	S.S.W.	1	Bright and hot.
,, 23	26° 44'	34° 13'	70		30·07	75·7	77	Z.	0	Bright and hot; dead calm; passing showers.
,, 24	27° 31'	33° 58'	40		30·02	74·3	73	Z.	0	Bright and hot; passing showers.
,, 25	28° 42'	33° 46'	72		30·00	73·6	78	W.	1	Bright, hot, and sultry.
,, 26	29° 11'	33° 23'	35		30·03	73·6	77	N.W.	1	Bright, hot, and rather sultry.
,, 27	30° 18'	32° 40'	77		30·00	71·4	80	W.	1	Bright, cool wind.
,, 28	32° 14'	30° 51'	149		29·99	71·1	78	W.N.W.	3	Bright, cool, fresh wind.
,, 29	34° 57'	27° 19'	242		29·94	67·6	72	N.N.W.	5	Bright, with cool fresh breeze; St. Mary's N. 42° E. 150 miles. The Lizard N.E. 1,350 miles.
,, 30	31° 33'	23° 23'	195		30·10	67·2	77	N.E. by N.	5	Bright, with strong cool breeze.
,, 31	34° 9'	20° 23'	150		29·98	65·5	67	N.E. by N.	3	Bright, cool wind.
June 1	34° 48'	21° 25'	64		30·08	68·7	62	Z.	0	Bright and warm; dead calm.
,, 2	36° 14'	21° 14'	87		30·08	68·5	83	S.W.	4	Bright; steady rain after 3 p.m.

THE METEOROLOGY OF THE OCEAN.   327

June 3	37° 3′	19° 14′	100	30·18	65·5	83	N. by E.	......	Bright, with cool, light airs. Lizard N.E. ½ N. 1000 miles at noon.
,, 4	37° 19′	18° 52′	21	30·20	68·3	78	S.E.	1	Bright, warm, and calm.
,, 5	38° 12′	18° 22′	58	30·10	68·7	84	W.S.W.	1	Bright, hot, an l calm.
,, 6	39° 4′	17° 32′	65	30·13	67·6	85	S.	light airs	Bright, warm, and calm.
,, 7	39° 52′	16° 48′	54	30·16	68·6	81	S.E.	light airs	Bright, warm, and calm.
,, 8	40° 56′	15° 50′	78	30·18	64·5	87	N.W. by N.	5	Bright, strong cool breeze.
,, 9	41° 26′	12° 22′	261	29·94	60·5	80	W.	5	Dull and cool; showery.
,, 10	46° 38′	9° 40′	175	29·70	57·9	97	S.W.	6 to 7	Dull; strong cool breeze; Start Pt. N. 49° E. 352 miles; Ushant N. 59° E. 220 miles.
,, 11	49° 22′	4° 55′	254	29·72	56·9	75	......	......	Moderately bright; strong cold breeze; showery. Start Pt. N.E. 70 miles at noon; sighted 6.30 p.m.
,, 12	......	......	......	......	......	......	......	......	Dull; strong cold breeze; showery evening. Anchored off Margate 4.30 p.m.
,, 13	......	......	......	......	......	......	......	......	Dull, cold, and showery. Off Gravesend at 10 a.m.; reached S.W. India Docks 8.30 p.m.

TABLE II. (continued).

Summary of Meteorological Observations.

	In.
Barometer (corrected for temperature) at noon—Mean	29·99
Highest (25th March)	30·21
Lowest (12th March)	29·38
Range	·83

	Deg.
Temperature of the air in shade at noon—Mean	69·5
Highest (7th May. Lat. 0° 7' N., Long. 20° 59' W.)	85·0

N.B.—This was the highest temperature at *any time* during the voyage.

Lowest (11th June, in English Channel)	56·9
Range	28·1

	%
Relative amount of humidity in the air at noon (100 representing complete saturation)—Mean	76

(On only one day—27th March—was the air completely saturated.)

Least amount of relative humidity (3rd and 15th and 24th March, and 6th of April)	60

(At no time during the voyage did the wet-bulb of the Hygrometer read more than 8 degrees lower than the dry-bulb.)

Wind.—The *Direction of the Wind* indicated in the foregoing tables is its *true* bearing at noon.

The Force of the Wind at noon (estimated according to the Beaufort scale, in which 12 represents a hurricane, and 0 a calm)—Mean	3
Greatest (at 3.30 p.m. 12th March, during a gale)	10

During the voyage three gales were encountered; (1) A moderate gale on 21st February; (2) A whole gale on 12th March; (3) A strong gale on 27th March. The sea during this last gale was unusually turbulent, rising in irregular heaps all round the ship. Several heavy squalls were met with after this date, but none worthy the name of a gale.

On twenty-eight days during the voyage, either calms or light airs prevailed at noon.

Surface Temperature of the Sea.—During the voyage the surface temperature of the sea was found but seldom to differ more than 1 or 2 degrees from the temperature of the air in shade. On one day, however (6th April), while in the Agulhas current, it was observed to be $6°·7$ higher than the shade temperature of the air. Between noon and 4 p.m. on the day following the surface temperature fell from $71°·7$ to $61°·7$, or $10°$ in four hours.

Remarks.—During the voyage seventy-eight days were recorded as bright, thirty as dull or cloudy, and ten as moderately bright.

Rainfall.—No rainfall measurements were taken during the voyage. On reference, however, to the daily register, it appears that during the *day-time* unusually heavy rain fell on two days; either heavy or steady rain on eight days; that ten days were showery; and that on six other days there were light showers —leaving *ninety-two days which were quite fine.*

Fog.—On the 27th February a rather dense sea fog prevailed during the greater part of the day; but on no other day was it at all foggy.

CONCLUSION.

THE HEALTH-VOYAGE OF THE FUTURE.

IN the hope that shipowners may eventually see their way to carrying out some of the suggestions that are from time to time made by medical men and others, with a view to extending the usefulness of sea-voyages for the purposes of recreation and health, I will venture briefly to sketch out my own ideas as to what a health-voyage should be, both as regards the ship in which it is to be made, and the route to be chosen.

For the present I will not consider the question in its commercial aspect, but will revert to that point before closing these remarks.

First, then, as to the ship itself. It should, I think, be either a wooden or a composite vessel. Ships built of iron have several drawbacks of a nature to be specially felt by invalids. Owing to the readiness with which changes of temperature are conveyed by metal, iron vessels are hotter in warm weather, and colder in cold weather, than ships with wooden sides. They are also less dry, because, whenever the sides of the vessel are cooled down by a decrease in the outside temperature, moisture condenses on their inner surface. It is possible also, as suggested by Dr. Faber, that nervous patients are affected by the magnetic currents that doubtless exist in large masses of iron.

The question as to whether the health ship of the future should be a simple sailing vessel, or should receive some assistance from steam, is a difficult one. There is no doubt in my own mind that under any circumstances such a ship should *primarily* be built and rigged as a sailing vessel; but, provided it could be done *without in any way affecting the size of the cabins*, the addition of engines of moderate power would be an undoubted advantage. Steam should, however, only be employed when absolutely required—in the equatorial calms, for instance, or when a succession of light or contrary winds are likely to render the voyage long and tedious. Steam would also be exceedingly useful when going into or out of port.

As regards size, I think the ship, if a sailing vessel, should have a registered tonnage of about 2,000; if provided with engines, she might be somewhat larger, say 2,500 or 3,000 tons.

The cargo of a ship intended for the use of health-seekers should be selected with the greatest care. All articles, such as hides, horns, wool, sugar, etc., likely to give rise to noxious emanations or offensive effluvia, or liable to contaminate the bilge-water, should be rejected. The bilges should be most carefully cleansed and disinfected at every available opportunity, and every means should be taken to keep the hold of the ship sweet and wholesome.

We now come to what are perhaps the most important considerations of all from a sanitary point of view—viz., the size, arrangement, and ventilation of the cabins. I am strongly of opinion that, except in those cases where an invalid travels with a friend or an attendant, each passenger who goes to sea for health should have a cabin to himself. In the best of the Australian sailing ships the cabins intended for two passengers are almost as large as can be expected, some of them being 10 feet by 11 feet, with a height of 7 or $7\frac{1}{2}$ feet. These dimensions might with advantage be increased to a slight extent, giving the double cabins a minimum size of about 10 feet by 12 feet.

The single cabins would of course have to be larger in proportion than those intended for two occupants. These should be about 10 feet by 8 feet.

The ventilation of the sleeping cabins is the problem which of all others is the most difficult to solve. In fine weather, when the ports can be kept open, and particularly if a good breeze is blowing, the air of the cabins is very fairly renewed by the currents which are set up between the port and the ventilators in the side of the cabin; but in bad weather, when the ports are shut, or in a dead calm even when they are open, any one who has been to sea knows how hot, stuffy, and unpleasant the cabins become. The arrangement for the admission of fresh air is comparatively simple. A tube of iron, zinc, or other material, carried through the deck, or communicating in some other way with the outside of the ship, and having the mouth curved downwards and valved, to prevent the admission of sea water, is all that is necessary. I have seen this arrangement in some ships, and, as far as it goes, it is a satisfactory one. But it is of little use to provide for the admission of pure air, unless means are taken to remove that which is vitiated, and thus to set up a circulating current of ventilation. This is the difficult point; but I believe it to be capable of satisfactory solution. In the first place, each cabin should communicate by a ventilating aperture in its upper part with a tube at least three or four inches in diameter. The tubes from the various cabins should converge to a common trunk, proportionate in size to the number of cabins to be ventilated. It now only remains to find means for the rapid exhaustion of the air from the main ventilating shaft. In steamers I think this might be easily accomplished simply by carrying up the shaft in close juxtaposition to the funnel of the vessel. The heating and consequent rarefaction of the air in the ascending ventilating shaft would cause a strong upward current, which would probably quite suffice for the ventilation of the cabins.

In sailing vessels a different plan would have to be adopted. The air might in this case be abstracted from the ventilating shaft by means of a turbine-wheel worked by the donkey-engine which is now found in most first-class passenger ships. It would not of course be necessary at all times to keep this apparatus in action. In fine breezy weather, when the ports could be freely opened, it would not be required; but in rough weather and calms it would be of the greatest service.

In making choice of the route for a health-voyage, there are two objects to be kept in view. First, to place health-seekers under the most health-giving conditions possible as to climate, temperature, etc. Second, so to arrange the voyage, by calling at a few places of interest on the way, as not only to render it as little monotonous as possible, but also by this means to obtain periodical supplies of fresh provisions, fruits, etc.

There can, I think, be little doubt that, as regards advantages of climate, no voyage can be compared with that to Australia or New Zealand. The reasons for arriving at this conclusion have been fully given elsewhere. The two great drawbacks at present to this voyage are its monotony and the cold and rough weather experienced, in the case of sailing vessels, in the latter part of the outward passage. Let us consider how far it would be possible to overcome these objections.

After leaving the English Channel the ship might at once shape her course for Madeira. In the case of a vessel provided with auxiliary engines, a call at this island would at all times be an easy matter; but with a sailing ship it might not under all circumstances be practicable. A couple of days at Madeira would give the passengers an opportunity of stretching their legs on shore, and enjoying the beautiful scenery of the island, and would be doubly welcome after the Bay of Biscay, with its usually unpleasant accompaniments. Madeira would be, as it were, a sort of introduction to the calmer and more enjoyable portions of the voyage; and here the steward could lay in a plentiful supply of fruit, eggs, and fresh provisions generally, sufficient to last for the next week or two.

Without going much out of her course, the ship might pass sufficiently close to the Canaries to enable the passengers at any rate to get some general idea of the principal features of the islands, with perhaps a glimpse of the famous Peak of Teneriffe.

The second point of call might be the Cape Verde Islands, which lie close to the ship's course on the outward voyage to Australia. Here a further supply of fruit, etc., could be obtained, sufficient to last through the equatorial calms.

A call at the Cape of Good Hope would involve a considerable deviation from the usual track of a sailing vessel, but nearly all steamers touch there as a matter of course to take in coal. In the case of a health-voyage, it would be extremely desirable under any circumstances to touch at the Cape, and any loss of time that this might involve would be more than compensated by the advantages to the passengers. A week's stay at Cape Town would form a capital break in the monotony of the latter part of the voyage, and would give the steward another opportunity of filling up his stores of fresh provisions before starting on the final stage of the journey.

After leaving the Cape, the route chosen might be almost identical with that usually adopted by sailing ships, except that the easting should be made four or five degrees to the north of the latitude usually selected—

viz., in about 40° S. instead of 45° S. Such a latitude, whilst sufficiently bracing to exercise the full invigorating effects upon the constitution for which this part of the voyage is conspicuous, would at the same time avoid the boisterous and ungenial weather generally experienced farther to the south.

A good ship, furnished with an auxiliary screw, to be used only in calms and light head-winds, or in the immediate neighbourhood of land, would probably make the voyage to Australia, including stoppages, in about ten weeks. This, according to the testimony of all who have had an opportunity of studying the subject, is, as nearly as possible the best time for a voyage to last in the case of health-seekers who wish to derive the maximum benefit from the ocean climate. Those, however, who have less time at their disposal, or who from other causes are unable to take so long a voyage, might with great advantage avail themselves of such a ship as far as the Cape, returning from thence direct to England.

As regards the homeward voyage from Australia, it would not be possible to suggest any great improvement upon the usual route taken by sailing vessels returning to England by way of the Cape of Good Hope, and calling at Cape Town and St. Helena, although perhaps a slightly more southerly latitude might be chosen for the first part of the course, in order to obtain the advantage of a somewhat more bracing climate. It would, however, add to the interest of the voyage to touch at the Azores, in addition to the places already mentioned; and this could be done without any material deviation from the homeward track. The greatest drawback to this otherwise delightful passage is, in the case of a sailing vessel, its length—often extending to 120 days. In a ship with an auxiliary screw this disadvantage would of course be in a great measure overcome, and the passage might be shortened by several weeks.

There are one or two points with regard to the arrangements on board such a ship as I have endeavoured to describe, which may be mentioned in passing. There should, if possible, be some little selection made with respect to the passengers. For instance, no case of far advanced or hopeless illness should be taken, not only for the patient's own sake, but also for the sake of his fellow-voyagers. A sea life, as has been repeatedly pointed out, is better suited for completing a tedious convalescence, for warding off threatened illness, or for invigorating the jaded and overworked, than it is for confirmed invalids. At the same time, all due provision should be made for the efficient treatment of any case of illness that might occur in the course of the voyage. A ship of this kind would of course carry a surgeon, and preferably one with considerable previous experience of the sea, and a practical knowledge of ocean hygiene. One or two trained nurses, male or female, might with advantage be taken. These, under ordinary circumstances, would act as stewards or stewardesses, but could be told off to their nursing duties, if required. One or two airy and secluded cabins should also be set aside for the reception of any patient who might require special treatment. The arrangements as to washing the decks, etc., should be under the same regulations as in government emigration ships.

The amusement of the passengers on a health-voyage is a matter of considerable importance; but a considerate and enterprising captain, seconded by the surgeon and other officers, would do all that can be done in this way, without suggestions from others. There should be some sort of a library for the circulation of books under proper regulations. A piano and perhaps an organ would of course also be provided for the use of the passengers, and a band might be organised among the stewards and men, to be employed on festive occasions, such as deck dances. Some part of the ship would be arranged so that it could be used for public entertainments, such as concerts and theatricals; and scenery of a simple character would be provided for the latter. Social games of all kinds, but especially those that can be played in the open air, would be organised and encouraged. I may mention that nearly everything I have suggested is already done in some of the best Australian ships.

The food-supply would of necessity be a matter of the first importance. The great desiderata are, (1) to keep up the supply of fresh provisions—vegetables, salads, milk, eggs, butter, etc.—as much as possible during the whole voyage; (2) to endeavour not so much to place a great variety of dishes on the table every day, as to provide a varied bill of fare from day to day; (3) to supply provisions of the best quality only, and to set before the passengers plain, wholesome, and well-cooked dishes, suitable alike for invalids and those in health, rather than to attempt any high flights of culinary art. An ice-house should in all cases be provided. The delights of cold water, cooled wines and iced provisions generally can only be duly appreciated by those who have felt the want of these luxuries during the hotter portions of a voyage.

Just a word upon the financial aspect of the question before concluding. Shipowners would ask themselves— as they are entitled to do—whether a ship of this kind would answer as a commercial speculation. Would the public be willing to pay a sufficient advance upon the present rates of passage-money to render it worth while for owners to incur so many extra expenses,—to make such a sacrifice of space, and such a selection of cargo, as would be involved in carrying out the suggestions that have been made? This question I am of course unable to answer with any authority, and I apprehend it could only be settled by actual experiment. One thing, however, is clear: the public must be prepared to make extra payment for extra advantages. The present charges, even in the most important steam lines, are exceedingly low, and it is a fact that a passenger can live on board one of these splendid vessels almost, if not quite, as cheaply as when stationary in a good hotel on land—thus practically paying little or nothing for his travelling expenses. In sailing lines this is still more conspicuous; and when the voyage is protracted beyond its usual limits, it is almost impossible to believe that the fare can cover the cost of maintenance. Speaking with the diffidence arising from a very imperfect knowledge of this part of the subject, I am myself inclined to think that an advance of, say, 40 to 50 per cent. upon existing fares for the return voyage to Australia might cover the extra expenses of the owners, and should be cheerfully paid by the public for the improved accommodation and many additional advantages afforded them.

APPENDIX A.

OUTFIT REQUIRED FOR A VOYAGE TO AUSTRALIA.

CABIN REQUISITES, ETC. (*necessary only in sailing vessels.*)
>Deal berth-place, *or*
>>Portable iron bedstead, *or*
>>Cot or sofa to stand or swing.
>
>Portable washstand and fittings.
>Looking-glass.
>Mahogany rack with water bottle and tumblers.

∗∗∗ *The above articles are furnished by the* OWNERS *in nearly all sailing lines.*

>Horsehair mattress and bolster.
>Horsehair or feather pillow or pillows.
>Sheets (?).
>Blankets.
>Pillow-cases.
>Counterpane or railway-rug.

∗∗∗ *Bedding is now provided in several sailing lines.*

>Towels.
>Table napkins (?).
>Portable easy-chair.
>Water can.
>Foot-bath or portable sponge-bath.
>Cabin lamp.
>Bookshelf.
>Carpet, rug, or matting for floor (?).
>Curtain for door, ditto for berth (?).

CABIN REQUISITES (*continued*).

> Cabin pocket.
> Soiled clothes bag.
> Swing-tray (?).
> Table (?).
> "Storm basin" (?).
> Pictures (?).
> Hooks for clothes.
> Portable chest of drawers, *or*
> > Trunks, boxes or portmanteaux.
> Store box (?).

NOTE.—In several lines of sailing ships the bedding, linen, towels, etc., and all *necessary* articles of cabin furniture, are now provided, if desired, for an extra payment of about £5.

CLOTHES, ETC.

> Woollen suits, thick for cold, and thin for warm weather.
> Thin merino coat for cabin wear (?).
> Two overcoats,—one thick, one thin.
> Flannel shirts (with collars ?), some thin.
> Linen shirts (not recommended for voyage).
> Under-waistcoats and drawers.
> Collars, socks (cotton and woollen).
> Handkerchiefs.
> Boots (one thick pair for rough weather).
> Shoes, leather or canvas.
> Flannel pyjama sleeping suits.
> Night-shirts (?).
> Scarves, woollen comforters, etc.
> Hats or caps, cloth. Straw hat (?).
> Suit of waterproofs (?).
> Brushes, sponges, etc.

STORES AND SUNDRIES.

> Candles for lamp.
> Soap.

STORES AND SUNDRIES (*continued*).
  Liebig's extract of meat (?).
  Preserved milk (?).
  Cocoa (?).
  Aperient medicine.
  Effervescing citrate of magnesia (?).
  Spirit stove and methylated spirit (?).
  Portable or pocket filter (?).
  Writing materials.
  Housewife.
  Tools, nails, hooks, etc. (?).
  Books.

In the above list, articles not absolutely necessary are indicated by a note of interrogation.

APPENDIX B.

NAMES AND ADDRESSES OF SOME OF THE PRINCIPAL SHIPPING FIRMS.

"Anchor" line of steamships, Liverpool to India *viâ* Suez Canal (also to New York). Messrs. Grindlay & Co., 55, Parliament Street, S.W.; and Messrs. Henderson Brothers, 18, Leadenhall Street, E.C.

Anderson, Anderson & Co.'s line of sailing ships from London to the Australian ports. 5, Fenchurch Avenue, London, E.C.

British India Steam Navigation Company. Lines of steamers for India, Persia, east coast of Africa, Queensland, etc. Agents, Grey, Dawes & Co., 13, Austin Friars, E.C.

"Castle" line of steamers, London to China, Japan, etc., *viâ* Suez Canal. Messrs. Thomas Skinner & Co., 5, East India Avenue, E.C.

"Colonial" line of steam and sailing vessels for Australia. John H. Flint, 112, Fenchurch Street, London, E.C.

Cunard line of steamships, Liverpool to New York, etc.

Messrs. W. and W. S. Cunard, 6, St. Helen's Place, E.C.; and 28, Pall Mall, S.W.

Devitt & Moore's "Australian" line of sailing ships, from London to the Australian ports. 89, Fenchurch Street; or F. Green & Co., 13, Fenchurch Avenue, London, E.C.

Donald, Currie & Co.'s Colonial Mail line of steamers from London to Madeira, South Africa, etc. 3 and 4, Fenchurch Street, London, E.C.; 23 and 25, Castle Street, Liverpool; 11, Commercial Buildings, Cross Street, Manchester.

"Ducal" line of steamships, London to India *viâ* Suez Canal. Grinday & Co., 55, Parliament Street, S.W.; and M'Diarmid Greenshields & Co., 112, Fenchurch Street, E.C.

"Elder" line of steam and sailing ships from London to Adelaide. Trinder, Anderson & Co., 110, Fenchurch Street, London, E.C.

Gavin, Birt & Co.'s "Thames and Mersey" line of sailing ships from London to the Australian ports. 27, Leadenhall Street, London, E.C.

Gellatly, Hankey, Sewell & Co., agents for steamers to India, China, Japan, etc., 51, Pall Mall, S.W.; and 109, Leadenhall Street, E.C.; also at Manchester and Liverpool.

"Glen" line of steamships, London to India, China, and Japan, *viâ* Suez Canal. McGregor, Gow & Co., 1, East India Avenue, E.C.

Green's, Messrs., "Blackwall" line of sailing ships for Australia. F. Green & Co., 13, Fenchurch Avenue, London, E.C.

Houlder Bros. and Co.'s line of sailing ships from London and Liverpool to the Australian ports, etc. 4, Oriel Chambers, Water Street, Liverpool; and 146, Leadenhall Street, London, E.C.

Inman line of steamships, Liverpool to New York, etc. William Inman, 22, Water Street, Liverpool; Eives and Allen, 99, Cannon Street, E.C.

Ismay, Imrie & Co.'s "White Star" line of sailing ships from Liverpool to the Australian ports, etc. 34, Leadenhall Street, London, E.C., and 10, Water Street, Liverpool.

"Messageries Maritimes de France" line of steamers from Bordeaux to Brazil and River Plate; also from Marseilles to India, China, etc. London Agency, 97, Cannon Street, E.C.

M'Ilwraith, M'Eacharn & Co.'s "Scottish" line of sailing ships for Queensland ports, etc. 34, Leadenhall Street, London, E.C.

Money Wigram & Son's line of steam and sailing ships to Australia. Messrs. Morgan and Allport, 7, Leadenhall Street, London, E.C.

New Zealand Shipping Company's line of sailing ships from London to the ports of New Zealand. 84, Bishopsgate Street Within, London, E.C.

"Orient" Steam Navigation Company (Limited) line of steamers to Australia. Managers, Messrs. F. Green & Co., 13, Fenchurch Avenue; and Messrs. Anderson, Anderson & Co., 5, Fenchurch Avenue, London, E.C.

Pacific Steam Navigation Company, Liverpool to Brazil and River Plate. 31, James Street, Liverpool.

Pacific Mail Steamship Co.: American route to Australia, New Zealand, Japan, etc. European offices, Windsor Chambers, Great St. Helens, London, E.C.; C. Clark & Co., agents.

Peninsular & Oriental Steam Navigation Company. 122, Leadenhall Street, London, E.C.; and Oriental Place, Southampton.

"Passengers" line and Albion Shipping Company's sailing vessels for New Zealand ports. Shaw, Savill & Co., 34, Leadenhall Street, London, E.C.

Potter, John, & Co.'s "Victoria" line of sailing ships, from London to the Australian ports. 15, Great St. Helens, London, E.C.

"Red Cross" line of steamers from Liverpool to Brazil. Messrs. R. Singlehurst & Co., Redcross Street, Liverpool.

Royal Mail Steam Packet Company, Liverpool to the West Indies, Brazil, and River Plate, etc. J. M. Lloyd, Secretary, 18, Moorgate Street, London, E.C.; and J. R. Linstead, Canute Road, Southampton.

Taylor, Bethel & Roberts, Messrs., "London" line of sailing

ships from London and Liverpool to the Australian ports. 110, Fenchurch Street, London, E.C.

Thompson, Geo., & Co.'s "Aberdeen" clipper line of sailing ships from London to the Australian ports. 24, Leadenhall Street, London, E.C.

Union Steamship Company (Limited), Southampton to Madeira, South Africa, etc. Oriental Place, Southampton; and 11, Leadenhall Street, London, E.C.

APPENDIX C.

I. *Table of approximate equivalents for estimated force of wind. (Scale 0 to 12).*

Force.	Beaufort Scale.	Velocity. Miles per hour.
0	Calm	3
1	Light air, or just sufficient to give steerage way . .	8
2	Light breeze ⎫ or that in which a well-conditioned vessel, with all sails set, and "clean full," would go in smooth water from ⎧ 1—2 knots	13
3	Gentle ,,	3—4 ,,	18
4	Moderate ,,	5—6 ,,	23
5	Fresh breeze ⎫ or that in which she could just carry "in chase" "full and by" . ⎧ Royals, etc. . .	28
6	Strong ,,	Top-gallant sails . .	34
7	Moderate gale	Topsails, jib, etc. . .	40
8	Fresh ,,	Reefed upper topsails and courses	48
9	Strong ,,	Lower topsails and courses	56
10	Whole gale, or that with which she could scarcely bear close-reefed lower main-topsail and reefed foresail .	65
11	Storm, or that which would reduce her to storm-staysails	75
12	Hurricane, or that which no canvas could withstand .	90

II. Table of Relative Humidity.*

Dry-bulb Thermometer Reading.	DIFFERENCE BETWEEN READINGS OF DRY AND WET-BULB THERMOMETERS.																			Dry-bulb Thermometer Reading.
	$\tfrac{1}{2}°$	1°	$1\tfrac{1}{2}°$	2°	$2\tfrac{1}{2}°$	3°	$3\tfrac{1}{2}°$	4°	$4\tfrac{1}{2}°$	5°	$5\tfrac{1}{2}°$	6°	$6\tfrac{1}{2}°$	7°	$7\tfrac{1}{2}°$	8°	$8\tfrac{1}{2}°$	9°	$9\tfrac{1}{2}°$	10°	
deg.																					deg.
40	96	92	88	84	80	76	73	69	66	63	60	57	54	51	49	46	44	42	40	38	40
42	96	92	88	84	81	77	74	71	68	65	62	59	57	54	52	49	47	44	42	40	42
44	96	92	88	85	81	78	75	72	68	66	63	60	57	54	52	49	47	45	43	41	44
46	97	93	89	86	82	79	76	73	70	67	64	61	59	56	54	51	49	47	45	43	46
48	97	93	90	86	83	79	76	73	70	67	65	62	60	57	55	52	50	48	46	44	48
50	97	93	90	86	83	80	77	74	71	68	66	63	61	58	56	53	51	49	47	45	50
52	97	93	90	86	83	80	77	74	72	69	67	64	62	59	57	54	52	50	48	46	52
54	97	93	90	87	84	81	78	75	72	70	67	65	62	59	57	55	53	51	49	47	54
56	97	93	90	87	84	81	78	75	73	70	68	65	63	60	58	56	54	52	50	48	56
58	97	94	91	88	85	82	79	76	73	71	69	66	64	61	59	57	55	53	51	49	58
60	97	94	91	88	85	82	79	76	74	71	69	66	64	62	60	58	56	54	52	50	60
62	97	94	91	88	85	82	80	77	74	72	70	67	65	62	60	58	56	54	52	50	62
64	97	94	91	88	85	83	80	77	75	72	70	68	65	63	61	59	57	55	53	51	64
66	97	94	91	88	86	83	81	78	76	73	71	68	66	64	62	60	58	56	54	52	66
68	97	94	92	89	86	83	81	78	76	73	71	69	67	65	63	60	58	56	54	52	68
70	97	94	92	89	86	84	81	78	76	74	72	69	67	65	63	61	59	57	55	53	70
72	97	94	92	89	87	84	82	79	77	75	72	70	68	66	64	62	60	58	56	54	72
74	97	95	92	89	87	84	82	79	77	75	73	71	68	66	64	62	60	58	56	54	74
76	97	95	92	90	87	85	82	80	78	76	73	71	69	67	65	63	61	59	57	55	76
78	98	95	93	90	88	85	83	80	78	76	74	72	70	68	66	64	62	60	58	56	78
80	98	95	93	90	88	85	83	80	78	76	74	72	70	68	66	64	62	60	58	56	80
82	98	95	93	90	88	85	83	80	78	76	74	72	70	68	66	64	62	60	59	57	82
84	98	95	93	90	88	85	83	80	78	76	74	72	70	68	66	64	62	60	59	57	84
86	98	95	93	90	88	85	83	80	78	76	74	72	70	68	66	64	62	61	60	58	86

* Abridged from the "Table of Relative Humidity," by E. E. Dymond, Esq., F.M.S., published in the Quarterly Journal of the Meteorological Society, vol. vii., p. 2.

INDEX.

"ABERDEEN" Line of Australian Packets, 62
Adelaide, City of, 235; port, 236; climate of, 236
Africa, South, *see* South Africa.
Agulhas Bank, 194; current, 192
Air at sea, purity of, 5; on land, impurities of, 5
Albatross, 173
Alps, Southern, 240, 259
Amsterdam, Island of, 123, 194
Amusement Committee, 93
Amusements at sea, 88
Anderson, Anderson & Co.'s Australian packets, 62, 341
Ascension, Island of, 197
Atlantic route to Australia, 41
Auckland, 251
Auroras, 145
Australia, Voyage to, 38, 77; various routes to, 38; ports, 63, 181, 226, 229; discovery, 202; area, 203; population, 203; divisions, 206; aborigines, 203; rivers, 203, 208; mountains, 204; form of government, 204; productions, 204; railways, 206; colonies, 206; cities, 216; health resorts, 216; climate, 46, 207
Australia, South, *see* South Australia.
Australian sailing-lines, 60, 339; steam-lines, 58, 339
Azores, or Western Islands, 198

BALLARAT, 220
Barometer, 9, 303, 310, 315; observations of, in the tropics, 310; in the southern hemisphere, 311; daily range, 311
Barracouta, 160

Bass' Strait, 180, 222
Bathing at sea, 130
"Bells," The, 86
Berth, Hints on choosing a, 66
Birds, Sea, 172—shooting, 91
Bloemfontein, 290, 296
Bonito, 160
Brazil, Voyage to, 29; climate of, 31; healthiest season in, 46
Brisbane, 235
British India Steam Navigation Co., 36, 341
"Bull-board," Game of, 91
"Burying the dead horse" 97

CABIN, Fitting up, 68, 74; furniture and requisites, 69, 339; ventilation, 130, 331; choice of a, 66
Cabins, Size of, 49, 66, 331
Calms of Cancer, 106; of Capricorn, 113; equatorial, 110
Campbell Town, 225
Canary Islands, 121
Cancer, Calms of, 106
Cape Colony, 280; population, 280; rivers, 281; mountains, 281; productions, 282; ostrich farms, 282; diamond fields, 283; railways, 284; wines, 282, 285; ports, 283; climate, 293
"Cape doctor," The, 294
Cape hen, 177
Cape Horn, Homeward Australian route, *viâ*, 187
Cape of Good Hope, Healthiest season at, 46; voyage to, 33; homeward Australian route *viâ*, 188
Cape Otway, 180
Cape pigeon, 177
Cape Town, Description of, 283; suburbs, 284; hotels, 286; con-

veyances, 285 ; population, 286 ; climate, 293
Cape Verde Islands, 121
Cape wines, 282, 285
Capricorn, Calms of, 113
Cargo, selection of, 331
Chess tournaments, 93
Christchurch, 247
Cities of Australia, 216
Climate, Ocean, Curative effects of, 2, 118 ; meteorological tables of, 316; equability of, 8, 312 ; sedative influence of, 8 ; bracing effects of, 10, 118
Climate of Australia, 46, 207; of South Africa 292; of New Zealand, 267
Closet arrangements in steamers, 134 ; in sailing vessels, 134
Clothing, Hints as to, 72 ; for voyage, 72, 339; for the tropics, 135
Cloud, Estimation of, 308
Cobb & Co.'s coaches, 297
Colds, Tropical, 136
Cold weather at sea, Effects of, on invalids, 10, 118
Colesberg, 296
"Colonial" line of Australian packets, 60. 63, 341
Constantia, Village of, 285 ; vineyards of, 285
Constellations, Southern, 144
Consumption, Effects of a seavoyage in cases of, 14; statistics of, 15
Coronas and haloes, 146
Cradock, 296
Crew, etc., of sailing vessel, 86
Cricket, Game of, at sea, 90
Crossing the line, 95
Crustacea, Net for capturing, 167

DARLING DOWNS, 213, 235
"Dead Horse," Burial of, 97
Devitt and Moore's, Messrs., sailing ships, 62, 342
Dew at sea, 313
Diamond fields, South African, 283
Diet, Management of, at sea, 127
Disease, Influence of Australian climate on, 215 ; effects of South African climate on, 300

Diseases, List of, benefited by sea voyages, 14
Doldrums, The, 110
Dolphin, Description of the, 153
Dunedin, 248
Durban, 288
Dust, Constituents of, 5

EAST LONDON, Port of, 288
Eclipses of the sun, 146
"Elder" line of Australian packets, 62, 342
Elizabeth, Port, 287, 295
Equatorial calms, 110
Exercise, Importance of, 128

FISHES, Deep sea, 155 ; shoals of minute, 163
Flying-fish, 162
Food, Quality of, at sea, 82
Furniture, Cabin, 68, 339 ; in sailing vessels, 69 ; warehousing in colonies, 183

GALES south of Cape, 115
Games, Open-air, 90
Geelong, Town of, 220
Gipp's Land, 210
Graham's Town, 295
Green's, Messrs., sailing ships, 60
Gulf-weed, 200

HALOES and coronas, 146
Health, Management of the, at sea, 124 ; in the tropics, 134
Health resorts of Australia, 216 ; of South Africa, 292
Health-voyage of the future, 330
Health-voyages, List of, 23
Helena, St., Island of, 195
Hobart Town, Description of, 226 ; climate of, 214, 227 ; excursions in neighbourhood, 228
Hokitika, 249
Homeward routes from Australia, 186
"Horse latitudes," 107
Houlder Bros., Messrs., Australian packets, 59, 63, 342
Humidity of air at sea, 8, 305, 312
Hurricanes, Area of Mauritius, 192, 314
Hygrometer, Use of, at sea, 305, 312

INDEX.

INDIA, Healthiest season in, 45; voyage to, 35
Indian Ocean, South, Climate of, 191, 316
Indian route to Australia, 39
Invercargill, 249
Iron v wooden ships, 55, 330

JACKSON, Port, Harbour of, 229

KAURI-PINE, 242; gum, 242

LAND sighted on outward voyage, 120; on homeward voyage, 194
Languor tropicus, 137
Launceston (Tasmania), 223
Letters sent by sailing vessels, 102
Line, Crossing the, 95
Liverpool Plains, 235
London, East, Port of, 288

MADEIRA, Island of, 121, 331
Maories, Description of the, 252
Marine Zoology, 148, 199
Mauritius hurricanes, 192, 314
Meals at sea, 79, 81
Melbourne, Description of, 216; hotels, 183; public buildings, 217; public gardens, 218; gutters, 218; vehicles, 218; climate, 219; hot winds, 219
Meteors, 146
Meteorological observations in Australia, 207; in South Africa, 290; at sea, 303, 316; in New Zealand, 269
Meteorological journal, 308
Microscopical objects, Marine, 166; method of obtaining, 167, 169
Mollymoke, The, 176
Mosquitoes in Australia, 219, 229
Mother Cary's chicken, 172
Mutton bird, 177

NAPIER, 251
Natal, Description of, 288; capital, 288; population, 289; productions, 289
Natal, Port (*see* Durban)
Nelson, 249
Nervous complaints, Effects of sea voyage upon, 17, 118
Net for marine objects, 167

Newcastle, Meteorological observations on board, 315, 316
New Plymouth, 250
New South Wales, Climate of, 211; population of, 208; cities of, 231; rivers, etc., 203, 208
Newspaper on board ship, 93
New Zealand, position, 238; area, 238; discovery, 239; history, divisions, 239; government, 240; geographical features, 240; harbours, 241; productions, industries, and exports, 242; railways, 244; cities and principal towns, 245; the Maories, 252; scenery and points of interest, 257; the volcanic district, 260; hot lakes and geysers, 260; forests, 263; flowers and fruits, 265; animals and birds, 265; reptiles, 267; fishes, 267; climate, 267; lines of ships to, 63, 339

OBSERVATIONS for latitude and longitude, 87
Ocean, "Regions", of the, 105; fishes, 155; meteorology, 303, 316
Ocean climate, Curative effects of, 2, 118; meteorological observations of, 303, 316; equability of, 8; sedative influence of, 8; bracing effects of, 10
"Old Wives," 161
Orange Free State, Description of, 289; population, 289; principal towns, 290; high-lying plains, 290; productions, 290
"Orient" line of Australian packets, 58
Orient steamship, description of, 59
Ostrich farming in South Africa, 282
Otway, Cape, 180
Outfit for sea-voyage, 72, 339
Outfitters, 74, 183

PACIFIC route to Australia, 39
Pacific Steam Navigation Co., 30, 343
Paramatta river, 232
Paramatta, Village of, 232

Passing ships, 100, 198
Peninsular and Oriental Company, 36, 38
Phosphorescence of the sea, 169
Pietermaritzberg, 288
Pilot-fish, 156
Pink and white terraces of Rotomahana. 261
Porpoise. The, 153
Ports, British, 76 ; Australian, 63, 181. 226. 229
Port Elizabeth. 287, 295
Port Jackson, Harbour of, 229
Port Natal (*see* Durban)
Port Phillip, Harbour of, 181 ; the "Heads," 180
"Portuguese man-of-war," 168
Potchefstroom, 291
Pretoria. 291
"Prickly heat," 137
Provisions, Quality of, at sea, 82; quantity required for long voyage, 85

QUEENSLAND, 208, 235 ; climate of. 213
Quoits, Game of, at sea, 90

RAILWAYS of Australia, 206 ; of New Zealand. 244 ; of South Africa, 284, 297
Rainfall. Observations of, at sea, 309, 313
"Red Cross" line of steamers to Brazil, etc., 30, 343
"Regions" of the ocean. 105
Requisites for cabin, 69, 339
"Rip," The, 181
Rotomahana. Pink and white terraces of, 261
Routes to Australia, 38
Royal Mail Steam Packet Co., 23, 30, 343

SAILING lines, Australian, 60, 339
Sailing vessels, Size of, 55 ; advantages, 48 ; various kinds, 54 ; course of Australian, 104, 186 ; arrangement of, 56, 79 ; dimensions, 57 ; quality of food in, 82; crew, etc., 86
Sailors, Amusements of, 94 ; songs, 99

St. Helena, Island of. 195
St. Paul, Island of, 123, 194
Sandhurst, 220
Sandridge, 181
Sargasso Sea, 200
Saw-fish, 159
Sea-air, Purity of, 5 ; special properties of, 7
Sea, Surface temperature of the 308 ; colour of the, 139 ; phosphorescence, 169
Sea-birds, Shooting, 91 ; various kinds, 172
Sea-sickness, Management of, 124
Sea-water, composition of, 142
Season. Best, for sailing, 46 ; healthiest in various countries, 44
Seasons in southern hemisphere, 45, 117
Servia, Description of. 52
Shark. Description of the, 155 ; various kinds, 155 ; parasites of, 157 ; fishing for the, 157
Shaw, Savill & Co., line of Australian packets, 63, 343
Ship, Speaking a, 105 ; choice of a, 48 ; arrangement of, 56, 79, 331 ; dimensions of, 56, 79
Ships, Passing, 100, 198
Shooting stars. 146
"Sights" for latitude and longitude, 87
Sobraon, Meteorological observations taken on board the, 315, 320 ; description of, 57
Soiled linen, Disinfection of, 133
Soland goose, 173
South Africa, Colonies of, 279 ; diamond fields, 283 ; ports, 283 ; climate, 292 ; high-lying plains, 290, 298; conveyances, 297 ; coast of, 194 ; productions, etc., 282, 289
South Australia, Climate of, 210 ; population, 208 ; rivers, etc., 203, 208
Southern Alps, 240, 259
Southern constellations, 144
Steamers, Rapid development of, 51; advantages and disadvantages of, 48; general description of, 51; description of *Servia*, 52 ; de-

INDEX. 351

scription of *Orient*, 59; quality of food in, 82
Steam lines, Australian, 58, 339
Stores, Private, for voyage, 75; list of, in sailing ships. 85
Storms, Distribution of, 313
Sunsets at sea, 147, 199
Sword-fish, 159
Sydney, Description of, 231; public buildings, 231; public gardens, 232; population, 208; hotels, 233; fruit, 233; climate, 233
Sydney harbour, Description of, 229; extent of, 233

TABLE BAY, 195
Tasmania, Description of, 222; cultivation of fruit in, 229; towns, 223, 226; climate of, 214
Temperature of the air at sea, 8, 312; of the surface of the sea, 308
Thermometer, Use of, at sea, 304, 307, thermometer screen, 304
Thresher-fish, The. 152
Time, Method of indicating, at sea, 86; alteration of, with latitude, 87, 117
Tongariro Mountain, 260
Trade-winds 108, ; north-east, 108; south-east, 112
Transvaal, The, 290; population, 291; productions, 291; principal towns, 291
Trinidad. Island of, 122
Tristan d'Acunha, Island of, 122
Tropical complaints, 136
Tropics, Management of the health in the, 134; clothing in the, 135

Turtle, The, 164

VENTILATION of cabin, 131, 331
Vertical sun, 147
Vessels, Various classes of, 51, 54
Victoria, Climate of, 209; population, rivers, etc., 208
Voyage to West Indies, 23; to Brazil and River Plate, 29; to Cape of Good Hope, 33; to India, *viâ* Suez Canal, 35; to Australia, 38, 77
Voyages, List of, 23

WAKATIPU, Lake, 241, 258
Wanganui, 250
Warwick, Town of, 235
Water, Fresh, quality of, at sea, 82; sea, composition of, 142
Waterspouts, 146
Waves. Height of, 143; peculiarities, 143
Wearing apparel, 72; for voyage, 72. 339; for tropics, 135
Wellington, 246
West Indies, Voyage to, 23; healthiest season in, 23, 44
Westerly winds, Region of, 106, 114
Whale, Various species of, 148; habits, 150; food. 150; enemies, 152; parasites, 153; blowing of the, 151
Whale-bird, 177
Wigram's, Messrs., steam ships, 60
Wind, Determination of direction and force of, 309
Wines, Cape, 282, 285; Constantia, 285; Australian, 205

ZOOLOGY, Marine, 148, 199

PRIZE MEDAL, LONDON, 1862.   SILVER MEDALS, PARIS, 1867—78.

PANCREATIC EMULSION

OR

MEDICINAL FOOD,

PREPARED BY

SAVORY AND MOORE,

FOR PERSONS SUFFERING FROM

CONSUMPTION and where there is a tendency to other **WASTING DISEASES**, attended with loss of power to digest and assimilate food.

PANCREATIC EMULSION will always take precedence of Cod Liver Oil, by reason of its introducing the STABLE SOLID FATS INTO THE SYSTEM, instead of the evanescent fluid fats or oils.

No Oily Emulsions of any kind, not even Cod-Liver Oil itself, can supply the kind of fat necessary for sound and vigorous human life. In addition to this, all the Oily Emulsions are liable to rancidity, and most of them are highly objectionable, in consequence of the saponification, and ultimate putrefaction, produced by the *Chemical Agents used instead of Pancreatic Juice.*

PANCREATIC EMULSION is the *NECESSARY FOOD* OF THE CONSUMPTIVE, and the most reliable form of nutriment for counteracting the tendency to Phthisis and other Wasting Diseases.

PANCREATIC EMULSION may therefore be regarded as Chyle obtained by nature's own process. In certain cases both Cod Liver Oil and Pancreatic Emulsion are required —one to supply the blood with oil or liquid fat, the other with the more stable solid fats; but it cannot be too strongly urged that both PANCREATIC EMULSION and Cod Liver Oil are *not to be regarded as Medicines, but as articles of diet*, without which patients, with their defect of health, will as surely starve as healthy persons would if deprived of the most nutritive part of their food. **Bottles, 2s. 6d., 4s. 6d., and 8s.**

ASTHMA, BRONCHITIS, AND DIFFICULT BREATHING,

arising from Affections of the Respiratory Organs promptly relieved, and Paroxysms averted and subdued, by Inhalations of DATURA TATULA in either of the forms for use—viz., Cigars, Cigarettes, Tobacco; also as Pastilles and Powder for burning.

Dr. Barker "On Diseases of the Respiratory Passages and Lungs."

"I have myself suffered several times from attacks of sub-acute Bronchitis, attended with painfully suffocative sensations toward bed-time, which have been immediately relieved by smoking for a few minutes some cigars made from the DATURA TATULA, by SAVORY & MOORE, of Bond Street, and equally beneficial results I have known to be produced in many other cases. This species of Datura appears to supply every want. Messrs. SAVORY AND MOORE also prepare the same plant for smoking in the ordinary way, and in some respects this is to be preferred. I consider it a remedy of great power and usefulness."—*From* DR. W. G. BARKER, M.B. LOND., *Senior Medical Officer to the Worthing Infirmary.*

SAVORY AND MOORE,

Chemists to the Queen, H.R.H. the Prince of Wales, H.H. the Khedive of Egypt, etc.,

143, NEW BOND STREET, LONDON.

BRANCH HOUSES: { 29, CHAPEL STREET, BELGRAVIA; 1, LANCASTER GATE, HYDE PARK; BRIGHTON—86, KING'S ROAD.

NELSON'S
PURE BEEF TEA.

SOLD IN HALF-PINT PACKETS.

Samples and Prices on application to the Manufacturers,

GEORGE NELSON, DALE, & CO.,

14, DOWGATE HILL, LONDON, E.C.

GOLD MEDAL, PARIS, 1878.
FIRST DEGREE OF MERIT AND MEDALS, SYDNEY, 1880, MELBOURNE, 1881.

FRY'S COCOA
EXTRACT.

Guaranteed pure Cocoa only, deprived of the superfluous oil.

"If properly prepared, there is no nicer or more wholesome preparation of Cocoa."—*Food, Water, and Air*, DR. HASSALL.

"Strictly pure, and well manufactured in every way."—W. W. STODDART, F.I.C., F.C.S., City and County Analyst, Bristol.

J. S. FRY & SONS, BRISTOL AND LONDON.

ALLEN & HANBURYS'
"PERFECTED" COD-LIVER OIL.

The OIL for DELICATE STOMACHS. Does not cause the usual nausea or after-taste, and can be borne and digested by the most delicate.

This Cod-liver Oil is manufactured from fresh and selected Livers at ALLEN & HANBURYS' Factory in Norway. It is prepared by an altogether new and special process of their own, and presents all the medicinal and nutritive qualities of the remedy in their highest degree of excellence. Sold *only* in capsuled bottles, bearing ALLEN & HANBURYS' fac-simile signature and trade mark—a plough.

EXTRACT OF MALT.

See **The British Medical Journal, May 1st, 1880; The Medical Times and Gazette, Nov. 22nd, 1879; The London Medical Record, Nov. 15th, 1879.**

The value of EXTRACT OF MALT as a nutritive and restorative agent for delicate and exhausted constitutions is now fully acknowledged by the medical profession, the extract being rich both in muscle and fat-forming elements. It promotes, moreover, in a special and peculiar manner, the solution and digestion of all farinaceous foods, and is therefore a valuable remedy in those diseases which arise from an imperfect assimilation of these substances. The presence of the active and valuable constituents of the Malt, unimpaired and in a concentrated form, is secured in ALLEN & HANBURYS' EXTRACT, by a special process of their own, and evaporation *in vacuo*.

DOSE.—From a desert-spoonful to a table-spoonful with or immediately after meals. EXTRACT OF MALT forms an excellent adjunct to COD-LIVER OIL.

In Bottles, at **2s.** *and* **3s. 6d.** *each.   Trade Mark—a Plough.*

NITRITE OF AMYL CAPSULES.

FOR ANGINA PECTORIS, SEA-SICKNESS, &c.

ALLEN & HANBURYS' supply Glass Capsules containing about 4 grains each in boxes (holding six capsules) at 2s. per box.

Dr. A. H. JACOB, of Dublin, says:—"I have tried ALLEN & HANBURYS' Nitrite of Amyl Globules in two cases of Amaurosis, with excellent results."

Extract from a letter on Sea-sickness to the LANCET, Aug. 10th, 1878:—"I now always recommend patients to carry the drug in capsules, such as are manufactured by ALLEN & HANBURYS, which may be broken, and their contents dropped upon a handkerchief as required.—CROCHLEY CLAPHAM."

The above and any other of ALLEN & HANBURYS' special preparations may be obtained from Chemists throughout the colonies, or from

ALLEN & HANBURYS,
PHARMACEUTICAL CHEMISTS AND WHOLESALE DRUGGISTS,
PLOUGH COURT, LOMBARD STREET, LONDON, E.C.
Large or Small Medicine Chests or Cases fitted to suit any requirements.

INDIA, CEYLON, JAVA, QUEENSLAND, BURMAH, PERSIA, EAST AFRICA, &c.

BRITISH INDIA STEAM NAVIGATION COMPANY
(LIMITED).

BRITISH INDIA ASSOCIATION.

MAIL STEAMERS FROM LONDON TO

CALCUTTA	...	Fortnightly.	JEDDAH	Fortnightly.
MADRAS	....	,,	ALGIERS	,,
COLOMBO	...	,,	ZANZIBAR	Every Four Weeks.
RANGOON	...	,,	BATAVIA ..	,,
KURRACHEE	..	,,	BRISBANE .	,,
BAGHDAD	...	,,	ROCKHAMPTON	,,

Delivering Mails, Passengers, Specie and Cargo at all the principal Ports of **INDIA, BURMAH, EAST AFRICA, QUEENSLAND,** and **JAVA.** Every comfort for a tropical voyage.

Apply to **GRAY, DAWES, & Co.,** 13, Austin Friars; or to **GELLATLY, HANKEY, SEWELL, & Co.,** Albert Square, Manchester; 51, Pall Mall, and 109, Leadenhall Street, London.

J. ALLEN & SON'S PORTABLE TURKISH BATH.

CAN BE USED FOR HOT AIR ONLY, HOT AIR AND VAPOUR COMBINED, OR FOR A MERCURIAL OR ANY MEDICATED BATH.

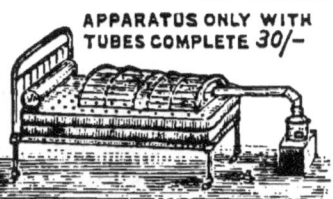

APPARATUS ONLY WITH TUBES COMPLETE 30/-

FOR RHEUMATISM, GOUT, ECXEMA, LUMBAGO, SCIATICA, AND SKIN, LIVER, AND KIDNEY AFFECTIONS.

APPARATUS FOR BED IN BOX WITH PAIR OF WICKER FRAMES 45.s FULL PARTICULARS WITH MEDICAL AND PRESS OPINIONS POST FREE.

APPARATUS FOR USE UNDER CHAIR, WITH BEST CLOAK TINNED IRON SUPPORTS IN BOX 50/s

21 & 23, MARYLEBONE LANE, OXFORD STREET, LONDON.

Also Inventors and Manufacturers of
BRONCHITIS' KETTLES, INHALERS, THROAT SPRAYS, VENTILATING CROUP KETTLES, INVALIDS' BATHS, INFANTS' AND INVALIDS' FOOD WARMERS, &c., &c.

Catalogues for 3 Stamps.

THE LANCET says:—"This instrument is very complete. Every precaution has been taken to make an accident impossible. It is portable, it is cheap, and it acts promptly," &c.

MEDICAL EXAMINER.—"It is not, perhaps, going too far to say that such a contrivance as Allen and Son's Portable Turkish Bath should find a place in every well-regulated household."

"The new route *via* San Francisco is yearly becoming more popular."
Times, 19th July, 1876.

AMERICAN OVERLAND ROUTE

TO

Australia, New Zealand, China, and Japan,

BY

CUNARD, INMAN, WHITE STAR, ALLAN, AMERICAN, ANCHOR, GUION, NATIONAL, FRENCH, GENERAL TRANSATLANTIC,

AND OTHER STEAMSHIP LINES TO

NEW YORK, PHILADELPHIA, BOSTON, QUEBEC, PORTLAND OR BALTIMORE,

And by the Union and Central Pacific Railways to

SAN FRANCISCO,

There connecting with **Steamers of the Pacific Mail S.S. Company**, sailing on the 1st of each month for

YOKOHAMA AND HONGKONG,

And by Steamers of the same Company sailing every fourth Wednesday to

AUCKLAND & SYDNEY,

CALLING AT HONOLULU.

FIRST-CLASS FARES FROM LIVERPOOL TO

HONOLULU	30 days	... £62 0 0	YOKOHAMA	40 days	... £87 0 0
AUCKLAND	42 "	... 70 0 0	SHANGHAI	42 "	... 98 0 0
SYDNEY	45 "	... 70 0 0	HONGKONG	42 "	... 92 0 0

Agents—

CHARLES CLARK & CO.,
Windsor Chambers, Great St. Helens, London, E.C.

HENRY F. GILLIG & CO.,
449, STRAND, W.C.

THE WHITE STAR LINE
ROYAL AND UNITED STATES MAIL STEAMERS,

SAILING WEEKLY BETWEEN
LIVERPOOL & NEW YORK,

Are distinguished by the following characteristics:—

All of them, without exception, are among the largest of Ocean Steamers.

They are nearly new and of their original dimensions.

They are of unusual strength, each being built in seven water-tight and fire-proof compartments, and the two principal decks in all of them being of iron, sheathed with wood.

Their fine model, full power, and excellent sea-going qualities, have made their passages famous for speed, comfort, and regularity.

The Cabin accommodation is all situated in the centre of the ship.

The Saloons are unusually spacious, and occupy the whole breadth of the vessels.

The Ladies' Saloon and the Smoke-room are each of commodious dimensions and handsomely furnished.

Electric Bells communicate with Stewards from each berth, and in each vessel are Piano, Library, Bathrooms, Barber's Shop, &c.

Baggage not required in State-room is stored in a room immediately under Saloon, to which passengers can have ready access.

These vessels are fitted to carry a limited number of *Steerage Passengers*, the accommodation being of the very highest order.

The lighting, ventilating, warming, and sanitary arrangements are all of the most effective description, and are unsurpassed in any vessel afloat.

The foregoing descriptions apply to all the **White Star Steamers,** *and not merely to those most recently built.*

NOTICE.—The Steamers of this Line, both on the Outward and Homeward Passages, take the Lane Routes recommended by Lieut. Maury, U.S. Navy.

For Freight or Passage apply to
ISMAY, IMRIE, & CO.,
34, LEADENHALL STREET, LONDON, E.C.; AND 10, WATER STREET, LIVERPOOL.

Royal Mail Steam Packet
COMPANY.

WEST INDIES AND PACIFIC
(via PANAMA).

COLON or ASPINWALL, SAVANILLA, MEXICO, CENTRAL AMERICAN, NORTH and SOUTH PACIFIC PORTS, SAN FRANCISCO, JAPAN, CHINA, and BRITISH COLUMBIA.

The Company's Steamers leave Southampton, with Her Majesty's Mails, on the 2nd and 17th of each Month, conveying Passengers and Parcels, also Specie and Goods, under through Bill of Lading.

An additional Steamer leaves on the 11th of each Month for Barbadoes, St. Lucia, St. Vincent, Grenada, Trinidad, La Guayra, Porto Cabello, Curacao, Savanilla, Carthagena, and Colon, and on the 23rd for Antigua, St. Kitts, Jamaica, and North and South Pacific.

The Atlantic Steamers now run through from Southampton to Colon (Aspinwall).

BRAZIL AND RIVER PLATE MAIL STEAMERS.

The Royal Mail Steam Packets also leave Southampton on the 9th and 24th of each Month, carrying Her Majesty's Mails, Passengers, Cargo, Specie, etc., for Lisbon, Cape de Verdes, Pernambuco, Bahia, Rio de Janeiro, Santos, and River Plate (calling also at Cherbourg, Carril, and Vigo). During Quarantine Season in the River Plate for vessels arriving from Brazilian Ports, Steamers proceed direct from Europe to the River Plate without touching at the Brazilian Ports.

For particulars apply to J. K. LINSTEAD, Southampton, or to J. M. LLOYD, Secretary, Royal Mail Steam Packet Company, 18, Moorgate Street, London.

AGENTS:—In Paris, GEO. DUNLOP and Co., 38, Avenue de l'Opera; Havre, MARCEL and Co.; Hamburg, H. BINDER; Antwerp, F. HUGER; Bremen, EGGERS and STALLFORTH.

CAPE OF GOOD HOPE, NATAL, AND EAST AFRICAN ROYAL MAIL STEAMERS.

Weekly Service to the Cape of Good Hope and Natal.

UNION STEAM SHIP COMPANY
(LIMITED).
ESTABLISHED 1853.

THE MAIL STEAMERS of this Company (under contract with the Cape of Good Hope Government) leave Southampton every alternate Thursday, and Plymouth the next day, conveying Passengers and Goods to Cape Town, Mossel Bay, Port Elizabeth (Algoa Bay), Port Alfred (The Kowie), and Natal, and Passengers only to East London.

THE STEAMERS IN THE INTERMEDIATE SERVICE leave Southampton every alternate Friday, and Plymouth the next day, conveying Passengers and Goods to East London and Natal, and calling at Cape Town and Port Elizabeth to land Passengers only.

All steamers call at Madeira, and St. Helena is called at at stated intervals.

FOR RATES OF PASSAGE MONEY OR FREIGHT apply to any of the following Agencies, or at the COMPANY'S OFFICES, ORIENTAL PLACE, SOUTHAMPTON, and 11, LEADENHALL STREET, LONDON.

Bristol	H. R. James, 8, Queen's Square.
Hull	H. J. Barrett, 17, High Street.
Liverpool	Stumore, Weston & Co., 20, Water Street.
Manchester	Keller, Wallis & Co., 73, Piccadilly.
Plymouth	H. J. Waring & Co., The Wharf, Millbay.
Glasgow	F. W. Allan & Co., 15, Gordon Street.
Edinburgh	A. O. Ottywell, 2a, Shandwick Place.
Dublin	{ Carolin & Egan, 30, Eden Quay. { H. W. Donnelly, 30, College Green.

South African Royal Mail Service.

The Castle Packets  Company's Steamers

(Carrying Her Majesty's Mails)

BETWEEN
LONDON AND SOUTH AFRICA,

Convey MAILS, PASSENGERS, and GOODS from ENGLAND to CAPE TOWN, MOSSEL BAY, ALGOA BAY, PORT ALFRED, EAST LONDON and NATAL, sailing from LONDON every alternate TUESDAY, and from DARTMOUTH every alternate FRIDAY. Extra Steamers are despatched from London and Dartmouth as may be required.

Loading Berth—East India Dock Basin, Blackwall, E.

Steamer.	Tons.	Steamer.	Tons.
"GARTH CASTLE"	3,705	"DRUMMOND CASTLE"	3,700
"KINFAUNS CASTLE"	3,507	"GRANTULLY CASTLE"	3,489
"WARWICK CASTLE"	2,957	"CONWAY CASTLE"	2,966
"BALMORAL CASTLE"	2,948	"TAYMOUTH CASTLE"	1,827
"DUBLIN CASTLE"	2,911	"DUART CASTLE"	1,825
"DUNROBIN CASTLE"	2,811	"DUNKELD"	1,154
"LAPLAND"	1,269	"MELROSE"	840
"ELIZABETH MARTIN"	1,246	"FLORENCE"	695
"COURLAND"	1,241	"VENICE"	511

The Royal Mail Steamers call regularly at Madeira, and touch at St. Helena and Ascension at stated intervals.

Passengers embark either at London or at Dartmouth. All heavy Baggage must be shipped in London. Twenty cubic feet allowed to each Adult Passenger, freight free.

The Third Class Railway Fares to London (Emigrants' Rates) of Second and Third Class Passengers is paid by the Company.

For dates of Sailing, Freight, Passage, or any further information, apply to

DONALD CURRIE & Co.,

3 AND 4, FENCHURCH STREET, LONDON, E.C.; 25, CASTLE STREET, LIVERPOOL; and 11, COMMERCIAL BUILDINGS, CROSS STREET, MANCHESTER; or to JAMES CURRIE AND CO., LEITH, and 40, ST. ENOCH SQUARE, GLASGOW.

THE
NEW ZEALAND SHIPPING CO.,
(*LIMITED.*)

Head Office—CHRISTCHURCH, NEW ZEALAND.

Capital Subscribed £250,000

,, Paid up £125,000

Despatch regularly every month, to the principal Ports in the Colony, the following or other equally fine first-class Iron Clipper Ships, fitted with every convenience for Passengers, and commanded by men of well-known experience:—

RANGITIKI,	1188 Tons Reg.		WAIRO,	1015	Tons Reg.
OPAWA,	1075	,,	WAIKATO,	1021	,,
WAIMATE,	1124	,,	RAKAIA,	1022	,,
WAITANGI,	1128	,,	PIAKO,	1075	,,
WAITARA,	833	,,	OTAKI,	1015	,,
MATAURA,	853	,,	ORARI,	1011	,,
HURUNUI,	1013	,,	WANGANUI,	1077	,,
WAIPA,	1017	,,	WAIMEA,	848	,,

PAREORA, 878 Tons Register.

FARES:

Saloon (including Bedding, &c.) . . £52 10s.
Second Cabin £25
Steerage . . . . . £16 & £18.

Children under 12 Years of age pay one-half fare: Infants under Twelve Months free.

Saloon Passengers are supplied with a liberal dietary, including Live Stock, but not Wines, Spirits, or Malt Liquors, which can be had on board at moderate and fixed charges.

For full particulars apply at the Company's Offices.
84, BISHOPGATE STREET WITHIN, LONDON, E.C.

O. R. STRICKLAND, Manager.

MESSRS. GREEN'S
BLACKWALL LINE

OF

STEAM AND SAILING SHIPS

FOR

INDIA AND AUSTRALIA.

Carlisle Castle,	Superb,	Viceroy,
Melbourne,	Shannon,	Windsor Castle.
Renown,	The Lord Warden,	

MESSRS. DEVITT AND MOORE'S
Australian Line of Packets

SAILING FROM LONDON.

SOBRAON	. Captain Elmslie.
PARRAMATTA	. Captain Goddard.
LA HOGUE	. Captain Wagstaff.
SOUTH AUSTRALIAN . . .	. Captain Barrett.
ST. VINCENT	. Captain Ismay.
RODNEY	. Captain Louttit.
&c. &c.	&c.

These favourite passenger traders have large airy cabins, and are fitted with Bath Rooms, Piano, and every necessary comfort, including Bedding and Cabin Fittings. They offer unequalled advantages to passengers travelling for health, and a surgeon is carried with each vessel. For plans, terms, and all particulars, apply to—

F. GREEN & Co.,
13, FENCHURCH AVENUE, LONDON, E.C.

ORIENT LINE OF STEAMSHIPS
TO AUSTRALIA.

DIRECT SERVICE
BETWEEN
LONDON AND AUSTRALIA
IN FORTY DAYS.

One of the following magnificent full-powered steamships belonging to the Orient Steam Navigation Company, Limited, and the Pacific Steam Navigation Company, is despatched every **fortnight** for Adelaide (Semapore), Melbourne, and Sydney, taking passengers for all ports in Australia, Tasmania, and New Zealand, and for the Cape of Good Hope :—

STEAMSHIPS.	TONS.	NOM. H.P.	CAPTAINS.
Austral	5250	1000	....
Chimborazo	3847	550	J. F. Ruthven
Cotopaxi	4028	600	R. Studdert
Cuzco	3849	550	J. Murdoch
Garonne	3876	550	O. Hillkirk
John Elder	4152	550	G. F. Dixon
Liguria	4666	750	G. N. Conlaw
Lusitania	3825	550	A. Charlton
Orient	5386	1000	W. F. Hewison
Potosi	4219	600	C. E. Darley
Sorata	4014	600	A. J. Cooper

These vessels are specially constructed for long ocean voyages, and are fitted with every convenience for the comfort of passengers.

FARES.

First Class, 50 guineas and upwards; Second Class, 35 guineas and upwards; Third Class, closed cabins, with two berths, 20 guineas each; Third Class, closed cabins, with four berths, 18 guineas each; Steerage, open berths, for Men only, 15 guineas each.

Special terms for return tickets, and abatement for families.

F. GREEN & CO.,
13, *FENCHURCH AVENUE, LONDON, E.C.*
AND
ANDERSON ANDERSON & CO.,
5, *FENCHURCH AVENUE, LONDON E.C.*

For Freight or Passage apply to the latter Firm.

COLONIAL AGENTS :—

JOSEPH STILLING & CO., Adelaide.
GIBBS, BRIGHT & CO., Melbourne.
G. S. YUILL, Sydney.

www.ingramcontent.com/pod-product-compliance
Lightning Source LLC
Chambersburg PA
CBHW030406230426
43664CB00007BB/776